Raving Lunacy

Also by Dave Courtney:

STOP THE RIDE I WANT TO GET OFF

Raving Lunacy

Clubbed to Death
Adventures on the Rave Scene

Dave Courtney

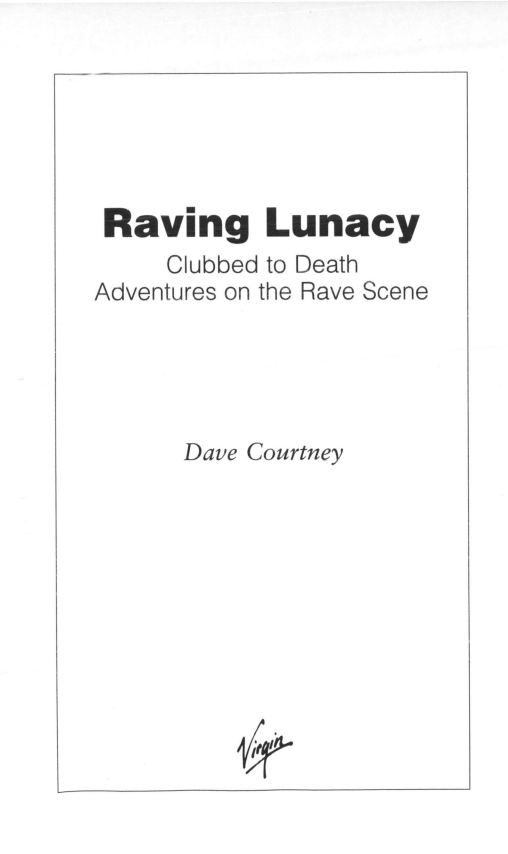

First published in Great Britain in 2000 by
Virgin Publishing Ltd
Thames Wharf Studios
Rainville Road
London W6 9HA

Photos courtesy of Jocelyn Bain Hogg and the author

A catalogue record for this book is available from the British Library.

ISBN 1 85227 901 X

Typeset by TW Typesetting, Plymouth, Devon

Printed in Great Britain by CPD, Wales

*To all the club people past and present (and those no longer with us);
to all doormen, club owners, dancers, dealers, DJs and ravers.
And to the women, the unsung female strength behind every successful man.*

Jennifer

Rave on.

DC 2000

Contents

'Hello You!'   1

1   This is What it is   4
2   Everything Begins with an 'E'   9
3   Underneath the Arches   18
4   Rave On   38
5   *Ssmo*king!   51
6   Loved Up   55
7   The Spirit of Ecstasy   68
8   Bleaching   78
9   Back to Futures: Crazy Mondays – Bleaching part II   96
10 Let's Have a Whip Round!   108
11 Club Nutter: Funny Glen, Mad Jack & the African
    Exorcist   125
12 Fuck the Suntan . . .   151
13 Clubbed to Death   171
14 Jesus Saves – Courtney Nets the Rebound   184
15 The World's Most Dangerous Babysitter   192
16 Bushwacka!   209
17 One Nation Under a Groove   220
18 Carry on Abroad   237
19 Bang up to Date   246
20 Two Tigers Walking Down the Street   266
21 At the End of the Day . . .   270

    Index   272

'Hello you!'

Yeah, hello! I'm back. Well, come on, you didn't think I had nothing more to tell you, did you? Oh, shut up! I ain't even started. I've got more tales than Crufts, more stories than Jeffrey Archer on a truth drug.

Speaking of old Jeffrey, that reminds me, I ran for Mayor of London, y'know. Straight up, I did. And I asked for Jeffrey Archer as my second-in-command. Because anyone who's that good at making up alibis . . . I wanted on my side.

But more of that later.

So, if you've bought this book cos you really enjoyed my last one, *Stop The Ride I Want To Get Off*, then thanks for your support. And I will wear it always. But, if you haven't bought this and you've just borrowed it from a mate or you're loitering in WH Smith's having a free read – YOU TIGHT BASTARD!

This one then, *Raving Lunacy*, is based around all my clubbing days. From Disco chickens to Hardcore ravers and everything in between. Rave music and the dance scene, when it first happened, gave me a new lease of life. When I discovered it, I just loved it. And I learned that I actually knew how to fucking dance. Which I never knew I did. Well you can't be good at everything, can you? Michael Jackson, for instance – good dancer, bad babysitter.

So, anyway, what a shocker; I went from thinking I was this flat-footed, big-nosed, bald geezer to being a loved-up Fred Astaire and John Gotti all rolled into one!

In *Stop the Ride* . . . I tried to write a book that was honest about the life of crime and to show there is such a thing as good baddies as well as bad goodies. Some of the stories in

1

Raving Lunacy tackle another taboo subject: drugs on the club scene. I ain't recommending either crime or drugs but all the people who've been there and experienced it will know the things I've said are true; all the people who haven't lived it might get an insight into worlds they haven't been part of or understood.

I do know that in my new line of business, the entertainment world, being honest and open about taking the odd little stimulant might hinder me, but I feel it is necessary that I tell the God's honest truth and be a bit of a pioneer in bringing the world back into reality. Because one thing I definitely ain't is a hypocrite. I'm not promoting the use; I just fully understand why people do it.

In this book you'll find the usual Courtney collection of colourful characters – blokes with hooks for hands, gun runners, Page 3 stunners, funny nutters, bent coppers, pill poppers, kickboxing Rastas, erotic dancers, exotic chancers, gangsters, scousers, Acid housers, fun lovin' criminals and, of course, raving lunatics. And all the usual stories of sex, drugs and a white Rolls.

In fact, there's only one other book I can think of that's got more fighting and fucking, and that's the Bible. Well, Adam and Eve were the original Big Bang, weren't they? It's a little light on jokes, though, the old Good Book.

I make loads of little Frankenstein monsters, I do. Without meaning to. Geezers that get swayed by the old 'gangster myth' thing and put on the suit, get the jewellery, shave the head, smoke the cigar and all that. They dress like one but when it's time for action, they just get gobbled up. And that ain't what I want you to take from me. If you learn anything from my books it's just to go out and have a good time, in your own way.

Laugh and the world laughs with you (unless you're at a funeral), cry and you cry alone. Another one of them little home truths I learned off my nan. Another thing I learned very quickly in life is this: don't put on an act. Cos clever people can see through it and they might not like what's behind it, or what (more importantly) they *think* is behind it. I talk to my missus, my mates, bank robbers, bank robbers' wives, policemen, judges, lawyers, and whoever, in exactly the same way.

And exactly the same way I talk to you.

The police think I'm still bang at the old villainy lark so I've still got a 24-hour blue shadow, and I don't mean when I miss shaving my head. Will they never learn? You'd think they ain't got better things to do than follow devilishly handsome magazine writers (that's me, by the way). Now that I'm a regular in *front*. I always knew I had plenty of it but I never thought I'd end up in a magazine named after me.

I live life for the laugh of it and have a fucking good time. I pull out every stop I know, quite a few stops that you probably haven't heard of, and also a few you wouldn't even want to touch.

But by the time you've finished reading this you'll at least know how much fun you can have if you put your mind to it.

Stay clever!

Dave Courtney
OBE

1 This is What it is

So anyway, I was in the Ministry of Sound having a blindin'
time and I went up to the bar. I was proper buzzing. While I'm
stood there waiting for my drink I said hello to this geezer stood
next to me. He looked like he was having a good time as well.
He nodded back and I said, 'Top night?' He went, 'Yeah . . .'
then said, 'Look at this . . .' and took his fucking eye out! *Pop*,
straight out the socket and *plop*, right on to the palm of his
hand. That fucked up my little buzz for a second, I can tell you.

'I hope that's false,' I said, 'or you've just maimed yourself.'
He started laughing and gave it to me to hold. It was glass but
it was fucking warm as well. Horrible. So I threw it in the ice
bucket on the bar and gave it a shake. Oh, *stop* it! I'm joking,
I didn't do that. As if I would . . .

I gave it back to him and said, 'And if you can take the other
one out as well I'll give you my house.'

What a cunt, though, if that geezer got so stoned one night
that he tried to take out the wrong eye? How he'd larf! Come
to think of it, that hollow socket behind the glass eye would
be a wicked place to hide a little stash when you were going
through Customs, wouldn't it? Just a thought. They can't
touch you for it.

That's one of the freakiest things I've seen in clubland,
though. I don't mind women flirting with me but I've never had
a geezer give me the eye before. HA! Well, that ain't strictly
true, actually. This bloke in a fetish club once asked me to
whip him! But I'll get round to that later.

Which reminds me, it was also at the Ministry that there was
this gay fella who used to work in the cloakroom. Now this

geezer was always *always* asking me for a dab of whizz. Always. It ain't no secret that I indulge in the odd dab myself. Obviously not a secret to this geezer anyway, cos he was forever trying to leech some off me. To the point of being annoying.

So one night, when I knew he was gonna do it again, I put my hand down the back of my pants and stuck the tip of my finger up my arse. Seconds later, without fail, it was, 'Dave! Dave, oh give us a dab of stuff, will ya?' I said sure. Dipped my finger in it and put it in his mouth.

His face scrunched up a treat. He went, 'Mmmm! Strong innit?' I thought; You bet it is, I had a fucking curry last night.

Anything you can think of happening, and even some things you can't, have at one time or another happened in a club or at a rave. In clubs, at some point, I've seen people shot, shagged, smashed and stabbed; off their trolleys, out of their trees, on their knees, off their tits (and on someone *else's*); having the best of times and sometimes the worst of times, but never bored.

This is what a nightclub is, this is why villainy and nightclubs run hand in hand. When you're a villain you've not got a nine to five job so there's no getting up in the morning. That actually means you can go to bed when you want. And if you're in villainy you should be having more money than anyone else, and there's only a certain amount of things you can spend it on.

A nightclub was somewhere where you could actually go more than anyone else, and the fact you had a few more quid than everyone else made you a little celebrity in there. If you went to any one club, or the same clubs, long enough you got that 'unity' feeling as well. Everyone in there knew your name and what you did and made you feel special. That's true of the speakeasies that American gangsters had in the 20s, the Krays had in the 60s with all their club connections (which everyone knows about), right up to present day. The clubs change and the music changes but the feeling stays the same.

The nightclub is a place for a naughty man to peacock his feathers, to show off your ladies, and your garments. Trying to make other people jealous is a very unconscious thing we all do, I'm afraid, and it is true; even by going 'I like that car', you know other people will like it as well. Or you buy a nice suit cos you know other people are gonna say, 'That looks really nice on you.'

Nightclubs are places where you can do all that. Once you've actually learned how to express yourself, the club scene is the place you can explore and express that.

The gangster element took a long time to get into the raving side of clubbing because it was looked upon as bad. Most gangsters thought drugs was drugs was drugs, meaning that they thought smoking puff was the same as injecting heroin in your eye. All bad. What gangster would like to take a substance that would drop his guard when he spent his whole life trying to be sharp? So they were the last people to get turned around to it. But, when they did, they grabbed it with both hands.

I remember when I first saw the rave scene and thought, Fucking hell! If I hadn't been sort of forced into it through work I would've never gone there by choice. Also in the rave scene it was about everyone together and sort of losing themselves, which ain't a villain's natural way. They all strive for their little bit of individuality.

What came with clubs and drugs. If you were into villainy then the rewards for getting into the drug game were so vast that whatever other kind of villainy you were at, this fucking drug game was knocking it in the air. It did drive a dividing line between the old and the new – those who moved with it and those who wouldn't. But the ones who wouldn't, found it hard not to, because the profits were so big, and everyone else they dealt with was dealing in it.

The amount of bird they started giving out, though, just completely shocked everyone. It was the way that the law created a deterrent – shock sentences. *Twenty* years for smuggling! That's fucking barbaric. Fifteen years for having a key of charlie in your car. Eight years for selling some wraps in a pub. It's been going on for so long now that no one bats an eye, but back then those sentences were new. Twenty years for bringing over some puff! Fuck me.

It didn't stop many, though, because such a small percentage were being caught. Truth is, selling drugs is far more addictive than taking them. Big time.

But the feeling of unity in the rave scene was similar for the punters as the feeling that the chaps, or naughty men, had always had.

One of the knock-on effects of clubland changing for the villain/club thing, though, was that the unity which existed in the old scene was deeper than a lot of that on the new club scene. In some ways I think mates were an awful lot matier then than now. Then, you dressed up in a nice suit, went out with your mates and spoke to them for *eight* hours; and you'd been with them all day as well. So you really knew these blokes. It's very hard to grass someone up if you know them well. But you could go raving with someone for two years and know jack shit about them. You've took drugs with him but don't really know him. There's good and bad.

And back then you had a better chance of getting a shag cos the club shut at two, so you'd still have time to do it! Now the club don't shut till ten in the morning. You can go with your mate and barely speak to him till you come out, but you'd took a pill which meant you could turn to the geezer next to you, who you don't know, and say, 'I'd die for you. You're top, you are!'

I've had people say to me, 'Did you feel you missed out because you didn't have the rave scene when you was younger?' – and this is said to me by a twenty-year-old who's never had a slow dance in his life! Because how can you slow dance when you're whizzing off your tits? So I honestly think that the ravers have missed out by not having slow dances like we used to have at the end of the night when I was younger. A slow dance to get that bird in a clinch and let your fingers do the walking. When the lights went down you could hear bra straps going off like gunshots.

There again, my mum would say I missed out by not having Glen Miller and his orchestra. Every generation thinks they had it the best, don't they? I've been lucky enough to have the best of two generations. Mine and yours. I've straddled the gap, so to speak. Many times, actually, come to think of it!

The thing is, once you've been raving you can't do any other dance. It fucks you up that way. Once you'd been raving you couldn't move to any other music, your body just instinctively went into it. Which could be fucking embarrassing when you went to a mate's wedding, let me tell you – everyone else is out on the floor doing the Dance Like Your Dad routine and you're up on a table doing the ravey-hands movements and shouting, 'Commme-*onnn*!' to Barry Manilow or Chris de Burgh's 'Lady in Red'. Auntie Maureen starts mouthing to the bride, 'Is Dave all right?'

Having said all that, though, raving definitely did far more good than bad. And if you were the right age when you got into it then you just got fucking blown away, mate. I was older than most but still youthful in my attitude to having fun, so I got it with both barrels!

Not so long ago there was a little meeting between the old and new. It was after a Kray twin benefit party. It ended about one o'clock and everyone wanted to go on some place else. The only club I could think of was the Aquarium, which was a place down Old Street. So I took some of London's most notorious faces, Freddie Foreman, Frankie Fraser, Roy Shaw, Charlie Kray, Joey Pyle and Tony Lambrianou. And this was Sunday night which is Garage night and very black. We were the only white folks in there. Freddie, Frankie, Roy, Charlie, Joey and Tony walked in, all suited up smart, and everyone turned 'round and thought, Fuck me, the fucking Mafia have turned up! A lot of the crowd couldn't get their heads around it. You could see them, sort of freaking out as these older white guys walked around as cool as fuck. As it happens, the chaps all had a smashing time. Frankie smashed a bottle on someone, Tony smashed a chair . . . oh *shut* up. I'm joking. But they did actually have a fucking good time in the end.

I've known both. The old-school way and the new skool way. So I can rave with a bird all night and then in the car home undo her bra in the dark with one hand while I'm lighting a cigar with the other. I won't tell you what I steer with, but God bless Viagra.

2 Everything Begins with an 'E'

I've always said you can't blame 'lack of swings and round-abouts' on my little start in it all. My life was one big fucking playground. I think it was because when we were learning to write the alphabet at school I only got so far as the letter 'e' before I got bored and set the desk on fire. So that letter always had sentimental value to me. And the local fire brigade.

I was married by now but I'd also been shot. No connection, by the way, I didn't marry a hitlady. So there was always those two sides of my life – the home bit with the kids and family, and the other bit with the villainy. And the clubbing part of it, waiting in the wings to turn into the third piece of my life. It hadn't gone really big yet. But whatever the music fashions were I was always a clubby person cos I liked people. That's it in a nutshell.

I was actually working at a club in Langley, Slough, called Queen's (or The Queen Mother Reservoir Yachting Club, to give it its full name) when Acid House first came out. Not that I didn't already have plenty on my plate at the time that I needed any extra stimulation – what with regularly nicking yachts and speedboats from the reservoir, having nightly fights with gypsies from the massive gypsy site next to Queen's, or being shot at by irate drug dealers. That kinda thing.

Working the door of Queen's was a tough one because of the gypsy site next door. If they were barred, they'd find out where the doorman lived and go beat him up there. In his living room. So they needed some out-of-town boys for the weekend door work. I got the job from a geezer called John Boy, who I'd first worked with on the door at Tattershall

Castle. At that time John Boy was Doorman No. 1 in London and he was, and still is, a legend in that field. This was at a time when doormen were doormen. Then, if you got beat in a fight you got the sack for getting beat and the firm hired a better fighter; now, if you get in a row and hit someone you get sacked for *that*. Then was a time that made individual stars of certain doormen. Now you just get famous firms.

Vinoo was the guy who ran Queen's and brought us down from London to deal with the gypsy rows. And Vinoo was, and is, the absolute bollocks and the best guv'nor for a doorman to work for. He'd come to court for you, get you bail, get you witnesses, vouch for you and pay you three times as much. But, because of all that, he also expected more back.

Queen's was a sparky little club, always something going on. Or a gun going off. Some funny little things happened there. One night I went into the kitchen to roll some joints. I'm not the best joint roller in the world so I'd do six or seven at the same time and put them in a fag box. So I'm in the kitchen and it's dark.

I laid out six large Rizlas then six lines of puff, before the fag, so I could see how much was in. I did six joints but there's loads of bits scattered on the work surface so I scooped them all up and made another joint. Waste not, want not, as my nan used to say. Whenever she rolled a joint.

Back out in the club and everyone's dancing and this bloke asked me for a pull on the joint. I didn't really want it going in his mouth and then mine so I gave him one out of the cig packet. He lit it, inhaled, paused, smacked his lips, looked a bit puzzled but carried on dancing. Then he took another drag, stopped dancing, licked his lips again and stood there thinking about it. I'm watching him thinking, Fucking hell, is he for real?

What is he, I thought, a top joint connoisseur? I was expecting him to come over and go, 'Mmmm . . . a fruity little number with surprising bite,' like some kind of wine tasting-type bollocks. I now know this guy is tripping off his box. He must be.

Anyway, he did come over and said that the joint tasted like cheese and onion. I thought, Maybe it does on your planet, matey, but I'm still down here on planet Earth. Christ, can I pick 'em. I'd only ended up talking to someone who probably thought he was being stalked by a big piece of cheese and a big onion.

So he carried on and on about it, asking me to have a go. So finally I took it off him. Now I'm doing what I didn't want to do in the first place, sharing his joint.

Even before I got it to my mouth the smell hit me. I thought, Fuck. I took a puff and got the full taste – cheese and fucking onion. I immediately clicked what had happened; he'd got the 'scooped up' joint off the kitchen work surface, along with the sandwich leftovers! Now the geezer's looking at me, all expectant. I've got to say something.

'Yeah, yeah, you're right,' I said, 'it is cheese and onion. Why, did you want the salmon?' His face just bent a bit, all puzzled. I took out the packet again, 'I've got all different flavours here, mate. Salmon, prawn cocktail, curry, spicey chicken. You should've said . . .'

You know what? That ain't a half bad idea, is it? I bet some prick nicks that one off me. Just remember where you heard it first.

It was at Queen's that I met a young geezer called Wolfie who went on to become a really good pal of mine. He was only eighteen at the time and a real happy kid, into raving. The scene had just started and Wolfie was already bang into it. In fact, it was Wolfie who gave me my first trip, come to think of it. I was actually working at the club at the time, and Queen's had the sort of decor that was already lairy enough to fuck with your brain, without taking some fucking psychedelic mind-fucking drug on top. The carpet came alive with snakes, all writhing about chasing each other, and the wallpaper was covered in spinning diamonds and throbbing flowers. And that was the normal decor *before* you'd even taken anything.

But everything did go a bit mental when I had that acid. Wolfie just thought it was fucking hilarious (as he would, not being the totally fucked one) watching me walk about the club like I was in zero gravity. He said I looked like the first man on the moon, taking these massive, divvy steps about the place. One small step for a man, one large leap for a fucked doorman!

I went off in search of some drink and got caught nicking some champagne by my boss Vinoo. You could say Vin wasn't known for his generosity. He even bought a black and white dog cos he thought the licence was cheaper. No, I just made that bit up about Vinoo to get the dog joke in. Vinoo was actually very generous. I eventually emerged from the Darkside Of The Dancefloor like Neil fucking Armstrong returning to earth. 'Euston, we have a problem.' I just headed for this young fella I could see laughing his nuts off at me and hoped for the best.

It was me and Wolfie that spiked these local police. The Old Bill up there were as thick as pig shit. They were proper turnip-faced bumpkins, these cunts. They drove a Vauxhall Astra diesel, for one thing. What the fuck you gonna catch in that? Some cunt on a space hopper with the wind behind him was a dead cert to get away.

Over summer we'd have all-night barbecues at Queen's on the veranda and these dopey police would call on their rounds at midnight and then later at two. So this time these two plods came around. I offered one a drink and he refused cos he was on duty but said he'd have a burger. Fair enough. I went to get a burger. Now the geezer doing the burgers and hot dogs was also the geezer that sold the speed . . . and I bet you're doing now exactly what I did then, ain'tcha? Putting two and two together to get a big fucking four! – *Yes!* How could I resist? I felt it was almost my duty, my *duty* as a silly cunt who likes seeing other people be silly cunts, to do it.

So there's the burgers, a dollop of mayonnaise, a good sprinkling of amphetamine sulphate, a piece of lettuce and a dab of mustard all put expertly together in a sesame seed bun. I believe it was what they would call in your local burger joint (if the cook was a whizzhead) a Quarter Ouncer. Me and the hot dog man were fucking wetting ourselves.

So the coppers walked off munching on these burgers and saying thanks. I said, 'No, thank *you*. You are very very welcome, officer!'

An hour later the diesel Astra comes up the hill, going a fair bit faster than usual I can tell you. The windscreen wipers were on as well, and it was dry. Not a good sign. They both jumped out of the car like a couple of Keystone Cops. Their hats are off, their ties are loosened, top buttons undone and red sweaty faces. If I hadn't known better I would've thought they'd been shagging each other in the back of the squad car. One of them said, 'I think I'll have one of those beers now, mate.' We were going, 'OK, Sarge, whatever you want.' I was cracking up so much I had to go inside.

Eventually they left but they realised at some point that they'd been spiked – I think it was when they found themselves doing 50 mph in first gear with all the windows down and the radio on full blast chasing an aeroplane's wing light over a field. Or was it when they broke the Astra Diesel In Reverse Taking A Roundabout land speed record? But when they got back to the club it was too late. We'd all fucked off. So they had to wait until the next Saturday to catch us.

A week later some other police came up to the club and started saying there had been allegations made that these geezers had been drugged. I told them that everyone here was so fucking tight that if we spiked anyone we told them later and charged them. Wolfie went, 'Yeah. We say, "You buzzing yet? Well I spiked you earlier so you owe us a tenner!" '

For some reason I was put down as the leading suspect during Langley police station's inquiry into the infamous Great Spiked-Burger Mystery. Personally, I think it was Colonel Mustard in the drawing room with the cosh, but they had it down as Dave Courtney in the kitchen with a wrap. No charges were brought. And those two coppers are now married. To each other.

While I was at Queen's I'd get gypsies continually offering me knock-off gear. Because Wolfie was a real go-getter, a right little money maker, I gave him the keys to my garage to stash the stuff I got from the pikeys (as we called the gypsies). Also, Wolfie used to bring any knock-off gear he got, to sell to me. Which all worked out fine until he nicked a lorryload of shoes from outside some exhibition at Earl's Court. I bought this lorryload of shoes off him and they all turned out to be just the left ones! For display. I said, 'Oh, that's *fucking* great! Now I just need to find three thousand one-legged geezers who each want one Hush Puppy!' He even said it was my fault cos I didn't ask what was in it! Another bad one was a whole container load of corned beef hash. I don't even like corned beef. Reminded me of prison, corned beef hash, fucking hated it.

In fact, come to think of it, a lot of Wolfie's gear was pretty useless. A big bag of broken stereos, that was another one. And how about this, a machine for making bread. He brought me a load of fucking *bread*-making machines. What am I gonna do with that? Sell it to the Hovis family?

One of the best earners I had, though, was this massive container load of Pampers. When there's a baby in the house, what is the single most important thing? *Yes!* Getting the revolting smell of baby bab as far from the gaff as possible. Correct. And how many mums are there that want good quality, cheap nappies? Thousands, mate, let me tell you. And I made the acquaintance of quite a few, one way or another. Mum's the word when Dad's away, as they say.

I drove between the clubs that I was working in a big black Daimler hearse that I'd bought. I'd have the bench seats in the back full of doormen, flying up the West End at 90 mph leaving a trail of expensive aftershave and spliff smoke. Anyone in the car following ours went home smelling like a sophisticated Rastafarian.

This hearse came in very useful one day, for nicking paving slabs. I had quite a big house in East Dulwich at the time and cos a friend of mine was doing pub clearances I got loads of stuff from him and built the hugest beer garden in my back garden that you could imagine. With all the nicked bricks and wood and tables and chairs and umbrellas it ended up looking like something in fucking Hawaii! I had a brick barbeque so big you could've housed an immigrant family in it and a grill so fucking wide you could've fed the five thousand from it.

So, up the road, the council were putting red paving stones in the middle of ordinary ones and every time I passed from work I'd stop, open the boot of the old Daimler hearse and fill it with these slabs. One day, though, I went a paving stone too far and got seen and nicked by the Old Bill. And get this, I was actually nicked by the tallest policeman in Britain. Straight up. And he was as well – straight *up*! I forget his name – Shorty, I think – but he was fucking enormous: about seven foot! Talk about the long arm of the law. He could've probably truncheoned you to death with his dick. Best bit was that when he saw me and nicked me he was riding around on a pushbike! What a freaky fucking sight that was. He looked like he'd just nicked a kid's bike.

My first proper experience of a rave was towards the end of Queen's. I also went to work in a big city club called Heaven, at Charing Cross Road. It was one of the very first raves and it was Richard Branson's promotion. It was run by him, and he'd been to America and heard the Garage scene over there and brought it here.

I did the door there with Oliver Skeet, Ken the Dog, Big Scotty, Big Chris, Steve Bogat, Andy Finlater, Warren, Mickey Green, Lone Wolf, Herbie, Carlton, Billy Isaac, Dave Dunn, Amon Ash, Matt and Keith and Robbie. I was the old-fashioned doorman type, bow tie, dinner suit, didn't like to sweat. And this was the first time I'd seen proper ravers. I'd heard about them but never seen them close up (which makes it sound like I'm doing the commentary on some wildlife programme).

So my first sight was thousands of these nutters all jumping around waving their arms in the air, blowing whistles, taking their shirts off and dancing on just about everything you could balance a body on. This was the mad early days when people wore gloves and goggles and swimming caps, wore the smiley face T-shirts and put fluorescent paint on their faces. I swear I saw some cunt on the dancefloor with juggling balls. Bit different from the old Cinderella Rockerfella disco.

On top of all that it was a night called 'Spectrum', which was a gay night. Nothing like being thrown into the deep end, is there?

So I'm walking through the middle of all this in the old dinner suit, looking like an uptight penguin with piles, and all around me there's these giddy fuckers completely off their trolleys. I'd never seen so many blokes hugging outside of (or on) the football pitch after a goal. It weren't just because it was a gay night either, as I thought at the time. Es had finally hit town but they just hadn't hit me yet.

Only thing I was hitting was any fucker unlucky enough to come up and try and hug me. If anyone even accidentally touched me I was brushing them away, so an outright hug got a clump. Which is a bit embarrassing to have to admit, but I really was not at all used to it.

Anyway, after walking around Heaven for a few hours, I worked out that these people were pretty harmless. In fact, they were a lot less trouble than your average Saturday night, pissed-up punters and boozy losers who have nine pints, two fights, one curry and think they had a blinding time out. Ravers were having too fucking good a time to get into trouble, or even want to. I just stood back then and took it all in.

What struck me was that people were paying astronomical prices for things you'd normally give away, or at least get cheap – water, ice pops, Coke, Ribena, Lucozade. In my world if you'd ever gone out with a mate before and he'd said, 'I'll have a Ribena', you'd have fucking hit him just for *that*. I'd never heard of one of my mates going to a club and going, 'Yeah, mineral water please, guv!'

It didn't take Einstein to work out the profits in a club like this, what with the door fee, the pop and the water. That was me sold on the business side. The other bit of it, the having fun bit, came pretty soon after. I thought, What are these things then, these Es? So me and Wolfie went out clubbing and I tried one.

Nothing happened, or it just seemed I was waiting a long fucking time, so I took another one. I didn't think it was the actual E doing anything at all, I just thought it was me getting into the music! (Which I came to realise is as good a definition of being 'on a good one' as any.) So, I was sitting there waiting for this 'thing' to happen to me. Because everyone had seen the news on the telly calling Es 'the love drug' and saying everybody was shagging on it, supposedly, all that sort of bollocks.

What actually happened was I just had a real good jump around, dancing and heating up. Anyway, when the lights came on six hours later I'd been properly on one, mate. I could actually see, straight away, what it was all about. Because before then, or up until very recently before then, I'd been very, very anti-drug. I just thought drugs are drugs are drugs and didn't like any of it. I thought it was all bad and meant loss of control. And loss of control amongst my crowd and in my world was frowned upon. So, I just wasn't having any of that scene. Till then.

For the first time I could actually see what the attraction was cos I had fucking enjoyed myself, big-time, and I *felt* like I'd enjoyed myself as well. Cos that ain't always the case, is it?

You can be somewhere where you know you're supposed to be having a good time, but you don't.

Like all the things I do, if I can justify something to myself then I will go ahead with it. And after doing an E I hadn't died or gone home and nicked my Mum's video to flog or tried to fly off the top of a block of flats, or any of the other stuff they said in the news – I'd just had a blinding time, danced all night, said hello to hundreds of people I didn't know and gone home a fucking happy bunny.

That night out and my nights working at Heaven were a real, proper eye-opener for me, in more ways than one. That gave me the fuel to get on the road to being a club promoter. It looked like fun and money to me and I wanted some of that. I got together with Wolfie straight away and started making plans to get my own place. And I did. And it did become, even though I say so myself, a bit of a fucking legend as it happens . . .

3 Underneath the Arches

So I was bang into raving now, almost an instant convert, and I found this venue for a club of my own. Down in south London, near the Elephant and Castle, I found a viaduct arch beneath the mainline railway track running over John Ruskin Street. I bought it from Ginger John and Tony from the tyre shop in Underhill Road.

We turned this arch into the club, hence 'The Arches'. Then we set about doing it up.

I wanted to get it up and running really quickly without spunking any money on it. Now it's really fashionable to have a trendy little club with no decor and bare walls, 'mimimal' they call it. Well, we had a phrase for that kind of look as well: 'fuck all spent'. And here into the picture enters someone who was an invaluable part of the 'fuck all spent' look, as well as being a really close friend of mine – Mr Ray Bridges.

Right, I've just decided, I'm going to totally digress here a bit if you don't mind (and if you do mind – *fuck* off and read Enid Blyton!), so I can tell you about old Ray. He's a real gem, is Ray, and well worth hearing about.

Me and Ray first met years and years ago when we worked at the council depot in Grove Vale. He was a mechanic and I was a dustman. Everyone's always shocked at first by that little snippet, that I used to be a dustman, but I know you ain't cos you read it my life story *Stop The Ride I Want To Get Off* (Virgin, £6.99, out now). Oh, I am shameless, aren't I? More plugs than B&Q. Anyway, if you didn't read it, catch up at the back will you?! Because I will be asking questions later.

So, because Ray was a bit sparkly himself and getting a bit of a reputation as a hot potato up at his own depot, they moved him down to ours at Grove Vale. Which wasn't a smart move cos all it did was move that little hot potato from the frying pan and right slap-bang into the fucking fire, mate.

Grove Vale depot was a naughty, naughty place. There was actual *families* of villains working there, whole fucking generations! They were all nice blokes but real facey fellas. It was villains wall-to-wall. There was a security hut full of guns and shotgun shells, for fuck's sake! It was a brilliant place. The Old Bill used to raid it regular and lock the gates so no dustcarts could get out. How many council depots have you heard about being regularly raided by the police?

And *that* was the place where they sent Ray to keep him out of trouble. Oops! Slight mistake there, I think. It was a different world from where he'd been and all the better for it. Ray fitted right in and me and him hit it off straight away. He was the best qualified worker there out of anyone, most O and A levels and diplomas and all that stuff, but the best move Ray ever, *ever* did – and this was the thing that made me realise we were gonna be big pals – was when he tricked Johnny Clay into blowing himself up.

Johnny Clay was this big, twenty-stone, unpopular bully of a man. The reason why people took an instant dislike to him was cos it saved time; you knew you'd end up hating him eventually, anyway.

So, one day when we were all in the yard on a break, Ray filled a party balloon with gas from one of the welding bottles. Then he pinned it to the end of a broom handle so it would be well out of harm's way and started waving it about in front of Johnny Clay's face – y'know, bopping him on the nose with it and banging it on his head. Now you know when someone does something like that, it's really funny when you're watching it, more so cos it's really childish, but it can be fucking irritating really quickly if you're on the receiving end. But you just smile about it cos you'd look like a prick not to.

Anyway, Johnny Clay's stood there, and he's also smoking. Did I mention that? In that position I'd defy anyone, even the most patient saint in the Bible, not to eventually use that cigarette. So we've got a balloon full of inflammable gas and Johnny with a fag in his hand. Need I say more? OK – one word . . . *BANG!* After about five *seconds* Johnny Clay popped the balloon and it blew up right in his face! We all jumped back together, like we were formation dancing or something. It was like the fucking Hindenburg disaster all over. A Hiroshima of the head!

All we could see was this big, fat, blackened face with red blinking eyes and flames and smoke coming off the hair. It was the closest I've ever seen to a human version of the old *Tom and Jerry* joke where a bomb goes off in the cat's face. Oh, it was *fucking* funny, mate. When I think about it now I can still smell it. He was off work six months.

Ray's timing was good too because that was on the day before Christmas. So merry fucking Christmas, Johnny! Ray came across all the innocent afterwards, saying, 'Well I didn't know what was in the balloon, did I? I can't check what gas is in it!' The cheeky, cheeky cunt.

That was *right* up my street, that little stunt, the way Ray dealt with someone he didn't like. So I knew me and Ray would get on like . . . like Johnny Clay's hair on fire, come to think of it. And we got up to loads of little escapades from then on. One time I needed a new kitchen so I went out and found one of these show homes on a new housing estate. It had everything in. I made a few calls and Ray was the unlucky punter that day who was in, or answered the phone, and I asked him if he wouldn't mind helping me un-fit this kitchen. Unfortunately I did neglect to tell him that it was from a Barratt show home, but he figured that out for himself when he pulled up outside. Also, one more thing, at the time I was driving an Austin Champ British army jeep painted in camou-flage and covered in flags – a skull and crossbones and a Union Jack being just two of them.

So, brazenly driving down the motorway in this army jeep with a ripped-out kitchen hanging out the back and the skull and crossbones flying, it was pretty difficult to blend in. I think because it just looked too ridiculously obvious that we'd nicked it, that made everybody think we hadn't. Ray followed on behind at what you might call a 'discreet' distance.

In fact, that's why Barratt brought in that helicopter they used in the adverts – it was to chase after me and Ray when they got wind of us robbing from their show houses.

That was in the proper Del Boy days when my house looked more like a warehouse. It was floor to ceiling with contraband. Boxes of dodgy perfume (Chanel No 4 was one of the clever ones), TVs, videos, bootleg tapes, five thousand pairs of moody Levi's, Barratt house furnishings, stuff like that.

Roy was in visiting me in hospital, one time, after I'd gone in with some battle wounds, and I looked over and saw this bloke being brought up from surgery. They wheeled him in and left him and he was still out. I suddenly recognised him as a geezer I'd been after for ages. For the life of me I can't remember, all these years later now, what it was he'd done, but I do know that I was fucking fuming about it so it must have been bad. Anyway, he's just laid there. I thought, What a touch!

I went over and pulled the curtains round the bed. I think he was having his wisdom teeth out, something like that. Not serious but they used to put you out for it in them days. I let him have it in the nuts with a few right good punches. Pummelled them a treat, like two little speedballs in the gym.

I wasn't there to see it but I *know* that geezer will have woken up holding his nuts in agony. And he only went in for his wisdom teeth. I bet he thought, Oh no, they must have turned the trolley round before they took me down.

One of the geezers on the dust with me was this fella called King John who was also a DJ. And that's about when I got into DJing. Nothing like it is today. You'd just have a box of 50s rock'n'roll and 60s pop music, and some flashing lights. The only scratching you did was when you fucked up putting the needle on.

I got a gig – through Peter and Paul Wilson (whose sister Linda was my first real relationship) – at a place in Croydon called Dr Jim's. I got there and found I was the only white geezer in a club full of black people dancing to reggae. I thought, These don't look like Elvis fans to me! But I was booked so I played. You ain't seen nothing till you've seen a Rasta try and jive, believe me. Completely destroyed the myth of all black people having rhythm, anyway.

The first place I DJ'd in was The Railway Signal pub. The Railway was the place me and my brother and my mates were that New Year's Eve night of the now-infamous Chinese

Waiter Swordfight Incident that got me three years. But even before that it was a fucking mad pub. It was, how can I describe it? . . . 'hostile' would be a good word. Even the women in there were dangerous. The barmaid had a black belt in Death. The first question in the pub quiz was 'What you looking at?'; the tabletop football figures all had their legs snapped off, that kinda place. If there was no one in there but two mates then they'd beat each other up. If you even looked like you *looked* like you deserved a slap, then you'd get one. And if a geezer couldn't think of a reason to beat you up then *that* would annoy him so much he'd beat you up for it!

So what could possibly go wrong one Christmas when they had a fancy dress party there? Apart from a massive fight breaking out between the whole fucking pub. It was funny because a geezer, Mark Tobin (RIP – motorbike crash – don't ask!), that was barred from the place went dressed as the Mummy so you could only see his eyes. He was at the bar giving the thumbs-up to the landlord who really hated him.

Ray went as a soldier, which was funny considering his later experiences in the TA (tell you in a minute).

So, this massive fight kicked off, probably because one geezer looked at another one's girlfriend who just happened to be dressed up as a chicken – a proper 'You looking at my bird?' moment. It was mental cos in the middle of this big, cowboy-type brawl you'd look around and see Frankenstein nutting the Pope, Father Christmas having it with Dracula, the Mummy fighting two cowboys, Marilyn Monroe kicking Hitler in the nuts and the Christmas tree fairy coming second place to the back of a fucking horse.

I went as the Incredible Hulk. Painted all green, barefoot in ripped clothes, and with bits of a black wig cut off and stuck on as eyebrows. I was having a fight with a geezer called Mark Lambert (who was actually a friend) and he was dressed as a nun, so I couldn't help but look like a fucking bully, could I? Not one you can really afford to lose either – Dave Courtney? Yeah, that geezer who got a kicking from Sister Mary . . . that one?

Anyway, because I was barefoot, my feet ended up cut to ribbons on all the smashed glasses. Half an hour later I walked into casualty and they were all there, weren't they! All sat on the bench waiting for treatment – sailors, cowboys, mummys, nuns, and me the Incredible Hulk limping in. We were all still trying to look hard as well, even though we were dressed in the divvy gear. Fucking hard to look menacing when you're a chicken with a bent beak, mate.

Yeah, so Ray had the bright idea of joining the Territorial Army to see how much plastic explosive and detonators he could nick. Don't ask me why, I'm sure it seemed a bright idea at the time. But he spent three fucking years in the TA! Get that. *And* he then got nicked for trying to nick the explosives!

He must've got away with some, though, because he later used it in another one of my favourite stories. You know the Elephant and Castle district in south London? Well, Londoners do, obviously. It's a famous little place and there actually is a statue of an elephant balancing on a castle on top of a building there. Famous landmark of London. And Ray blew it up. Blew the fuck out of it. Why? Well, y'know, it was Wednesday . . . he was *bored* . . . he just happened to have some explosives under the bed. Usual thing.

It made the news big-time because the police and politicians thought it was an IRA warning about a mainland bombing campaign that they were due to start! And I'm sat there at home watching the news thinking, No . . . that's *Ray*! Mental.

Anyway, what I was trying to get around to before you distracted me was about Ray and the Grove Vale depot crew. There were some outlandish characters there. All with properly chequered pasts. One terrific fella called Chrissy Thompson. Top man. In a way it actually made us, being around people like that.

So when I started the Arches and I needed stuff doing cheap or for nothing and I had to get paint, scaffolding and stuff like that for fuck all, I knew where to go. Back to the depot to see Ray and the chaps. I picked up anything that was lying about, basically, and nicked stuff like scaffolding poles to make a gantry for the DJs. We built that and a lighting rig. I poached people everywhere from the depot to do electrical work on the lights and sound system and joinery on the doors. Cos I knew we was gonna have it large and fucking loud so we had to have about five doors to stop the noise. We had mattresses nailed to two doors and then another door behind that, all held together with a massive bolt through the middle screwed up tight. A real insulation sandwich.

I nicked loads of paint and just sprayed the whole of the inside of the arch with this black and red lead colour. It looked like you were walking into Hell.

For the toilets we dug a pit down and went into the mains outside. I just knocked a big fucking hole in the side of this mains pipe with a sledgehammer. Then we put a manhole cover over it, nicked some portable toilets from a building site up the road and put them in there as well, covered in brick cladding. And that was that – all done in a couple of days. I was bang into DIY well before it started becoming trendy!

The Arches was the first all-night, illegal rave in London – very *very* illegal. And we were jam-packed right from the word go. All the other clubs in London shut at about 2 a.m. but mine was still banging at 8 o'clock in the morning! So guess where everyone went? Straight to yours truly's. Loads of other club promoters and DJs came down (we even had celebrity limos outside) and it got to be this proper little legend of a place.

I'd leave the Limelight, where I was working, at two o'clock (Wolfie would be in charge at the Arches till I got there) and shoot straight down to the Arches with about a dozen other doormen in tow. We'd be in the cars ripping our ties off, already buzzing as we were driving down cos we knew what we were gonna walk into. By the time we got there the streets were already jammed with cars parked up and bumped up on all the pavements and people pouring in. I'd generally find Wolfie first to check everything was going OK.

We'd walk in and just stare, you couldn't help but just stop and stare for a bit before you did anything else. Under this great big curved, black and red railway arch roof there was the scaffolding gantry holding the DJ on the decks, massive speakers either side and the lights hanging above; and below that this heaving mass of lunatics just going completely mental, arms in the air, whistles and foghorns blowing, sweat and condensation running down the walls and bringing the red paint with it – so it looked like the walls were bleeding! Steam and joint smoke hung like a fucking fog, people were dancing on speakers and scaffolding – the whole building actually felt like it was jumping out of its foundations. And you just stood in the doorway and went *WOWWWW*! Fuck *ME*!

We had things that you'd never seen before at illegal dos. Because I ran it more organised, y'know it was a proper club to us, not a one-off. So we'd have a girl walking round in a *Playboy* bunny outfit with an ice-cream tray round her neck full of ready-rolled spliffs for a quid each! – 'Get yer joints 'ere!' And big plastic dustbins filled to the top with ice and free apples and ice-pops. Crates of beer and bottles of water, Ribena and Lucozade in ready supply. We'd sell water that was bottled on site, meaning there was an ordinary tap beneath the bar that we used to fill proper spring water bottles. Then, just as you handed it over the bar, the trick was to remove the cap so the punter couldn't tell the seal had already been broken. The heat and the noise were ridiculous. Even the hard-core ravers were blown away.

It was the naughtiest, most underground joint I'd ever seen, and wouldn't really see again until another place of mine called Crazy Mondays at Futures a couple of years later. Like Futures, at the Arches we had a mad mixture of people: from hardcore ravers, professional clubbers, black geezers, white geezers, plenty of women, football hooligan nutters going all smiley, hardnuts softened by Ecstasy and all the dancing doormen that followed me down there.

That was the funniest thing to me, to see dancing doormen. Before rave it wasn't the done thing for a bloke, a man, to dance like that: to lose it a bit and go mental. I know cos I was one of them. And because they were all a little bit unsure of it they came down to my place first, because they knew that's where all the other six-foot-two, bent-nosed clumps went to get out of it so it must be OK. And it fucking was! The classic one that everyone knows is when I was looking round the club for a mate of mine called Norman, and I found him on top of one of the speakers with his black jacket off, white shirt undone, sweat pouring off his shaven head and dancing his bollocks off. And this geezer was a solid sixteen stone hardnut doorman. Fucking wicked, mate.

I had names DJing there before they became superstar DJs like they are now – Danny Rampling, Carl Cox, Fabio & Grooverider, Brandon Block, Norris d'Windross, Carl Brown and loads more playing proper hardcore Acid House music.

We looked after everyone around there. The local residents in the flats around the club all got a knock on their door come Saturday night and a bottle of champagne for putting up with us. I had boys out in the street directing traffic so we didn't block off the market boys the next morning (that happened only once and they were fucking fuming).

The police weren't very happy but we just did *Not*. Give. A. Fuck. This was our place and we ran it how we wanted and everyone wanted us there because they'd never seen anything like it in their lives. The Old Bill were right down our list of priorities on who to please. They did call round to visit now and again, though, bless 'em.

The first time was funny because when they turned up we just creaked open this massive iron door we'd had built and looked at them through the iron bars of this shutter-gate (we kept that padlocked with a big chain). So, we just went, 'Yeah? Can we help you?' Really fucking cheeky and taking the piss. The copper said something like they'd come to close us down and shut the club. Me and Wolfie just looked at each other and then said, 'Erm . . . No, I don't think so. Not tonight,' and slammed the door. I thought, I am *not* getting dragged into it!

There was nothing they could do because they knew it would've taken them till Tuesday just to break in! So they just had to turn round, go back to the nick and say, 'Erm . . . *Sarge*!' They did get their own back, though, in a very big, big way.

Before that happened we did have a few calamities of our own. I'd put down a load of quick-drying cement with red dye in it to level out the cobblestone floor. It was a screed of cement over the surface but the dye had weakened the mixture. So when there was alcohol and water everywhere and everyone jumping up and down dancing it turned the cement into slush. But by the time everyone had nearly left at the end of the night the cement had started to dry again, so I couldn't do a lot about it. Other than turf everyone out in the middle of the night so I could brush all the cement out. Which I wasn't gonna do, obviously.

That also had a knock-on effect on another little hiccup we had. This one, the worst one, was when we found ourselves properly in the shit. This particular night it was pouring down outside, the street was running rivers. The sewers filled up and backed up but because there was this outlet where I'd banged a hole in the mains pipe, all the water came up there. And into the club. The first thing the water reached wasn't the toilets, but this manhole cover I'd put down. That manhole used to be the best place in the club to dance because of the vibrations. Even if you couldn't dance you just stood on it and cos it was metal it would just shake you into being a fucking good mover!

What was actually happening was that all this shitty water was bubbling up from the sewer and squeezing out of the manhole cover. It's all bubbling up and if someone hadn't been stood on it there would've been a big turd fountain. And when raving first started it was not like it is now, it was really, really manic, and everyone got completely off their heads in a way they don't now. And when I say everyone, I mean *everyone*! So people were so fucked that they didn't even really notice all this shit, but they were coming out into the light by the doors absolutely caked up to their knees in it! On top of that the condensation had really started to bring the red paint down off the walls big-time. Shit and red paint.

Wolfie saw all this and came up to tell me. Now I just thought it was the old problem of the floor cement loosening up – which I'd had people moaning about for months and was fed up of – I didn't know when he said 'shit' he actually meant shit. So I said, 'Oh, for fuck's sake, Wolfie, just deal with it, will you? I'm sick of hearing about it . . .' And Wolfie, being just this eighteen-year-old kid who'd moved up from Staines to run my club, and was living in my house, he didn't want to say he couldn't deal with it.

Wolfie didn't really know what to do. So, get this, he just got loads of people to stand on the manhole cover! Which stopped it coming out there but just drove it further along the pipe until it burst out the bogs. So there's a dozen people wobbling away on this manhole cover and, meanwhile, a fountain of shit is firing out the toilets. I pity anyone who was in that toilet at the time, I really do, because they must have got pinned to the fucking ceiling.

We called this emergency plumber but he didn't arrive. Called him again and he said he couldn't find us because it was all dead-ends and warehouses. I said, That's us! Number 13.

So he gets there eventually and he was this fifty-year-old geezer. He walked into the club and just stopped like he'd hit a glass door. You can imagine can't you, what it looked like to this middle-aged bloke? He just couldn't get his head round this place. He was like, What the fuck's going on here? To him it was all the telly news and newspaper headline horror stories about raving all come true in front of his eyes. And big Norman dancing on the speaker and smiling at him didn't exactly put him at ease!

I told him that if we switched off the music and put up the lights to allow him to work then all these people would fuck off home, so we couldn't do that. I put a little scrum of people around the plumber and hustled him through the crowds to the bogs. When we got in there was shit absolutely every-where, I mean everywhere. Oh, and *the SMELL! Fuck*ing hell. It was like the Devil had shit out hundreds of years of baby shit and diarrhoea into one small room – that's the closest I can get to it. Words don't even exist, really, to describe it. It made your brain *stutter*.

And this guy being a plumber, and it being his job, he got down on his knees, rolled his sleeve up and put his hand right on in! He's got his arm in up to here, trying to find a blockage. I told someone to put an amyl in the smoke machine. What happened whenever we did that was this – when you put a bottle of amyl nitrate in the smoke machine it just heated it up to a cloud and blew it out. You could direct it and give someone a massive blast of amyl! Their little legs would go ten-to-the-dozen like a clockwork toy. It was really funny.

I said to direct it into the bogs to try and block some of the smell, but what they did was point it down and blast the fucking plumber! A direct hit of concentrated 'poppers' on the old geezer. He just sort of ... stiffened, held it for a few seconds, twitched, kicked his feet quickly, and then fucking fainted. He's laid out, across the floor. There was already a wall of people stood round him with their backs to him so as to block what he was doing from view, and they just thought the geezer was fiddling with the pipes.

I came back in after a while and went, 'What's up with our plumber?' We got him up and slapped him round and he came around in a right panic, not surprisingly. He just wanted to run out.

Anyway, we eventually got something set up, some tubes knocked together as a flow pipe. And the Great Raving Turd Disaster was narrowly averted. Ha-*haa*!

I was supposed to meet Ray the next morning and when I didn't turn up he came round the Arches to see what had happened and found us all shovelling shit out. 'Good night, then, was it?' he said. Cheeky cunt.

Another time me and the chaps had just arrived from the other club we worked at and everyone was already mad at it in the Arches. So I'm stood there admiring the madness and this little seventeen-year-old kid with eyes big as dinner plates comes up to me. 'You look like a drug dealer,' he said (cheeky cunt), and then asked me if I had any.

Now, what I did happen to have on me was a bag of those liquorice torpedos, so I gave him a mauve one. He asked what it was. I said, 'it's a Californian Purple.' He said, 'Will you do it for a tenner?' I went, 'Oh go on then, it's the last one.' I couldn't believe I was selling a liquorice torpedo for a tenner. Probably only cost one tenth of a penny.

I watched him go back to the crowd and his mates. And the little scene that followed was all silent, like mime: he showed this 'Californian Purple' to his mate, his mate looked puzzled, the little geezer pointed over to us, his mate looked at us, and then turned back and obviously said 'But it's a liquorice comfort, you dickhead!' The little guy laughed, then went serious, then bit it in two and tasted the aniseed. Then his face just crumbled. Proper collapsed. It was fucking funny watching it, it really was.

Anyway, I went up to him and gave him his tenner back just for giving us such a good laugh. And I advised him not to take any Fruit Pastilles because there were rumoured to be some dodgy ones about.

We were going great guns at the Arches for the best part of a year but what really fucked it up was when we began advertising. None of this 'secret phonecalls and meet me in the car park' type stuff either. We did blatant, fuck-off, 'Here we are, come and get us!' style advertising. We didn't even need to, really, but I just liked the idea that it gave me an excuse to print loads of flyers and go public with it. Take me to my people!

I think what happened was that, because we'd been doing it so long and getting away with it, we sort of forgot it was all illegal! So we started with the flyers, half thinking we'd get away with it. Up until then I think the police had tolerated us to a certain extent, but when the flyers fluttered down from the helicopter you could say we were taking the piss. Which, of course, we were. That is our *job*, officer!

Another thing that fucked us was that fact that I didn't have any police officers on the payroll. That would always have been handy.

So they started putting undercover Old Bill in the club. Which we spotted quite easily, as it happens. They were always the frightened-looking ones in brown leather jackets and regulation haircuts, talking into their top pockets.

Wolfie used to have some proper fun with the undercover Old Bill. One time a couple of them knocked on the door and Wolfie went to see. They put it to him that for a little 'drink', as they called it – or 'backhander' as anyone else would call it – they'd see to it that the club didn't get in any trouble. Wolfie, seeing real wind-up possibilities here, asks them how many 'drinks' they usually get. The copper, by now thinking in terms of wads of cash, said, 'Usually about two.'

Wolfie went, 'Right. OK. I'll be right back.' He disappears inside and the Old Bill are left there rubbing their hands at the thought of this new little earner. But only until Wolfie reappears, hands them two cans of lager and says, 'There you go, boys. See you again next week!' And then he slammed the door on them.

Now that story's worth the price of admission alone, ain't it? I do wish we'd had CCTV cameras outside to catch that one. Fucking priceless.

Wolfie would also go around handing out Scholl insoles to the undercover police in the club. When they looked at him he'd say he'd heard they were a bit flat-footed.

This is when I had my dealings with Carter Street police station. Carter Street was notorious for being a hard and very, very naughty nick. That's where the Special Patrol Group were based. The SPG were like the SAS of the police, a renowned bunch of hardnuts. Their idea 'rights for the accused' meant hitting you with the hand opposite the left.

The SPG were the mob that arrested me after the Chinese waiter thing. They came to the door, all plain clothes, and didn't even say who they were. First thing I got when I opened the door was a smack in the mouth. *Then* the introduction. In fact, a smack in the mouth was the SPG's introduction.

Carter Street really was a naughty place, though. They'd fit you up, beat you up, verbal you up; anything and everything 'you up'. All the prison and legal reformers have stopped us from getting a good hiding now, but in those days you'd get a good hiding even before you got in the nick. Also, before they tape recorded everything like they do now, two coppers would just verbal you up. Then kick fuck out of you! Ahh, the old days . . .

And Carter Street was the nick local to the Arches. Lucky, eh?

It was a combination of things that led to the end of the Arches. Raving had got to the point where it was gripping the nation, or at least the young people, and scaring their parents and the authorities at the same time: so there was a general move to clamp down on all clubs. The specific bit that related to my club was the fact that we were advertising and we were also permanent, remember. We weren't doing one of them hit-and-run rave nights where you met in a motorway service station. Taking the piss out of the police didn't really endear us either. And the family of the plumber started complaining that he'd never been the same since that day.

So the Old Bill sent a little welcoming committee to us late Saturday night, early Sunday morning one August. Well, when I say 'little': there was a 'little' army of 150 police, with some fuckers called No 3 Area Territorial Support Group in flameproof overalls, bulletproof body armour and steel helmets with radio microphones, carrying an angle grinder, a hydraulic ram, sledgehammers and a thermic fucking lance! They'd obviously heard about our extra-thick matresses behind the door and the high-tog duvet we used as insulation. Silly cunts.

They burst in in all their fancy dress at about two in the morning like a bunch of SAS rejects looking for glory and a chocolate medal.

Two days later the *Independent* ran a full-page article about the raid with the headline THE PARTY'S OVER AT AN ACID HOUSE UNDER THE ARCHES – POLICE RAID IN SOUTH LONDON. It also used photographs of the police preparing for the raid before it happened, having a briefing, and pictures of the raid itself. What does that tell you? Obviously that they'd invited the press there to get them on camera so they could later use the press for their own propaganda. As they often do, but ordinary Joe Public don't even think it goes on. 'Invited media' they call it. They even had news cameras there – we were on TV A.M. for fuck's sake! What's that about?!

What that's about is reassuring the masses of England who don't really know what the fuck is going on, and because they don't know, they're scared – what frightens you is the unknown. So this little article and film shows our brave police charging into a rave and arresting everyone. Bound to look bad on film, ain't it? Never mind that it was mostly young kids bouncing around having a blindin' time. Even the naughty geezers in there, who were the only ones capable of having a row, were too busy just having a good tme.

Even the newpaper article said, 'The most offensive weapons sighted are packets of Rizla cigarette papers, most of them quickly dropped to the floor when the police burst in.'

So, the Old Bill charged on in shouting, pushing everyone around, slapping on these plastic one-use handcuffs on people left, right and centre. At the first sign of the raid everyone in the club just dropped what they had, if they had anything on them. The few who were dealers even threw their money away. Behind the bar wads and rolls of money lay on the floor!

The floor was covered with stuff that people had dropped but there was no way, absolutely no fucking way of knowing what belonged to who. But the coppers just went round picking something off the floor and then collaring the nearest likely-looking person they could see and saying, 'That's yours – I saw you drop it.' Which was a fucking lie. But they had to get some collars to show off for the cameras outside and make it all look worth while. Even the paper admitted it – '. . . quickly dropped to the floor when police burst in,' it said.

The *Independent* also said, 'They go straight for the known dealers.' Sorry, but when there's over a hundred and fifty people crammed in there (not one hundred like it said), how would you straight-off *know* who was who; and by the time you did know they'd have got rid of their stuff anyway. Which is when the coppers started picking stuff up off the floor and pretending they saw who dropped it. When there's no way they could have done so.

You notice I ain't even attempting to say that there was nothing in there and that people weren't on anything. Obviously there was. Course there was – it was a fucking rave. No drink, no pub. No drugs, no club. Same difference. I weren't involved in it but you knew it went on.

We did have a sign up saying ANYONE FOUND BUYING OR SELLING DRUGS WILL BE REMOVED FROM THE PREMISES. OK, the sign *was* in Chinese but at least we had one. And our Oriental ravers were very well behaved. Another sign said, IF YOU WANT THE CLUB TO SURVIVE PLEASE KEEP IT QUIET ON LEAVING! That one was for the undercover police.

The newspaper thing also describes a 'casually dressed young officer' bagging up the gear they found: some ecstasy tablets, LSD tabs, some cannabis resin and some weed. Big fucking deal. They quote the young copper saying, 'Not a bad haul. A bit of everything, about what you'd expect at a place like this.'

Then the best bit, the bit that kills me – he's quoted as saying, 'Don't know what the appeal is. I wouldn't come here on a Sunday night, would you?' Which is *exactly* why everyone else wanted to go to 'a place like that', you silly little cunt, because they knew it would be full of other happy, bouncy little ravers and *not* uptight, straight-arsed divs like you. For fuck's sake.

Funnily enough, about the only bit they did get right was when they said '. . . and the toilets were a disgrace!' Bang on with that one!

Talking about happy little ravers. Wolfie, for instance, had just popped two Es minutes before the raid happened. They hadn't come up yet, though, and it weren't until he was nicked and taken down at the station that the rush started – WHOOF! Big blood rush and tingles. Get *that*! He's sat there in the nick just off his tits! Wolfie turned to one of the coppers there, a high-ranking officer it was as well. 'Bit hot in here, innit, Constable?' he said, deliberately getting his rank wrong. The inspector said, 'Not half as hot as your Arches, son!'

One of the photos in the newspaper article showed an Old Bill grabbing Wolfie and a girl. Underneath the picture it said,

'Officers accost some of the 100 teenagers at the party.' Now, I was looking at that recently and I always thought 'accost' meant to attack someone, didn't you? So I looked it up in my dictionary (cos I am a writer now) and it actually just means 'to speak first' to someone, or the other meaning is, 'to solicit as a prostitute'! Fancy that. So how do we know which they were doing? In other words, 'Officers soliciting as prostitutes'. Funny that, cos I've never even called the police 'slags'.

They arrested twenty-six. Wolfie was one of them. Because I was still on my way down from the other club I got there late enough to miss the worst of it. Wolfie was roped in and said to be one of my 'lieutenants', as they called him. He stuck to his story about being the organiser.

If the original raid had been a farce then the trial was even worse. More of a pantomime, really, but with more horses' arses than usual. The judge, for instance, Hugh Morgan he was called. Or Huge Organ as our lot called him. Not that we thought he was a dickhead, or anything like that. Not at all, your honour. The prosecutor was someone we thought equally high of and he was called Mr Bates, so he became Master Bates, obviously. We were nothing if not predictably childish!

The trial lasted six weeks, believe it or not. Another opportunity for the press to go to town on the old 'Evil Acid House Music' riff they were so fond of. I wasn't allowed to be named so they just referred to me as 'Mr X', which casts a bit of a shadow on anyone they link with you, doesn't it? I ask you, 'Mr X'! I sounded like a fucking baddie in a Bond film. So that meant Wolfie was then had down as 'Mr X's trusted lieutenant', which don't sound too good does it? They couldn't call you something innocent sounding like 'Mr Y' could they? Well, at least they didn't call me Mr E, I suppose.

The trial was a joke, though. One of the jurors dropped out through supposed intimidation so they said we could carry on with eleven jurors or opt for a retrial with police-protected jurors. The police preferred the idea of the protected jurors because that always makes the defendants look worse. Then the two undercover policewomen who'd been in the Arches both gave different evidence. The first one said the defendants had been picked out in the cells, which sort of went in our favour because it ain't really a fair way of IDing someone is it

– pointing at them in a cell? The second copper changed stories and said the defendants had been ID'd at the time of arrest and that the first copper was mistaken! Can you believe that. *And* the cheeky cunts got away with it.

What with all that and the biased press coverage we knew the jury were gonna come back with guilties. We'd all been telling Wolfie not to worry because he'd only get a 'suspended' and a fine, or a few months at most. It's always worrying, to some degree, for the person who gets nicked, but you can usually predict how it's gonna go. You can usually guess what's going to be handed down, prison wise.

So we turned up at court the next morning with £1,800 to cover the fine and the judge gave Wolfie five years. Yeah, that ain't a misprint – *five* fucking years. For holding a party. It's basically no more than that is it, really? Holding a big fucking party. And Mr Hugh Morgan – who if there is such a thing as justice shouldn't have had a decent night's sleep since then – gave this nineteen-year-old kid, Wolfie, five years in prison. Morgan also handed down two-year, three-year and four-year terms to the other six who were found guilty.

We were just . . . absolutely gobsmacked, mate. People were getting less, in them days, for tying people up and raping them. Seriously, they were. Or someone would stab someone and cop a plea for manslaughter and get less. This was a big party we were talking about. No one got hurt, no one got raped, no one disappeared and turned up in the white slave trade, no one died, nothing even got nicked. Worse thing that happened was one night when loads of people went home with shit round their trousers.

But it weren't about what the party was and what the fitting punishment for that would be. It was about what would satisfy and help calm down the fears of conservative Britain. Because they were fucking scared by the new reports on raving and Acid House and Ecstasy and all the other things they didn't have a prayer of understanding.

The police had invested so much in the raid, not just money but all the publicity, that I guess the court had to come down hard to justify it all. And the police justify the harshness of their actions and the sentencing by using the media to whip up hysteria and prime the public for what they're going to do later. You might not want to believe that but it's true. And if you're a straight punter reading this then you've got to admit that I'm better placed to know whether or not this goes on. They were all out to set an example and they did. They didn't give a fuck whether it was unjust or not on Wolfie cos they just wanted to throw him to the pack.

The police knew it was my place but because they could only nick Wolfie they went to town on the old 'trusted lieutenant of a gangster' who must be treated accordingly. But Wolfie never said anything and got the bird, and did it. And that broke my heart, that did. It really did – broke my heart. Everyone on that scene just loved old Wolfie to bits.

They actually made him do four years nine months of that five-year sentence. Which is almost unheard of for something like that. To get no parole, or virtually no time off, no nothing. Over four years in prison for putting on a party. That's a lot, mate, a lot.

Strange thing was that I was due in court the very next day after Wolfie was sentenced to hear the verdict on a charge against me. This was the one where me and the boys down at Queen's saw off some cocaine dealers from the club. They got hurt, mostly because we beat the fuck out of them, and reported me to the Old Bill. (You know the full story from *Stop The Ride* . . .) Also, at this time the BBC were filming me for the *Bermondsey Boy* documentary and they filmed me getting dressed to go to court in the morning. I say in the film that my mate Wolfie got bird yesterday and I was gutted.

Ironically, right up until we got to trial for my thing I'd said that I'd done it. Then when we got there and I was up in front of the jury I explained why, saying I was responsible for safety in the club. So, then, that day, the day after Wolfie went down, I went to court and got a 'not guilty'. It was a funny fucking week that week.

You'll be happy to know, I'm sure, that Wolfie came out a better, stronger person than he went in. Like all smart geezers do who get time, he properly learned from it. And we're still great pals to this day. My two girls, Chelsea and Levi, were born while Wolfie was in prison, which wouldn't have happened if I'd got done for it and got the bird. So I owe him my two girls. How much more can you say than that?

The Arches was a big hit, though. Not just in money terms but the fact that it became the kind of place it did. It was right on top at the time when raving was just about to go really massive. I made loads of mates and connections on the club scene and ran lots more club nights afterwards.

But the Arches – that place opened a few doors in a few minds, that place did. And a few holes in a few sewer pipes as well.

4 Rave On

I put on a rave in a sewer. How *not* legal is that!

You see, before raving was legal and was still very much frowned upon, it was still held in all the illegal places. Because RAVING – in capital letters, like the newspapers printed it – was the new scare story.

Like rock'n'roll was in the 50s when Elvis first swivelled his hips and everyone went, 'Fucking hell! Swivelled his hips he did! The country will collapse!' And they all ran to bomb shelters. Then, same in the 60s with rock and protest songs and Jimi Hendrix playing guitar with his knob while smoking a joint, and then all that mad psychedelic stuff. And in the 70s everyone got a bee up their arse over punk rock.

Raving? Same story. Loud music plus new drugs plus kids loving it plus parents hating it equals everyone in danger, the country in peril, and the whole world blows up. That kinda thing. Raving was like rock, psychedelia and punk all rolled up into one big fuck-off party. No wonder it blew every straight parent's slippers off.

And the authorities talked about it in the same way as they've always condemned any movement they didn't understand. Practically saying it was Devil's Music, leading people astray, full of sexual innuendos – the same old crap they'd been saying about rock'n'roll 30 fucking years ago! Do me a favour.

You just wanted to say, '*Yesss!* The sex and drugs and music are exactly why we're interested in it, you silly cunts!' And music is sex, ain't it? Good music is sexy.

This was during the proper Summer Of Love time, as well. Smiley, happy acid people getting right on it.

So, anyway, I had a mate who was groundsman for a football pitch belonging to a college. Down in Slough. Around the edge of the pitch was a manhole and you went down the manhole into the sewer. I decided to put on a rave down there.

What is with me and manhole covers and raves, anyway?! Because this weren't long after the Great Manhole Cover Disaster at the Arches. Maybe I just liked to find an appropriate place for people to get shitfaced.

The sewer was disused (you'll be glad to hear) and the inside of a sewer is semi-circular, the floor is flat, and then there's a step that goes around the floor like the walkway at a swimming baths. So we just breeze-blocked up either end of it and had electrical cables running through. And we had a fucking rave in there! Nothing if not enterprising, eh?

We sprayed all of the inside with black paint to cover all the old dried shit on the walls cos no one – surprise, surprise – wanted to pick it off, and then we shot these paint balls every which way and splattered colours everywhere. The paints came from any mate I had who worked at Do-It-All or a car bodyshop. So it was the only rave venue splattered with 'peach', 'apple blossom' and 'honeysuckle', and also Escort red and Jaguar silver. Which was good cos it covered up the Arse brown.

'Oh, how artistic, Dave!', I hear you saying. Well, it fucking was actually, as it happens. At least not bad for a sewer.

When it was actually happening, and the rave was in full swing, the music sounded the bollocks because the acoustics were amazing. The sound just bounced everywhere. I think we actually invented Dolby Surround Sound! Yeah, the bouncing sound was the thing that done your head in most.

What we did when everyone turned up was have them wait in this sports/cricket-type pavilion on the grounds because if you could've seen a big crowd from the road it would have looked suspicious. Then we'd bring them over from the pavilion in batches of ten. It was really funny seeing all these ravers crammed in a sports pavilion and being led across to the manhole. It always reminded me of the scene from that film *The Great Escape* where all the British prisioners are lining up to escape from the German prison camp (and you should've seen me try and jump the perimeter fence on a motorbike).

There was only one way in and out and that was down this metal ladder underneath the manhole cover. What we had to do was keep wrapping the steps with masking tape because it had gone all rusty and sharp over the years. And that was all before you even fucking got in there – meet in the pavilion, run head down to the hole, jump down the hole and try not to cut your hands off. It must've been easier getting out of fucking Colditz than into our rave.

When you were down in there it was really worth it cos if you go through all that to get somewhere you are gonna make sure you have a fucking good time, ain't you? There must've been nearly two hundred people down there, though you could have fitted more in. And with the tunes bouncing round off the walls and attacking you from every side you didn't even need to be fucked on acid to enter another dimension. You'd see people looking around freaking out on the paint splats, thinking, 'That's the colour of my mum's front room', or 'I used to have an Escort XR3i that colour!'

Upstairs, up topside, the grass was bouncing. You could see it vibrating to the bass. It was fucking mad. You'd never seen so many musically-in-tune worms as on that football pitch. The snails didn't slither, they fucking boogied, mate. Next day after the event the whole of bleedin' Slough knew about it.

There's good and bad bits to putting on illegal raves. There were no flyers so it was all done by word of mouth. It went on but it weren't advertised so you had to be really careful who you invited because they might ruin the whole party. Talk about *The Great Escape*! – this was at the time when it was like a military fucking operation just to get to the rave. You'd have to ring a number and then they'd give you another number or a place to meet in some service station somewhere. Then you'd get there and have to follow someone on. But that was all part of the excitement for people. That they were doing something illegal.

Another mental one was called the Clink. It was in an old prison in Clink Street, just south of the river, near London Bridge. You could hire it out for a rave, but it is actually a crime museum in the day. They have waxwork models of Crippen, stuff like that. Each cell had a different theme. A poor man's Madame Tussaud's for crime.

They used to bung all the models in one cell, lock it up and then put painted backdrops up. That's why backdrops were invented. People think it was just to make the place look pretty but it was because most of the places weren't built for raves so you had to put up removable decoration. Then things moved on and promoters started using things like parachute silk to cover the ceiling. Things to make it different from a normal nightclub.

The Clink was wicked, though. Very druggy and very housey place, full of proper hardcore havin'-it-larger's in there. And it was good cos it had all these individual cells so it was like having loads of little VIP lounges. In a club you normally establish your own little corner anyway, don't you? Somewhere where people know they can usually find you if you get lost. So everyone in the Clink had over twenty individual rooms. Wicked. Bit odd for me, though, or anyone that had actually been banged-up to find yourself raving and smoking a joint inside a prison. Actually, come to think of it, not much change there then . . .

There used to be a geezer outside in a burger van selling hot dogs and burgers for £20. Now all you out-of-towners are thinking, 'I know London's dearer than the rest of the country but that's just fucking ridiculous!' Well, to tell you the truth, there was an E out at the time called a Burger. Yeah, you're ahead of me now, ain't you? So you'd go up to this converted ice-cream van that played fucking Popeye's theme tune and ask for a burger. The geezer would ask you if you wanted a cheap one or an expensive one. Then you'd give him your twenty quid and he'd give you a plastic burger box with a bun inside, and when you opened the bun there was your special filling – a little E called a Burger.

On a good night that little van turned over more than Piccadilly Burger King during rush-hour. Wicked little idea, though, ain't it? I thought so.

Over the road from the Clink was Shoom, which was another favourite of ours. Shoom weren't quite like the Clink cos the Shoom people had already been out in Ibiza and brought some of that back. Yeah, you walked into Shoom and the music hit you right in the Balearics.

I used to go to Shoom and the Clink with Darlington Dave, Norman, Steve, Funny Glen, Joe, loads of them. Oh, fuck me, yeah . . . Darlington *Dave*! Let me tell you this. Darlington Dave was the funniest geezer, an absolute fucking diamond.

He worked as a doorman and did some stripping as well. Not at the same time, thank fuck. He was a nice-enough kid but not the sharpest chisel in the toolbox, know what I mean? Which is why we also called him Divvy Dave. And he'd call himself that as well.

He'd ring me up and go 'El*lo*! It's me, Divvy Dave!' Sometimes in the middle of a coversation I'd have to stop it to take another call, or whatever, and I'd tell him to ring me back in two minutes. The phone would go, I'd pick it up and he'd say, 'El*lo*! It's me, Divvy Dave!' I'd say, 'I KNOW it's you Dave, I just told you to call back!' I knew it was him from his voice, immediately. I just didn't know anyone else who sounded like him!

He was fucking funny, though. One time back at Stormin' Norman's place we chopped out a line of Shake'n'Vac carpet cleaner and told him it was coke. He bent down and snorted one of these two lines right up. We started laughing and he thought it was cos he hadn't done both lines in one go.

'Aye, it's all right for you t'laugh,' he said, 'but I'm not a fuckin' junkie like some a you guys!' Then he bent down and did the other line! Half a packet of carpet powder straight up the hooter. He started fucking going red and his nose was running like Niagara. Even his eyeballs were sweating. Then he came out with an all-time classic. He smacked his lips as if he was tasting the stuff, and he said, 'Aye, lads. Yer can always tell good coke cos it tastes right minty at t'throat, like!'

I remember he sat down and started watching TV news about the Gulf War, and then he said, 'I'm getting a right rush coming on, lads!' Well, we were just all bent double laughing. Talk about 'do the Shake'n'Vac and put the freshness back'.

Which reminds me of when I was in Limelights, and this was at the height of the coke-snorting 80s, and as a joke I chopped out a line of Vim in one of the toilet cubicles. I came out and started washing my hands, waiting for someone to go in. This geezer did, snorted it and then came out all red-eyed and runny-nosed. I just said to him, 'You greedy cunt . . .'

But he was a breath of fresh air, was old Dave, because he was so . . . how can I put this? Erm . . . 'divvy'. No other word for it. But we all loved him to bits cos he was such good value for money.

The only time he weren't good value was when something he did cost me a packet. It was when I was doing car repossessions for Steve and Ricky. This one car that we'd pulled in was a big black Vauxhall Carlton Royale saloon, top spec, nearly new and worth over twenty grand. Divvy Dave's dad had died the week before and he asked if he could borrow it for the funeral. So I lent it to him.

A few days later he was at home having a row with his missus, and he was holding a kitchen knife at the time. He stabbed it into the table and cos his hand was wet it slipped down the handle and then slid right down the blade. His fingers were now hanging off and blood was squirting everywhere.

I visited him in the hospital. He was OK but his hand was fucked. I asked about the Carlton cos I'd been getting a bit worried about him getting it back in one piece. He gave me the keys and said it was down in the hospital car park. In the car park I saw this really battered motor and felt sorry for whichever poor cunt it belonged to. I went round the car park three times looking for the Carlton before I realised I was the poor cunt. Cos that battered motor was the fucking Carlton.

The interior was completely splattered with blood as well: on the doors, the roof, the dash, the seats, even in the ashtray. It was, literally, a bleeding mess; it looked like an abattoir on wheels; I wouldn't have pissed on it if it was on fire. Turned out that because Dave had half his fingers in his top pocket his bird had driven him to hospital. But Divvy Dave's bird couldn't drive and she'd hit about ten cars. The car wasn't even mine, of course, it was a repo.

When he got out of hospital, I called him about the car cos it cost me an absolute fucking fortune to put straight. He said, 'Aye, Dave, sorry 'bout that, mate. Tell you what, fuck my bird and just knock the money off.' Only Divvy Dave would've said that. And only me, Dodgy Dave, would've agreed it was a good idea.

So that bird of his fucked up the car but she helped unfuck-up a really dodgy situation a few years ago.

I took over doing the security on this really rough pub. It was a real war zone. Fucking hostile it was. Anyway, my boys on the door got done over by the punters there. I kept sending bigger squads down there but the same thing happened. I knew I had to sort it once and for all and organised for about 30 of us to go down there.

On the evening of it we rounded everyone up and then went to pick up old Darlington Dave. He only came out the house with his bird Tracey in tow, didn't he? I said, 'Dave, we're going for a row,' mate. He said, 'Saturday's always been my Tracey's day, Dave, you know that. She'll have to come.' Fuck me. So along she came. And she was a *Sunday Sport* and Page 3 girl so she didn't actually look ready for a ruck (no . . . *ruck*).

When we got there it was crammed with this crowd who'd been attacking my doormen. They looked ready to kick off. We ended up stood by the bar, backs to the walls, waiting to see what happened. No one dared move. We were pissing in bottles cos no one wanted to go to the bogs and risk getting a kicking. Things were getting pretty fucking tense and I thought any minute it was gonna explode.

Then suddenly we heard this weird noise, turned around and Dave was on the karaoke machine singing to Tracey! Slap-bang in the middle of all these hardnuts. He was singing 'Hopelessly Devoted To You' from *Grease*, and giving it the full hand-on-heart treatment: ''Opeless-lee deeevoated to youuuu . . .!'

I could not fucking believe it. Neither could the other mob. It actually broke the ice to see this nutter down on one knee singing. And because of that no fighting broke out. The savage beasts were tamed by Divvy Dave. Wicked.

After the Arches was closed down by the Old Bill I started doing open-air raves. I was bang into the old rave promoter thing now. And this was just before that idea of open-air things had really took off during the Summer of Love time. With me, though, it was out of necessity rather than some 'peace-love' vibe.

I didn't have a new venue yet so I bought a massive removal van with a diesel generator and drove in on to fields or grasslands. Tooting Common was one. Peckham Rye was another. And that is common land so you can use it for what you want really. The law was actually on my side for that one! Touch.

I'd open up the back of the lorry, set up the DJs decks and put these dirty big speakers outside. We'd get eight, nine hundred people up there really going for it. Speakers booming it all out. And cos I didn't charge no one the law had a job stopping me doing it. It just started attracting loads of gay blokes, which is something I hadn't counted on. But then it *was* the Common, the well known shag-spot for gay geezers doing some fresh air cruising, so I guess it made sense. They all came out of the bushes through the morning mist. It was like some gay zombie movie – *Dawn of The Living Fag*.

I weren't too gay-friendly back then, as it happens, cos in those early days I didn't know any better. I hold my hands up to that one. But I do know better now. My actual feelings along that pathway are very liberal now. And everybody knows, or should do, that the gay club scene often gets the new music first and helped bring on the rave scene. After being involved in the club scene in London for so long now you learn to live with and accept that community. And I've got gay friends, some who've come out and some who've not. So I got rid of my ignorance on that one.

Then again, a lot of them aren't just little campy people cos some of them are into the old bodybuilding lark. In fact, I've had a few geezers work for me – a couple still do – who are gay. But, believe me, they are very very handy in a row and could give me, you and anyone you know a fucking good hiding. Straight up. I can have a fucking good row but even trying my hardest I'd get a battering from these blokes. Just because a geezer takes it up the bottle don't mean he hasn't got any bottle. You certainly wouldn't call them 'puffs', put it that way.

I actually put a rave on in Sidcup (I thought I deserved a medal for that alone), and the only entrance and exit to the place was up and down this alley. So I got my mate Brendan to get a JCB and he dug a fucking great big dirty six-foot deep hole. Seven-foot wide. That was it. The only way in and out. And the only way the police could've got in would have been to fill it in. As we poured boiling oil on them! I only just stopped short of filling that mini-moat with water and crocodiles and constructing a drawbridge. Well, you can go too far (I've been there many times, and passed it).

Then I moved on and took on a place called the Fitness Centre, a gym on Southwark Park Road that, we turned into a club. The owner was Jim and he used to move all the apparatus away and put up backdrops. Then we'd have it as a club till six in the morning.

This is when my debt collecting got massive as well so I had money. I had untold money at that time. So the gay chatline really did pay off! No, it was the *Bermondsey Boy* documentary about me on the BBC that had kick-started my debt collecting in a big way. So big thanks to the Beeb. I almost feel guilty for never having bought a TV licence. Almost.

Going back to filming the *Bermondsey Boy* documentary: at that time I got charged with something that it looked like I'd get sent down for. Or so everyone thought. So the night before the jury decision the film makers took us out to this Chinese restaurant called Gracelands. They only had a fucking Chinese Elvis impersonator there, didn't they? Wicked. I don't even know any Chinese people who can *say* Elvis Presley, let alone sing like him.

There was me and over 30 other geezers in there that night, sat around all these tables pushed together. It was a right invasion. I was in the black trilby that I always wore at that time. I was proper suave and suffocated. This was supposedly the farewell party before I got sent down. The film makers encouraged us to behave really badly but, to be honest, we didn't need that much fucking encouragement.

My missus stood it for about ten minutes then she just stood up and said, 'I am NOT sitting here watching this!' and stormed off. As a mark of respect we quietened down for about ten, fifteen seconds and then got proper trolleyed! We got completely lagged and started acting up. We mugged the Chinese Elvis and nicked his mic; Stormin' Norman jumped into the restaurant window, pulled out this massive plastic lobster and stuck it down his pants, then staggered about screaming that he had crabs.

Funny Glen did the best one, though. By the window was this really huge fishtank. It was like a big glass coffin with all these exotic fish darting about inside. Glen stood up on a chair and, fully clothed, dived right into this tank. He just fitted. You could hear him under the water talking all bubbly, saying

'Here kitty, kitty!' to the fish. He swallowed a couple by accident trying to get back out.

The staff were going completely nuts but what can you do when nearly 40 big geezers are going rampant with your plastic lobsters and molesting your fish? You can do not an awful fucking lot, as it happens. Which made a change cos the only time I'd been jailed up until now was for the Chinese waiter stabbing thing a few years earlier.

Anyway, when Stormin' Norman started taking bites out of the wine glasses and crunching the bits in his mouth, that sort of went out as a warning sign to any cunt in the kitchen who had thoughts of running out with a machete. Again.

We were just messing about anyway. Nothing too serious. The lobster broke a claw and a few of the fish had to go into therapy but apart from that it was a good night.

The next morning we went to Crystal Palace park to relax before I went off to court. And there in the park a really weird thing happened. First off it was really busy cos there was a Capital Radio roadshow there, so it was packed. Not a spare foot. People picknicking everywhere.

Then this thing appeared. I can only describe it as a mini hurricane. That's what it was like – a tiny whirlwind. I bet they happen all the time and we don't see them. But because there was just so much litter and fag ends and crap about, all that shit got sucked up into this little whirlwind and made it visible. It was dark grey with dog ends and you could see it flitting about causing havoc.

It was bad enough that people were holding their kids to themselves until it passed. Funny Glen knew it wasn't strong enough to lift him so he just walked straight in front of it, proper playing the little park warrior! He was shouting 'Come on then! Try and wind me!' This thing got to him and he almost disappeared in the litter and crap and got smacked full-on in the face by this nappy! Fucking difficult to keep your 'warrior' dignity wearing a shitty Pamper for a hat.

After that Glen always referred to it as Hurricane Litterbin.

All sorts of other things had helped get me some infamy, or even fame by this time: the Chinese waiters' swordfight story; getting acquitted of shooting that hitman that was gonna shoot me; acting in the Paradise Club with Leslie Grantham; then getting on the front page of the *Sun* after that massive fight when I had my nose bitten off (won the row though). That kinda thing. All those stories in *Stop the Ride I want To Get Off* (Virgin, all good bookshops) – sorry, just can't fucking help myself.

And my raves got known and also notorious for being the naughtiest looking places. Because when I had the security companies and hundreds of blokes working for me, most of them would come to my raves. Maybe it put off some ordinary punters to see these guys, but even though they looked like they'd rip off your arms and legs and bang you on the head with the soggy end, they were all too busy dancing.

So because there was always a lot of doormen in there having a good time it became the place for other doormen to go and have a jump around, whereas they couldn't do it in front of other punters because they're supposed to be the law and order. Doormen would say, 'Let's go down Courtney's place, they're all down there.'

I'd also gone out raving at Labyrinth on Dalston Lane, which is where the Rat Pack and Kenny DJ'd, and Dungeons on Lee Bridge High Road where Devious D and Adrian Age played. The Dungeon was a Saturday night/Sunday morning rave and the only one at that time that went on till ten in the morning. There'd be people dancing on cars in the street!

In the Fitness Centre rave we had a right mixed bag there, mate, let me tell you, and all the better for it.

It used to be the hottest place. It was this windowless basement space made for about 30 geezers to work out in; not two hundred people to get off their tits. Fuck me, though, when it got going it just got so hot. As you walked down into it, halfway down the stairs you started taking really big breaths in case you couldn't breathe when you got to the bottom! You'd see people going redder as they came down the stairs thinking, Is this *really* a good idea?

It was like an oven. Plastic cups went all soft and bent out of shape. I paid five hundred quid to have these backdrops made but the heat just melted the paint and made it run. As you walked into the place your fag wilted in your mouth, just bent over all soggy. You had to crumble Viagra pills in your spliff just to keep it straight! No, the truth of it was that you couldn't even skin up cos the puff just fell through your Rizla. And every single night people collapsed and fainted. Just dropped, spark-out. The place was fucking dripping, mate.

There wasn't really anything like it until I did 'Crazy Mondays' at Futures, which even out-naughtied and out-scorched the Fitness Centre. But we'll come to that in a bit.

While it lasted the Fitness Centre rave was great but it had to come to an end. If ever there was a case of 'too many chiefs and not enough Indians', the Fitness Centre club was it. It was jam-packed with fucking managers, or people who thought they were. It was funny cos we were all bent-nosed scrappers really, but we were also bang into the whole loved-up pill thing as well. So you just befriended someone and made them your fucking partner!

Anyway, I decided I wasn't having any more of it cos we were all 'partners' until about six in the morning when they all disappeared and I had to pay the fucking rent. That wised me up on the old 'partners' market pretty sharpish. So I was getting cheesed off with the whole thing and decided to call it a day with the club. We had one more night and I'm really glad that we did because on that night something happened that was to change a lot for me – alter my whole perspective of things.

It was just like an ordinary night in there, or as ordinary as that place got – everyone going mental, people fainting, beer evaporating before you even got to sip it – that kind of thing; and then in walked this group of about a dozen women. Well, when I say 'walking' that's fucking underplaying it (which ain't like me, is it?) It was more like they *invaded.*

They came in dancing, bouncing around, singing, and playing trumpets! How's that for an entrance? Everyone started cheering. They were stars. Whether you knew them or not, they were stars. And at the front were two twin sisters Jennifer and Julia Pinto, and the rest were another four of the Pinto sisters and six or seven friends. They just didn't stop smiling, the lot of them, and Jen in particular.

Now everyone who knows me (and if you've read the last book I include you in that) knows that I am not a mushy person, but if there's such a thing as love at first sight – that was it.

Anyway, turns out that Jenny and her sister had their own dance, rap and MCing act going and they were in the club to play that night! I thought, 'Charming, no one tells me anything – I only fucking run the place!' No, I did know we had someone on but I hadn't booked it so I didn't know who. But when they played I was just blown away. I thought it was the horniest, *horniest* thing, watching Jen and her sister performing their act, dancing in unison. It was just the most natural bit of talent I'd ever seen in a club and I'd been to thousands of clubs. Jen and Julia were the most natural movers. Then and there I thought, I am not just gonna be a voyeur of *that*!

But what with one thing and another – delegating between chiefs and indians, seeing that all the fainters were resuscitated (I did volunteer for the odd kiss-of-life), making new 'partners' I didn't really want – I didn't actually get to speak to Jen and next time I'd looked for her she'd gone. Which put a bit of a dent in the night because I was still properly buzzing from watching her. Worst thing was I didn't know then who she was and how to get in touch with her. And as you might have picked up from how the place was run we didn't exactly have an official Events Manager with a booking rota.

To top it all this was supposed to be the last night of the Fitness Centre club! I thought, 'Oh, *thank* you, God. You cunt. Drop a little angel down on me and then whisk her away. What have I done to deserve this?' Erm . . . well, apart from that . . . and that . . . and oh, yeah, that other thing I did . . . and OK – just fuck off!

So, only one thing for it. I kept the club open for one more week in the hope she'd come back. Which she did. Danced right back in the next Saturday with a big smile like she'd danced right the way through the week without stopping. And that weren't too far from the truth, as I later found out.

That's why raving, and that whole scene, will always mean something to me. Because raving gave me Jennifer.

5 *Ssmo*king!

Let me tell you what I think the addictiveness of raving was, and still is (and this little explanation probably ain't going to be something you'd first expect). By raving I mean what you'd probably now call just clubbing, something like that, since the word 'rave' has gone in and out of fashion. But it's all the same thing. I'll still use the old word but you know what I mean.

What the rave scene actually meant – and you can call it what you want and have different strains of music and all that – but the reason for its success was that for the very *first* time in the modern history of Great Britain they actually made a building where people could go to smoke dope/cannabis/weed, whatever you personally call it. Me and mine, we just call it 'puff'. So now you know.

See, there's always been millions of people in this country – between about five and ten million they say – that smoke puff. But never had anywhere to officially or safely do it. And that's a fuck load of people waiting for something to come along. Most people hide it from their mum, their workmates, their boss, their kids, the manager of their pub. They can't show the world that they smoke it so they're always having it in secret. Even in the pub you couldn't smoke puff. If you did everyone looked at you like you were a proper *junkie*. It was horrible.

And if you looked up the list of laws against it, and the offences you could be charged with, and the powers the police had against you if you were caught with it – for something that is, when it comes down to it, just the leaves from a fucking *plant* – then you got some idea of why people who smoked puff could get paranoid. It weren't the puff, it was the laws against it that did your head in!

Then, all of a sudden, in the 80s, along comes raving and the rave scene and the whole drug culture thing that comes with it. Now, forget the hard drugs, cos that's another matter: what it was was for the first time ever there was this venue – y'know, be it a tent, a cellar, a warehouse, a club, whatever – where all these people who were normally doing something they'd have to hide in the shadows, could go to a place and smoke openly in front of loads of other geezers doing the same. Touch! It was the only place where no one looked at you, and you could go up and say, 'Got any large Rizlas, mate?' without them going '*What*!'

And THAT was the attraction of the building. The fact that they played music there, *initially*, was secondary. If they'd taken all the music out but kept the building, people would've still gone there and they would've called it a 'chill-out' room. Like they do now! They have them in clubs still. But that's just another excuse to go and have a smoke of puff.

And as puffing is addictive, so that room became addictive because you wanted to puff there more because you weren't hiding. Because you could do it openly it was like being set free. You didn't feel like a leper in society, like the odd one out.

That, actually, that one thing, was an awful big thing behind the rave scene; a real big booster that helped get it all started. Cos all the people that puffed were sort of like-minded people anyway, even though they might be from different walks of life, puffing was founded in the sort of anti-establishment, don't-give-a-fuck side of society anyway. And loads and loads of young kids were into it and they brought the music.

I mean, imagine that cigarettes now were thought of in the same way as smoking puff was then, and everyone had to hide their twenty Marlboro in a drawer, and only buy them from certain people and only smoke among friends hiding in someone's bedroom, stuff like that. Then this rave scene comes along where you could go and get a cig out, blatantly, light it up and do it with loads of other cheery, happy fuckers who were also glad to get out of their mate's bedroom! You would be well and truly pretty fucking chuffed, wouldn't you? Well, that's what it was like and so much other stuff sprang from that little foundation. 'A mighty tree grow from de roots!' as they say. Amen to that.

And in the beginning – fuck me, listen, I'm starting to sound all biblical now! – '*In the beginning . . . there was one word and the word was "puff".*' No, actually, it was 'God'. But not a lot of people know that God only rested on the seventh day of creation cos He'd been smoking puff all day and He thought, Oh, *fuck* it . . . I've done enough.

(Think we might have just lost a few of our Christian readers there, don't you? Fuck 'em. I'm a Satanist anyway. Not really.)

Anyway, in the beginning of raving they didn't clamp down on the drugs like they do now. The laws were more lax and getting out of it seemed more acceptable. Back then the thought of you being searched on the club door and your drugs being taken off you on the way in seemed fucking barbaric! You know? When you'd actually driven all the way there to stay till ten in the morning and smoke and get off your tits, and to look at each other and go ACEEEIID! with a load of other people who wanted to do the same and not feel stupid – and *then*, before that, if your gear had been confiscated . . . imagine.

Also, the feeling of not having to be embarrassed about being out of it in front of your mates or the geezer sat next to you, that was a big thing. Because before, in pubs and clubs, it weren't really like that. Now suddenly you were in a place where you could puff all night long.

That was addictive to those people, the feeling. That's why people go to football matches so they can stand in the middle of ten thousand blokes and go 'WHOAAAHHH!' It was the same as that. And you started to live for your raving or clubbing weekend like the football hooligan lived for his little clashes on a Saturday. (And if you Peace and Love clubbers could never understand the football hooligan then just think of it the way I've just described: their Saturday afternoon was your Saturday night.)

The authorities tried to work it out and got it all wrong and said IT'S DRUGS – RAVING'S BAD. They didn't realise that a lot of people didn't give a fuck whether you were playing Beethoven or Big Beats. That club was their fucking release. It meant that at the weekend you were the bollocks. A fucking millionaire. Another mistake the authorities make is that, while puff is illegal, dealers are essential. Howard Marks told me how true that is.

The feeling of unity and power and all-of-us together was a very powerful motivation in clubland, and a real proper buzz. That feeling's addictive and it keeps you going back. More so than any drug, really, cos that feeling *is* your drug.

And all the time without realising it had all started because of puff. That was one of the real deep motives behind the first wave of raving. Just because there was a safe, friendly building that allowed millions of people to smoke their little lump of puff. And then you only had to go once to get hooked on the building, or on whichever bit of what happened in there made you feel most free.

So you'd get people coming out in a kind of awe and thinking things like – I don't have to smoke puff and zonk out in the pub any more because I can do it openly *in that building*; I've never seen a bird dancing in a bra and pants except *in that building*, just ten quid away; I can't dance and neither can any of these other cunts but I take that pill and I'm king of the dance *in that fucking building*. Or a girl that liked black guys didn't have to walk down the street getting looks from people for just holding hands when in that building they could actually fucking snog without anyone batting an eye! And gays, who had to hide their feelings outside, could kiss in front of everyone and no one minded. In that building where the rave was.

That's why it was so popular, because it was so many different things to different people. That's why for young people it became almost their church. The real church would have rejected or condemned most of the people in that rave. So fuck God and put your arms in the air! – Chooooon!

Look back at the two most popular images on T-shirts and caps and bags, and anything else you could stick a patch on to help sell it: the yellow smiley acid face, and the green marijuana leaf.

Northern Ireland says it all about the whole thing. I put on club nights there. And raving made Catholics cuddle Protestants. When they came out the next morning they were shooting each other. But when they were *in that building* . . .

A lot of superstar DJs and a lot of big venues got the credit but . . . let me tell you – it weren't them that did it, mate. It was you lot.

6 Loved Up

After waiting, Jen came back to the club. I'd seen her dancing and rapping and MCing and I just buzzed off her and her talent. I said to her, 'I don't know if you have anyone, but I want you.' That's what you might call the direct approach. Which she appreciated.

Afterwards I took her to Woolwich Common and we just sat and talked for ages. Or I did. I had something to tell her. If I can see something about to happen or happening in the near future, what I do is tell someone that I've seen it already. Cos I hate going 'I told you so' or 'I knew this' after the event. Anyone can do that can't they, and it don't prove nothing. So, I say it in advance.

I said to Jen, 'At the expense of sounding like a right silly cunt at this moment, listen to me, because I don't want to say this in ten years' time knowing that I knew it now. But I think you are the perfect partner for me. And I'm afraid you're gonna have me wrapped around you for the rest of your life.

'And I ain't gonna say this again cos I sound like a wanker just saying it once, but believe me it will happen.'

Jen listened and understood it all, and believed me. Like I knew she would. And her belief meant as much as mine. I'd just met the person I needed to complete the rest of my dream.

Blinding first day, or what? Talk about jumping off the deep end. But don't it always feel the best when you do that and get a happy landing? Best fucking feeling in the world.

It weren't easy, though. Even ten years ago things were different from now when it comes to mixed-race relationships. I mean they weren't as accepted. Particularly in my world.

What I did went down like a turd in a swimming pool. A lot of the chaps were just saying, Why, Dave, why? Why have you run off with this black girl? They thought that raving had got me into drugs and got me off my head, and I'd run off and left my wife and kids for a sexy black dancer.

What I said to each of the ones that said that to me was this: 'I've known you long enough for you to give me a couple of days of your life. So I want you to come out with me on Friday and meet Jen, and I'll drop you home on Sunday. If, at the end of that time, you cannot see why I love her then I have not got the fucking words in my body to tell you. *But* if after that you don't want to talk to me, or you can't handle it, I don't mind any of it . . . but I know as a man with bollocks, you are going to understand.'

And they did. Jen won them over.

But still, a lot of the chaps thought I was a proper raving lunatic. They were believing the hype on telly about the whole rave thing. And the raver himself weren't exactly a good advert for the scene, know what I mean? A typical one wore odd Kickers, a belly bag, hat on back to front, sunglasses on in the middle of the day, a whistle, white gloves, jaw going ten to the dozen while ravey-hand dancing and shouting Acceeeiid! I mean, that image weren't exactly gonna win over the critics of raving, now was it?

It was at this time that I made the move to leave my missus Tracey and go live with Jennifer. Everyone did think I was making a serious mistake and going wrong. And had I not had a good woman beside me I might have gone off the rails – or got proper, totally fucking derailed – like some who did when they got into it right at the beginning.

The club scene's different now but then it was so intense it culted you, know what I mean? It took over your life like a cult. People actually gave up their fucking jobs to become full-time ravers. Never having had a full-time job, that wasn't a problem of mine – ha! imagine doing that, though; one minute you're a gravedigger, next you jack it all in and you're a rave ligger. (Maybe if you said it quick no one would know.)

Anyone who was slightly addiction-prone could find something in the scene to get addicted to. Fuck the drugs. There was the false confidence of getting to the rave, and then getting in;

the music, the freely smoked puff, the overcoming shyness. All that. All addictive that.

My mates got into it a bit at a time. And then a hell of a lot fucking quicker when they came out with me and Jen.

But what raving did for a lot of people was this – it helped reduce the racial problem in this country. True. Before raving came along, racism was an awful lot more ferocious and fierce than people might care to admit now. We're going back about thirteen, fourteen years to when raving first began and things *were* different then. Things were, literally, more black and white.

For instance, if you lived in Hampstead you went to school in Hampstead, you drank in Hampstead, and you barely saw a black face. And because you didn't see a black face they intimidated you. Then you got married, got a job and it was a little insulated world. But then raving came in and in that little tent or field or building where everyone met you'd find the white Hampstead geezers having it large with loads of different people, black, brown and whatever colour. And all off their heads having a good time. So the next time a Hampstead White sees a Brixton Black in the street he weren't half as intimidated cos they'd been out at the same rave together.

Now, that white geezer would've never, by choice, gone to Brixton to check out what the black community was like. But raving *forced* people to get together, to get integrated. Then, once they were there, they saw how much of that stereotype stuff was bollocks. So the white bloke would end up having a blinding time sharing a joint and dancing next to a black geezer.

It all happened a bit more gradually than I've made out, obviously, but still a hell of a lot fucking quicker than it would have if people had just been left to it. Get what I'm saying?

It made an awful lot of people kick that whole racist thing into touch. And talking about 'into touch' – even the football crowds were getting into it. The football boys were all loving it and all, getting right off their nuts and dancing their heads off. So a lot of that violence stopped cos every fucker was too chilled-out. Result! It is a fact that, as the raving culture grew, the football hooligan culture dwindled.

I mean, think about this. There was even a divide between north and south London! The north–south divide with the

Thames. But then with the intervention of raving it didn't matter that the Ministry of Sound was in south London, or the Paradise Club was in north London, everyone went there. So it knocked that on the head. Then people started travelling the country to go to clubs – coaches and convoys of clubbers on Ravey Away-days – so the whole north–south of England thing took a knock as well.

Meanwhile, any of the north–south, black–white barriers were coming down pretty fucking sharpish, thank you very much, between Jen and me. We moved into a block of flats in Woolwich, no carpets or nothing. It weren't no fucking palace, mate, that's for sure. But we never went anywhere and didn't feel like VIPs, funny as that might sound. You can't help but feel like a star when you're with Jen because she's just such a natural one herself. And she did that for me. She put three stone and eighteen inches on me. Meaning she just grew me.

Jen was, and is, such a proud, strong-willed woman. And I'd never had a proper relationship with a black woman before, nor could say that I had any understanding of black culture – even though I thought I did. But Jen just melted me.

And I wanted so much to be 'the best' for her that it made me do my best. You know, the way you sometimes do that, don't you? Try harder on someone else's behalf than you would for yourself. Cos people can be lazy when it comes to themselves. Letting someone else down always feels worse than letting yourself down.

I just wanted to be something that my missus was proud of and it just seemed to capture the public imagination. Although I, personally, don't think I'm different from anyone else.

So because I preached certain things to her, and she did *exactly* what she said she'd do, I had to do the same. Living with her began to make me practise what I preached because I didn't want to let myself down in front of her. Sometimes it's hard to get that kind of inspiration from yourself and you need to fall in love to do it.

Then, for a time, apart from all the ravey friends we had, we were very much, sort of, alone. Kind of caught between two worlds, you might say. When I left my house and family and kids, that was a lot, and then a lot went with all that. I was seen as running away to live with a young black girl and it didn't exactly go down well. It was about as popular as a fart in a spacesuit, to be honest.

All I had to do with Jen was show her to the right people. That's what my job was. Her talent would do the rest. We'd go to record companies: straight to the door, straight into the offices with the twins, Jen and Julia, in their hotpants. That's when this geezer asked if he could see them do a live show. He came up to Maximus and filmed them. Then he came around to see Jen when he knew I'd be out.

He said that he wanted her and her sister for the record company and that he'd put them up in a flat by the studio, give them twenty grand and a car *but* . . . 'but they had to drop the skinhead', in his words.

Oh how happy was I about that? Not very. I rang him up and said, 'Hello, it's the skinhead.' He hung up. So I went to his offices in Canary Wharf, big flash place, and asked to speak to the geezer. There were four or five of those little security guards in the foyer in those silly brown uniforms they wear. They looked like they should've been at Asda guarding beans and cornflakes.

The receptionist said to me, 'Yes, sir. Could you tell me what it's about?'

I said, 'It's about battering your boss, darlin'.' Then I said to the guards, 'Listen. I'm battering someone here today cos he just went round my missus's house and said leave your man and I'll give you twenty grand. I think it'll be a sensible choice if you let me clump him here in front of you where I ain't gonna go too far. If you don't, one – you'll have your work cut out for you, and two – I'll be forced to find him elsewhere. Because any cunt who knocks at *your* door and says, "Leave your man and I'll give you twenty grand and a BMW" is definitely lining himself up for a slap. Without a doubt.'

The receptionist went, 'He's not here!'

Anyway, he did come down into the foyer, eventually. He was a proper little maggot. Just a haemorrhoid with a crombie on. So weasly you couldn't even hit him. I said, 'You're such a maggot I can't even clump you,' and then he relaxed. So I gave him a quick slap round the chops and said, 'I lied.'

What a slimey thing to do, though, for that cunt to try to break up a relationship.

I did know I'd found my equal in Jennifer, though, and although she learned certain things from me, and certain ways, I actually drew on things she didn't realise she was giving me: her *will*, for one thing. Stubbornness can be a cunt of a thing but pride, in the right place, is a real fucking asset. And quite a rare thing as well. I knew how strong-willed Jen was and to have to buckle under and change some things for me was fucking hard for her. Fucking hard. She'd actually run away from home to be what she wanted to be.

And because I loved her a lot I stopped pushing me forward and concentrated on her. But the big doors were always shut. Like at the BBC. It made me realise that you've got to get someone in. It's like cracking a safe or doing a bank job – breaking into the establishment is always easier if it's an inside job.

And that big, main door – the one that leads into the mainstream of success – that door was shut to me because of my success in my other chosen area, villainy. I didn't realise it at the time because that notoriety had brought so many good things as well. The club owners would want me to come to their club cos I'm a good spender and bring a bit of an entourage. The doormen would like to see me there, the DJs would like us there cos my crowd all like a dance, and Jenny could just get up and dance and sing and rap so the DJs played her records. So the street people, the DJs and punters who actually made up the scene absolutely fucking loved us. But the big doors closed because Mr Radio 1 doesn't want to be seen playing a record associated with Dave Courtney.

I had a lot of younger friends that I could learn things from and an older set as well. The raving was a big thing for me: supplying the doormen, running the clubs and individual nights. But during the day I was putting people to work debt collecting and things like that. So a lot of the older set of my friends had been and were friends of the Kray twins.

So I thought I'd get in touch with the twins, Ronnie and Reg, and see if they minded my set of twins, Jennifer and Julia – or Jenny Bean and Sugar Baby: the Courtney Twins – doing a rap record about them. I took the girls to see them and they said they liked the idea, so it started from there. I started visiting Ron and Reg and we became friends. The track we did was called, 'They Took The Rap', co-written with Master P, and was about the injustice that had kept the twins banged up after 30 years.

The press didn't exactly need an invitation to write about us either. I mean, imagine, two naughty black twins managed by a villain in a black hat, singing their song about two naughty white twins – the most celebrated villains in British history. Just ever so slightly press-worthy I think you'll find. And me being one to always run towards a camera rather than away from it, we welcomed them all. I gangstered it up big-time and Jen and Julia out-naughtied everyone you could think of.

We even did a publicity shot in front of the place where Ron shot George Cornell, the Blind Beggar pub.

There was a protest rally held on behalf of the Reg and Ron in Hyde Park and Jen and Julia played there, leading the parade. Which would've been a massive contrast to another one we were lined up to play – the opening of Euro Disney in Paris! I think they found out just what the twins' act consisted of and decided they didn't want to risk arousing Mickey Mouse in case he jumped Minnie, or get Goofy in such a state he tried to fuck Donald Duck. And what the seven dwarves would've done to Snow White I dread to fucking think.

When Jen started doing the rapping we had a record launch at the Hippodrome. We had 2,500 personal friends and whenever she played she'd also have two hundred doormen there to watch her. Even my old mate Ginger, who works the security there at the Hippodrome, came in that night to watch Jen perform. Cos he likes perving over my missus, the dirty cunt. No, that's fine by me. We are here to please!

Once when I was at the Hippodrome me and the doormen saw a couple shagging in an alley on the security cameras so we broadcast it on a screen in the club for everyone to see. When the couple came back in they thought they'd been mistaken for a couple of stars because everyone started applauding!

That night was the launch party for another track Jen did called 'Who Is He?' This one was about me getting acquitted for shooting that geezer, and it featured sirens, gun shots and my voice saying 'Not guilty!' Just your average, family listening really. We were hoping to get it on the *Teletubbies* album! Jen was carried out on stage for that gig by Selwyn Cotterell, Mr Universe, and Big Noel, all around them more bodybuilders escorting her out. It was fucking wicked. You utilise what you've got around you, you see, and so whenever we did anything it was surrounded by muscle. Bit like my cock (he said hopefully . . .).

Terry and Bryan Adams recorded and produced it and also did a 'Dodgy Dave Mix' and a 'Dub Minder Mix'. It sold enough to get into the top ten at least – 18,000 copies – but it didn't make the top one hundred for some suspicious reason. Even without Radio 1 DJ support we did well because we had the support of the club DJs.

Meeting Jen just gave me a new lease of life and took ten years off me. Which was handy cos with all the clubbing we were doing, if I'd felt my age I would've been fucked. Ha! Going out is good for the soul. It really is. It can heal a few wounds as well. Listen to this.

There was this guy, Glen. Not Funny Glen, another one. He'd split up with his missus, he was a bit overweight, a bit shy, but actually a really really nice fella. Glen was really down though, about what had happened. His younger brother was going to raves, bang into it, and cos his homelife had changed now, Glen went with his younger bruv one night. Took a pill, got off his head and thought it was the best thing that'd happened to him. A whole new world opened up for him.

And, on top of that, as if that wasn't enough, on that very first night that he went to a rave who did he happen to bump into? That's right. Youurrrs truly! Oh, yes. The lucky little tart. I remember it well. Me and Jen were out and just fucking buzzing off life and each other, mate, and forget the rest. I was happier than a six-cocked Alsatian in a five-bitch kennel. The Third World War starting would've been a minor fucking interruption. We were going to the top. Which top? The very top.

So Jenny danced up to Glen and he just couldn't believe it; this beautiful black chick in hotpants wiggling in front of him. He looked over at me and just gave him the big 'OK'. Then we got chatting. I don't know why but I just felt the need to talk. Not like me at all, ay?

Turns out Glen was a wealthy geezer with a mansion down in Slough. It was snowing outside (well it wouldn't have been fucking snowing inside would it?) and he said he didn't want to go back to this big house by himself, and would we like to go with him? Oh fucking yes, mate, was the answer. Lead the way to the snow-capped mansion and we will follow. We are the Snowy Mansion Crew in full effect!

There was me and Jen, Seymour and Jackie, Fred the Fuse and Kerry, Danielle Montana the DJ, Danny Dolittle, Ray, Funny Glen, Johnny Jacket, Brendan, Creed, Bulldog Dean, Stormin' Norman, Warren, Warwick, Bez, Joey Pyle Jnr, Goldie, Big Lee, Big Barry, John Corbit and Big Mick (Charlie Kray's minders), Andy the Cab and Big Mark, Robert Hanson, Ian and Marcus and some other geezers and birds and well-known nutters too far out-of-it to mention.

We went down to Slough with an entourage of about twenty-five people in half a dozen cars. And we didn't lose one – a record for us. Usually something daft happens, like someone falls asleep at the wheel waiting at the lights. We just stop off and wake them up on the way back!

Now this geezer Glen must've been either expecting guests or he had developed one massive drug habit. He'd done what you usually only see in those films with Hollywood party scenes: he'd filled five glass fruit bowls full of grass, weed, hash, Charlie and whizz and there they were on this huge wooden coffee table in the middle of the room. How decadant does that look? No teabags in the house but glass pots full of pot.

And even though I know it's wrong I do have this habit of hogging the joint. It gets passed to me and I get talking and I just forget to pass it on. Honest, guv. It's a memory lapse, all right! So everyone thought they'd teach me a lesson by rolling a really really strong weed joint, really packed it up. By accident I caught them rolling it, all huddled round whispering and laughing. But as Darlington Dave would say, 'I said nowt!'

So back in this massive living room of Glen's where we were all chilling out, this joint is going around and everyone's only taking a little puff from it cos they know what's inside. And fuck this thing just being a joint, this was like pass the fucking parcel, mate! Daniella did her back in lifting it and Fred had to use both hands. A proper Camberwell Carrot. When I saw it coming towards me I nearly hit the Nuclear Strike button.

It got to me. Ta very much, don't mind if I do (as you well know). Now, I thought, I can do one of two things here. Take a puff and pass it straight on to Danny, which would completely fuck up their little plan, and completely fuck up Danny probably, from the strength of it – and bring new meaning to him for his surname, Dolittle. Or Dofuckall, as he'd have been after that. *Or*, or I can be the man here and do the old Greek Spartan warrior thing and jump right into the battle, sandals blazing and jockstrap on fire.

Guess which? Yes, you *know* that! I hogged that joint like it was my fucking life-support system. I disappeared in a fog of blue smoke but emerged a much better person, officer! Let me tell *you*. I'll have you know I smoked that carpet remnant of a joint and coped very well, thankyouverymuch. Much to everyone's disappointment I didn't melt into a cosmic puddle and start hugging the carpet or slip into a smiley coma. I did cope with it.

Having said that, though, half-an-hour later I *was* rolling around naked in the snow, so I ain't completely denying a possible connection. You decide. You can even phone a friend.

OK, what happened was this. I was looking out the kitchen window and I saw Glen's neighbour out in the garden. The house next door is as massive as Glen's. You know the kind of place: driveway so long it had a speed limit, front door like a castle drawbridge, garden so big it still had German pilots from WWII hiding out down the bottom of it, the bath came with its own coastguard and if the five-car garage was full of Ferraris you could always park in the dog kennel. It's the only gaff I'd seen that had 'His & Hers' helicopter pads. Every house I'd ever lived in would've fitted into this one.

So I sees the geezer next door pottering about the big chunk of south England he calls a back garden, putting bacon rind on the bird table. Which I thought spoiled the whole classy atmosphere. This geezer's got a beautiful house and then turns the birdhouse into a greasy caff. He could've at least put out vol-au-vents!

Everywhere was covered in this blanket of fresh snow. Completely untouched. I thought that looks very very very tempting. I think human beings must be either naturally destructive, or have a deep urge to make their mark, like leaving a sign. Because y'know when you see a freshly cemented floor or a fresh plastered wall, you spend about the first ten seconds thinking, 'Oh, ain't that good – how he's got that so straight and so flat and all that.' And then you spend the next half hour trying to resist the urge to fuck it all up by slapping your hand on it or jumping on it boots-first.

Or maybe that's just *me*. Ha. And here I am trying to pass it off as human nature. Worth a shot.

So, I stripped off naked, stark bollock naked, and put on these big green wellies that I found by the kitchen door. Oh, and one more thing – a baseball cap on back to front. Well I didn't want to go out with nothing on my head and look a complete div! Tut. I walked out into Glen's back garden and went, 'Morning', and he went 'Mor*ning*!' back.

That's a point, actually, while we're on it. Have you noticed that whoever says 'morning' first says it really quick, but whoever does the reply really drags out the second bit of the word – 'Mor*ninnng*!' True though, innit?

Anyway, the bloke was halfway through his 'Mor*ninng*!' as he was turning round to me. But when he saw me his little 'Morning' froze and took a sharp fucking downturn. Dropped his bacon as well. I'm naked and in only the cap and wellies, walking across to the fence and making chit-chat. Casual as fuck. Passing pleasantries, as you do in an English country garden.

'Cold for the time of year, squire, ain't it?' I said rubbing my hands together. 'Fuck me, you do spoil the sparrows round here don't you, mate?' I nodded at the bird table. 'I never saw as much bacon as that during my whole fucking childhood!'

This bloke didn't say much. Must've been in shock, ay? Why I can't think. Just because there was a shaven-headed, green-wellied, spliff-smoking totally naked stranger with knuckle-duster tattoos stood knee-deep in snow in next door's garden chatting about the weather. What *was* his fucking problem? Bleedin' snob.

Anyway, I decided to do a Basil Fawlty, y'know where he falls over, suddenly faking a war wound. I threw myself away from the fence and landed on the ground and started rolling all over the garden. Snow was flying everywhere. I was like a spinning top. I must have flattened a good twenty foot square.

I stopped and lay there on my back and I could see the neighbour from the corner of my eye. He's edged up to the fence for a better look but he just cannot believe what he's seeing. I got up, faced him, and then really deliberately went, 'Mmmmm . . . *nice*!' Then walked to the house and shut the door.

So, no, that big spliff earlier had no effect on me *whatsoever*! No, seriously, you know I don't need anything like that to make me do stupid things. I ain't got that as an excuse, 'The weed made me do it!', 'Yeah, but what about the other nine hundred and ninety-nine times when you were completely straight and still acted like a tit?' Oh, yeah . . .

So now Glen's house is really rocking. There's snow outside but inside we're keeping the home joints burning, and there's music on and people dancing round or chilling out. Glen's on a happy pill and he's now got twenty new mates who're cracking him up laughing. We didn't take the piss though. On the way down we'd called in at a service station and bought loads of food and loads of booze, cos we didn't know what his house was gonna be like. But I did know that if he's a geezer living by himself there's gonna be absolutely fuck all in the fridge.

We had a blinding time, really wicked. I was sat there chilling out in a big leather wing-backed armchair, surrounded by mates, in a mansion house in the country with snow outside, a roaring fire inside, a joint in my hand, Jenny sat in my lap, and I thought it just don't get any better than this.

It did get better, actually, but first it got worse. When we went to leave my Jag wouldn't start. And it's still snowing. Glen said, 'It's all right, take the Jenson.' I thought, I must've heard him wrong. He can't have said a 'Jenson'.

Jenson Interceptors were made in the 60s and 70s and were always one of my favourite cars. They are the nuts; a real big handsome beast of a motor with a seven-litre V8 block and a massive, curved back window. Fucking testosterone on wheels, mate. Anyway, Glen flipped the garage door back and there it was. A Jenson Interceptor! Bright red with a grey vinyl roof, chrome wire wheels and in perfect condition.

Glen chucked me the keys and I thought, I fucking *LOVE* you!

What a drive home that was. Our arses snuggled down in black leather, driving through the snow in this fuck-off, bright red, Santa's sleigh of a car. I felt like Father fucking Christmas on steroids I did. Blasting back up to London to bring goodwill to all men. And even more women.

When I got back home my phone had been cut off. I did tell the kids not to play with the scissors but would they listen, would they fuck. Anyway, about a month later I got this call from Glen. He sounded quite tentative. He asked if I still had the car. ''Course I have,' I said. 'Why didn't you ring me? I've been waiting for you to call!'

I think in the meantime he'd been worrying about what the fuck I might have done with the Jenson cos he didn't know me at all, really, and then he'd told a few people what he'd done and they'd gone, 'You gave it to Dave Courtney!?' and then probably told him loads of kind of bollocks that gets said about me by people who don't know me. But then Glen didn't know me well enough to know I'd look after his motor.

He was so pleased that I still had it in one piece that he forgot what a right diabolical liberty it was that I'd kept it for a whole month! And Glen is still one of my best mates to this day. Never saw his neighbour again, though. That bird table stayed suspiciously bacon-free whenever I turned up at Glen's house.

7 The Spirit of Ecstasy

Not wanting to sound flash or anything but I was driving along the other day in the Rolls, as you do, and there at the end of 300 foot of Old English White bonnet was the Flying Lady mascot, sparkling in the sun. Well, it would've been sparkling if it hadn't been for the blind nun impaled on it (they do loiter on those zebra crossings, don't they?)

Anyway, did you know the official name for the Rolls-Royce mascot is the Spirit Of Ecstasy? Which just goes to show why it took them so long to build each car. They were all fucked. You try assembling a walnut burr dashboard while you're buzzing.

Why the fuck am I telling you this? Don't know. I'm just trying to overcome my natural shyness by making conversation. I did actually overcome my shyness when I was about, oh, ten, fifteen seconds old. The midwife slapped me and I said, 'Pick on someone your own size you fat cunt.' She drop-kicked me into a crib and I've never been the same since. I was mentally scarred by being a Caeserean birth, though. For years I'd only leave a room by climbing out the window.

Anyway. Shyness is a real illness, a real fucking illness. People are properly crippled by it. A lot of people who would've like to have a dance didn't because they didn't dare. Which is sad. And when you're looking at everyone else enjoying themselves and you *can't* cos you think you'll look silly or you're not a good dancer, or for whatever reason it is that makes you shy, then you feel crap.

So someone really clever invented a pill that you can take to make you enjoy yourself as much as the person next to you (and if I was the person next to you then you had a *fuck*ing good time!) Ecstasy was only made illegal here in the mid 1970s, did you know that? And it was still legal in America right up until about 1985. Talk about Land Of The Free.

I'll tell you something, if there'd been more Ecstasy still available over there a few years later, and some of it had been pumped into the police force, the LA riots would've probably never happened. For one thing, it was the white cops beating up that black geezer Rodney King that kicked it all off. A lot more MDMA and a lot less Charlie amongst those cops and they would've probably just hugged him. So that would be my first job as the Drug Tsar – E-up the Old Bill.

But at whatever age they started raving, this was the first time the shy people and the not-so-sure people (i.e., 90 per cent of kids) felt like one of the chaps, like part of the gang.

So – and this is the vital bit – people were finding sanctuary in what they thought was just making them feel *normal*. Understand that – that's the real important part. People weren't left feeling freaky or mad or junkies because of Ecstasy – it just took away everyday restrictions and gave them a little taste of what they thought it was to be normal. Then that little taste gave them a proper appetite. And, let me tell you, it was a fucking nice feeling for them people to have once a week when for the other six days they were shy, or quiet, or sad, or bored, or whatever it is that stops people living.

It was like people realised, fuck me, you only go round once; what the fuck am I doing with my life? You could see it in their faces. They felt like they'd kicked a steel wheelclamp off each foot and grown ankle wings.

THAT is what was addictive. The feeling. Not the drug. The feeling, the place, the mates. The mates you met in the place to get the feeling. Ecstasy was an aid to that.

And that's why the people who will never understand the attraction of the drug thing will never understand the attraction of the drug thing. Ever. People who weren't or haven't been part of it; the police, the Drug Tzars, the government, the anti-druggers, your parents, your teachers; everyone not connected or clued-up. Because they don't know how *fucking good* you felt on that Saturday night.

Banning a drug is one thing. Trying to outlaw and ban a feeling is a fucking difficult thing to do, mate. You *know* that. It's impossible actually.

In a good club on a blinding night, or even in a so-so club on a wet Wednesday, if you were raving then you were surrounded by people who didn't care whether you made a prick of yourself or not. The place was full of people so elevated by it all, or so off-the-wall and stuck to the ceiling out-of-it, that who gave a flying fuck if you weren't in tune or on the beat! And most likely you were anyway cos you'd had an E!

It gave (and gives) the youth a 'gang' feeling. A unity feeling. That's something which every single person of that age grasps with both hands, cos when you're young you just fucking wanna belong, dont'cha? It's the buzz of the whole tribe thing. I saw that the 'Us and Them' feeling was massive. The rest of the world was thinking, It's bad! But the kids knew it wasn't and knew that the rest of the world had got it wrong!

Most everyone would go home after a night and their mum and dad would be finger-wagging and going, 'Oh, you just don't know how to enjoy yourself!' I know those kids were thinking, *What!* I don't know how to enjoy myself? Listen, inside they knew this: *Last night they went out; spent two hours getting ready, getting dressed, making calls – then piled out into a car already crammed with mates, all laughing and buzzing and the night ain't even barely begun yet. Then it does begin. You meet more mates in town in cars, music banging out; shouting hellos and see-you-theres. Pop your pill in the queue, shivering but you don't give a fuck, bounce into the club and slap-bang into a crowd of hundreds. Sweating, smiling, saying hi, hands in the air, water in your hair; buzzin', loving, Dove-ing. It feels so good that it seems to last forever and then BANG! it's over and you're moving out holding someone's hand. The sun's coming up, you're coming down. Heading back to crash at a mate's for more laughs over a joint and maybe a lovely warm shag with that saucy-looking thing that came back with you.*

And their mum was telling them they didn't know how to enjoy themselves! Well, fuck me for not curling up on the sofa with a TV remote, a pension plan and a Pot-fucking-Noodle!

It was so easy for anyone taking Es to justify taking them cos they saw what the legal drug, alcohol, was doing so much fucking damage. A load of people on E were a much healthier, happier prospect than a load of people that were pissed. People who took E knew they weren't as bad as their mate who drank Scotch or vodka or nicked pints all night long. And as a doorman I knew doormen would rather deal with ravers than pissheads. Having to fight off some raver trying to cuddle you is better than having to just fight someone.

On top of that, all the bollocks put out by the authorities was causing untold problems for clubbing people with their parents or girlfriends or whoever believed what they read. So it was easy for people to feel they were being unjustly treated by the government.

According to Them, the parents and the police, etc., you, the clubber, were wrong and they were right. Kids would be watching the telly news about some raver scare story saying, She Took One E And Died! Which made the Mums go, 'See!', and the kids wanted to say, Mum if only you *knew*. But you can't argue because you're arguing on the side of taking drugs and that's a no-win situation. You couldn't win an argument with people who couldn't possibly understand cos to them drugs is drugs, and I know exactly what that means because I was like that.

Young people, though, are very good at sorting these things out, contrary to what some older people think. They were actually on the ball about it. The authorities did a very amateurish job of putting out information and scare stories and they got absolutely no respect for it. Because as soon as you did one E you knew the scare stories were bollocks. Then no one believed anything else they heard!

They had an uphill struggle because for every person who'd say Es are bad there would be twenty people who'd go, Fuck off! And they were saying such bizarre things like, you're instantly hooked or you want to shag everyone or people were getting raped on it. Any eighteen-year-old knew that was bollocks.

The authorities aimed too high with the fear tactics, got a bad ricochet and shot themselves in the foot, big-time. Their own fear made them make an awful lot of mistakes when they first decided to put legal restraints on the rave scene. Their own fear made them a laughing stock. No one listened.

And if someone says don't do this, don't do that, then young people are, naturally, gonna want to fucking do it. It was the wrong punishment for the wrong thing cos all the kids that were going were rebels anyway. So to go, 'It's now illegal!', just made it more illicit and much more attractive. And that was more damaging than just trying to curb it. Just like Prohibition in America. They banned alcohol so then when you did have a drink it tasted ten times better!

I tell you what, the best way to have turned young people off raving would've been for the authorities and parents to welcome it with open arms. If ravers had seen their mums getting into it, shouting Accceeiid! and their dads wearing smiley face T-shirts, they would've run the other way screaming. Yeah, mums and dads going raving would have killed it stone fucking dead.

A prime example of how people thought, and how big the gap was between Us who understood and Them who didn't, was the death of Leah Betts. She quickly became the most famous case of a death on an E and the press jumped on it. Sorry to be the bearer of bad news but all that happened when the adverts came out saying that Apple Es killed Leah Betts was that you couldn't buy one for love nor money cos every raver wanted one. There was a lot of shit pills out there and those ads were just saying to people that Apples were pukka. (Can you even *imagine* trying to explain that to the police or Just Say No anti-drugs campaigners?! They would not have believed you in a million years.)

Then the market got flooded with fake Es stamped with apples cos they'd suddenly got a massive reputation. People were even making jokes about it – saying there was only 25 letters in the alphabet cos Leah Betts took the E. Horrible stuff like that. Kids knew that one E wasn't killing people, because they'd taken two or three or more and survived. Only the very very unlucky ones died, like Leah Betts.

I mean you can't, for one second, blame her old man and her mum for doing what they did; and their reaction was to throw themselves into the old anti-drug campaigning. Fair enough. Must be fucking hard to lose a child. But if people from that side of the fence read this and they learn only one thing it should be this – that they were never really fighting 'drugs' but the fact that drugs made their kids feel more normal. And that *feeling* was the drug. You try banning that.

Difficult one, that, ain't it? Difficult one to get your head round if you're not already there.

Also, it did, without any shadow of a doubt, chill out a lot of potentially violent people. An awful lot. At one point, a lot of hardnuts thought it was too mamsy-wamsy to dance. Like you were on too much of a 'look at me' trip, right? And when they got into raving and the whole scene they found it really easy to let go as well. Cos even a lot of them are shy too. Yeah, I know, there's a fucking lot of it about, mate. So they could go to these places and have a proper good jump around and no one gave a fuck.

And people forget, or if they weren't there they don't know, that football hooliganism was a proper big problem then. London, Manchester, Liverpool and Leeds were all kicking off big time. Geezers just kicking fuck out of each other and people were dying. Then Acid House and ecstasy came along and blew the whistle on a lot of that warfare. You'd actually see two blokes in opposing team shirts hugging each other on the dancefloor! Police overtime in the riot squad hit an all time low.

They just needed a bit of helping along in that direction, the toughnuts. And it's really hard to hit someone when you're smiling! Nature makes it more of an effort to growl than smile. Even God made it easier to smile. (Fuck me . . . I came over a bit Walt Disney there, didn't I? Not that anyone ever did come over Walt Disney I'm sure.) I've seen geezers that, three months before, I'd thought of as the scariest fucking creatures I've ever seen walk the earth and now here one is, in a club, off his head, and trying to fucking moonwalk! I'd be thinking *fucking hell*! This is the same bloke that I've seen headbutt someone for looking at his bird's drink, and here he is cuddling people and asking them to show him their ravey hand movements!

Now tell me that ain't a good thing.

I participated in the popping of the old love drug, as they called it, and got my boy scouts badge in cuddling everyone and thinking I was the best dancer in the world. When I was only second best! And Es definitely made me realise I've got rhythm. Before that, even though I liked it immensely I wouldn't have even attempted to get up and have a dance with those people. It actually made white guys be able to dance, for fuck's sake! I always wondered if black geezers got pissed off about that cos it meant they'd lost an edge!

It made everyone want to be friendly. But the drug didn't do that, you're like that anyway. Because every man, stripped of his façade, wants to go to the next man, 'All right?', and smile and give a thumbs up and get one back. Rather than the other bollocks, of who can stare each other out.

Without a shadow of a doubt it chilled out an awful lot of violent people. Ninety-eight per cent of people who'd taken something got something out of it. Many more than the few people who've perished. The problem arises when the raving wears off and you've got to get back to reality. Because it's an infectious thing, raving – or clubbing – there's places to go nearly every night which means it can fuck up your daytime job (you lose your job as a chef, for instance, cos you ain't got the strength to fondle an egg let alone beat it!)

The younger ones found that they wanted more and more of the club scene and then it became their life and they became 'A RAVER', capital letters, like in the newspaper stories. But the shy people started having it big-time as well! Wicked. So it brought an awful lot of people out of themselves. Raving made them do it but once they'd done it *once* then they knew they could do it without the gear. It turned more people off being shy, and off being violent, than it turned people into addicts.

The biggest, worse kept secret is this: the drugs didn't make everyone like that, *everyone is like that anyway*! The drug stripped everyone of their pretentiousness and fear. Everyone thought it was a love drug which it weren't, really, because behind all the bollocks everyone wants to be happy anyway. And *that* is what it was.

There's a few things that sum up the good bits of the club scene, y'know, that whole getting-clubby buzz and the getting ready and the going out, and meeting mates. All that. One of the bits that sums it up for me was what happened to this geezer I knew called Dean.

Dean was an overweight kid but not one of them that's confident with it. He was a right lovely geezer but, like so many people, he was shy. And he really really wanted to be in on the whole club scene but he weren't a clubby person. He loved it, though, the clubs, and he did things like tried to be a DJ, even a barman, just to be on the scene.

Now this was at the time of my Fitness Centre club when it was still bang-on, arms in the air raving. And that's why Dean loved it, because when he was in the rave he was still the shy fat kid with glasses but, like I said earlier, *in that building it was all right.* No one gave a fuck and he could jump around with the best of them.

But he wanted to be doing something on the scene.

This was also at the time when those Tango orange drink adverts were out. Y'know the ones with the big naked geezer painted orange and wearing a loin cloth, running round slapping people and getting slapped back on his head? Fucking funny those ads, and they were massive as well. One of the adverts had to be changed cos kids were copying the slapping thing in the playground and damaging each other.

So one night I said, 'I know. Dean, what do you think of the Tango Man?' He said he thought he was wicked. 'Well you be him then. Be the Tango Man. Just wear your pants, get painted orange and you'll be a fucking star, mate.' I asked him if he minded being slapped on the head and he said he didn't, he loved it.

I paid him a ton a night to be the fucking Tango Man. Now even with the offer of money you try persuading someone to run around a club naked apart from orange paint and Y-fronts. It wouldn't be easy would it? But Dean was in the right place at the right time. With the right body. And the right baggy Y-fronts.

First time he did it he got ready at our house. He stripped right down to his undies, we painted him orange, threw a cover over the car seat and drove down to the club. He was one very nervous Tango Man on his way down, mate, let me tell you. He was fucking fizzing. Me, Jennifer and the mates with us all geed him up, telling him he looked the absolute orange bollocks. Which he did, as it happens!

By the time we pulled up outside the club he was buzzing and proper up-for-it. When he jumped out the car people on the door and everyone in the queue looked 'round and went,

'Oh look! It's the Tango Man!' There was nearly a fucking riot! And in the club he just went down a storm. People were slapping his head and he was slapping theirs. He got drinks bought, girls sitting on his lap, geezers shaking his hand. He almost knew what it was like to be ME!

Listen, from then on I hired him out to raves and strip clubs, and lent him out to charity dos. He went to the openings of new clubs. He was loving it so much he would've gone to the opening of a gas bill.

And when you watched him get ready for a night, stripping and painting himself and everything, you could see he felt like Tom Cruise. He didn't fucking look like Tom Cruise, and I'm sure Nicole Kidman would've noticed the difference if she'd opened her eyes and seen it was Dean's orange cock she'd got in her mouth, but he *felt* like him. Y'know, like a star. And I've said that that's what clubbing is, haven't I? The feeling.

You couldn't help but get a massive buzz just watching him buzzing. He got real popular, old Dean. I thought, I have created a monster. A big orange monster. In underpants. Frankentango! I just hoped it didn't go to his head. I thought he might ask for his own tour bus, or a fucking Winnabago; or start making weird demands, like no one eats an orange in his presence, and asking for young, impressionable satsumas to be brought up to his hotel room.

So Dean became a bit of a star. He was the Robert de Niro of Tango Men. Or Marlon Tango. Fuck me, yeah – *Last Tango In Paris*! That was Marlon Brando's film. I just thought of that one. Oh I wish I'd thought of that at the time, we could've done a remake.

But after the Tango adverts stopped the future weren't bright and it definitely wasn't orange. I considered stuffing him in the blender to keep us in juice for a year but decided against it cos we all thought he was top. Then I had another idea. 'Dean,' I said 'what do you think of those round purple characters in the Ribena ads?'

This all reminds me of why orange has never been one of my favourite colours. When I was about fourteen my mate Colin Robinson used to call for me at night. I'd sneak out the bedroom window and me and Col would go out nicking. One night I went out nicking car wheels. I went out in my pyjamas but I put on a black crombie overcoat and black trilby hat, and loafers.

I was loosening the last wheel nut on this Cortina 1600E when Colin shouted 'Leg it! Old Bill!' and ran off up the street! I turned the other way and there was a police car right on me! I ran off across the park but cos I'd got all the wheel nuts and bolts in the crombie pockets I was weighed down. And cos the loafers were leather-soled I was skidding everywhere on the grass.

So what I done was I kicked off the shoes and undone the crombie and let it drop. Forgetting that the pyjamas I was wearing were bright orange! You could've seen me from fucking Big Ben. I tried to hide in the bushes but the coppers could see me throbbing like a Belisha beacon. That was awful. I've never forgiven that colour for getting me nicked.

It worked wonders for Dean, though. But because he was bright orange it would've taken a very very long weekend to get Dean 'bleached'. You know what bleaching is, don't you?

8 Bleaching

Anyways, so it was a Monday afternoon and me and Jenny were in bed for the first time since the Wednesday before. That's when we'd first set off out clubbing and since then we'd done this – been out five nights, done thirteen or fourteen different clubs (and as many stimulants), been to seven cafes and half a dozen off-licences in between, had numerous splifs, seen hundreds of mates, made loads more, and totally buzzed our tits off. We had been out nearly six days straight and over a hundred hours pretty fucking un-straight.

And lying there in bed I realised something . . .

I said to Jen, 'Babe? I don't know how this has worked out but . . . I've just figured out we're now on a five-day weekend and two-day *week*! It's all gone wrong.'

And fuck me sideways with a chihuahua if it weren't true. We'd gone one better than the three-day week and just invented the two-day one. 'Bleaching', they call it. When you're out for so long and don't see the sun for so long that your skin goes white. Good word that, innit? Sums it right up.

But that's what had happened. Our nightclubbing days, and nights, had slowly stretched to take over most the week. Five-day weekend, two-day week. This that really fucks up your job prospects but you have a blinding social life!

So, roll up, roll up, folks, I'm now gonna take you on the typical Five-Day-Weekender rollercoaster ride that we were doing at the time. I'll warn you now, though, it ain't suitable for those with dickie tickers, nose pickers, window lickers, pregnant ladies, newborn babies, nervous midgets, children, OAPs, MPs, anyone suffering from the

DTs, and all schizophrenics. So that rules out most of my mates, then.

And, if at any time it all gets too much for you and you want to shout *Stop the Ride I Want to Get Off!* (Virgin, out now in paperback – ha ha!), then feel free. I won't fucking listen to you but you can shout: it's always good to have someone to drown out the sound of those who are crying. Here we go. Hold on tight, it's gonna be a bumpy ride . . .

WEDNESDAY

On the night we'd start off with just what you might call a small advance party of me, my Jennifer and Brendan. We'd jump in the Rolls and Royce-on down to Wandsworth Road to Continentals. This was my place. But since I'd took it over I'd changed the name to the Place. As in the Place-to-be.

And that club, when I took it on, was a proper Yardie stronghold. They came with the building, fixtures and fucking fittings, mate, that's what they were. The guy who owned the building said that if I could run it for six months without any trouble then I could have it. So, my little dilemma then was what to do about potential problem on the Old Yardie front.

Well, once again, music was my saviour cos I decided to put on a rave night. That solved it, Bang! just like that. Well, imagine it, your average Yardie ain't gonna want to go to a rave now, is he? A chilled-out Yardie Bro not gonna really get into being surrounded by bug-eyed lunatics with their shirts off blowing whistles and shouting 'Tuuunnne!!'

Unfortunately it didn't work on all of them. Well, there's always one, ain't there, who just *has* to be different? Fuck me. Anyway, so this geezer walked in one night – tall, skinny black guy wearing a long coat – and tried to pull a fast one on me. He strolls in, reached behind the bar and poured himself a brandy, necked it and then leaned over and took 60 quid out the till. Now that, correct me if I'm wrong, is just ever-so-slightly taking the piss. And charging 60 quid for the pleasure.

I didn't see any of this, by the way, cos we're in a club rammed with people dancing and, it being my night, I'm mingling about making sure things are going smoothly; dancing around to check the dancefloor's safe, drinking shorts at regular intervals to check the optics are in good working order, y'know, that kind of selfless behaviour.

I had my back to the bar so it was Jen that actually saw the geezer lean over the bar and help himself. So she comes to tell me. I went and had a quick word with the guy that we leased the club off, just to check out what the situation might be.

The owner went, 'Oh, him. No, we just let that one do what he wants and he keeps the others away.'

I said, 'Wait a minute. It ain't your gaff tonight, mate. It's mine. This is my night and that's my 60 quid out the till and my brandy he's just nicked.' (And I do drink brandy as well, so that was a double 'fuck off'.) I thought, right! Start as you mean to go on, Dave.

I sees the geezer's now making his way out so I crossed the dancefloor and stopped him. I said, 'I think we've got to have a little chat, me and you.' He did the old rude-boy badman routine of kissing his teeth, and said to me 'Listen, man . . .', and he opened his coat and showed me the handle of his knife. Big knife. Looked like a machete.

Now if you get in them kinds of confrontations a lot, which I have, you learn how certain people do certain things. Some people clump you almost immediately cos they haven't got the words to argue; some guys start shouting and creating; other geezers pull out a piece and start growling; and some just show you the handle of their knife. And that one is the muggiest thing in the world to do, in my book. Twenty-four carat prat behaviour. I've had it happen to me many a time. And because life is a form of habits, you react the same way when certain things are done to you.

So this geezer's stood in front of me, teeth-kissing and showing me the knife, and everyone's staring over now cos it looks like something's brewing.

I looked at him and said, 'You're new to this, ain't ya?'

His face fell and he just looked at me like I'd really burst his little bubble, really spoiled his image of how he saw himself. Which I had, and all with six little words. 'Someone,' I said, 'has got to have sent you down here cos there's no way, no *fucking way* that you can pull that little stunt in here, matey.' Then I pulled out a gun I just happened to have on me, jabbed the barrel end forward and dented his forehead with it, one of my favourite little moves. I left it resting there.

See, cos we thought we were in for loads of aggro from the local Yardies, maybe even a big gunfight and all that, we had a proper little well-stocked arsenal down there. Shotguns, handguns, the lot. So I banged the barrel of this one I was carrying right into his forehead really hard so it left a little dent.

I said, 'If you even *look* like you're gonna use that . . . I shoot you.' His hand slipped off the handle. He died. He just died inside. His face went white (not easy), and he just stood there. 'You silly, silly boy,' I said. 'Go back and tell whoever sent you down here that if this is a little warm up for something, then I'm starting as I mean to go on. And if they want to send anyone down here to talk to me then they can.' I took the money off him and he left.

While I'm still inside the club, waiting in there and thinking he's gonna have some big pow-wow with his chiefs – or maybe gone to tell someone to come in for me – I told the doormen to keep an eye out. About fifteen minutes later one of them comes back down and asks me to go look at something upstairs. I went up thinking, what? Guys outside with guns? Blacked-out Merc parked across the street? . . .

When we get upstairs, they point up the street and this machete-carrying badman that came to rob me is only stood waiting for a fucking taxi home! I could not believe it. He tried to rob me and go home in a cab. What a cheeky, cheeky cunt.

Anyway, years later, me and Jen are in another club somewhere and this geezer came up behind me and put his hand on me and said, 'Remember me, man?' I really didn't. He explained that he was the guy with the knife from in the Place club. He went, 'You're the only man to bummy me!' which is like patois for 'being scared'.

I hadn't seen this guy approach, didn't remember him anyway, and he could've done anything to me really. Cos I hadn't seen him. He could've stabbed me, if he'd held a grudge. And I was fucking easy to spot cos by then I'd taken to wearing a black wide-rimmed fedora hat. (Flash? I don't know what you mean.) Because I didn't stop sweating I'd wedge it right down on my head. When I finally did take it off about a half a pint of liquid flooded out.

Anyway, then this geezer said that if I wanted him he would work for me anytime. I thought about it for, oooh, half a second before I said, 'No. You're shit.' Which I think had been proved by his escapade with the knife.

Anyway, so remember, we're still in the Place club and it's still only Wednesday night. Get that. Now is that or is that *NOT* one fucking way to start the weekend?! It is, ain't it? And we've still got five days to go. Ding-ding! those with heart problems – next stop.

THURSDAY

So we'd dance on at the Place until 8 a.m. Thursday morning then all pile in the car, along with anyone we'd picked up following in their car, and head back to Jenny's house. Our mate Brendan had already disappeared after copping off with a bird. Probably pulled her with his usual irresistible chat-up line of, 'Fancy a shag, darlin'?' which, more often than not, they did.

When we got to Jen's house the kids, Jenson and Drew, would get up, put music on and dance around the house. We'd just chill-out for the day with tea, toast and the odd medicinal joint, until Thursday evening. Jenny was also geting paid for singing in nearly every club we'd visit. So we were getting paid for going out! Everyone else got skinter, but cos of Jen, we got richer. Then just as you were probably settling down to watch *Top Of The Pops* on the telly we'd be getting ready to go out. Me, shaving my head again, Jen wriggling into another pair of sexy shorts. We tried it the other way round but decided it was better if I had the bald head and Jen wore the hot pants. Well, them tight leather gussets, they don't half fucking chaff.

Loads more people turned up at the house. Everyone would be getting ready. My mate Michael Santry would be there, dispensing from his pockets. That's how he got his nickname, Jacket or Johnny Jacket, because people would be running around the house looking for stuff they'd lost (or never had in the first place) – Rizlas, cigs, lighters, a pen, taxi cab card, pill, whatever – and Johnny would just dip into one of his jacket pockets and pull the thing out. Johnny Jacket! Everything but the kitchen fucking sink came out of that jacket. I once said I'd lost Pamela Anderson and was going 'round looking for her in the hope that Jacket would fish a big-titted blonde out of his inside pocket . . .

Then there'd be the sounds of cars pulling up outside playing music full blast, always full of people come to meet us and go on partying to the next place.

We left then with our clubbers' convoy getting a little big bigger. We'd head for a night called 'Delicious' at the Boulevard, Ealing Broadway with Daniella Montana, Creed, Johnny Ash, Lloyd, Floyd, Errol, Rocky and Mark. That was fucking top. At some point Brendan reappeared with another bird.

The Boulevard was the place where Jenny once caused complete havoc, by accident. We were all standing at the door ready to leave, Jen and me and my mates Luke, Paul and Glen. I realised I'd forgotten to leave something with someone so I said to Jen, 'Do me a favour, babe, please, and take this back in to Tony.' And I gave Jen the thing, a little canister like a mini-foghorn.

Now this was at a time when loads of ravers on the dancefloor had those little foghorn things that they blew to the music. I mean sometimes, with the foghorns combined with dry ice, you didn't know if you were in a club or Plymouth docks. Anyway, Jen walks in to give this thing to Tony, Boo, Paul and crew and she immediately gets back into the music and starts dancing her way across the club and pressing the button on the canister, thinking it was one of those foghorns. What Jen don't know is that it's actually a CS gas canister. So she's dancing across the club leaving a trail of people hitting the floor and grabbing their eyes, and cos of the music she can't even hear them screaming. And the gas cloud grew like a ball of fire until the whole of the club panicked and made a mad stampede for the doors.

Everyone came pouring out and I'm stood there talking to my mates thinking, what the fuck's gone on in there? Anyway, I carried on talking and Jen came out, unscathed, and didn't want to really interrupt to say something like, 'Look, babe, I've just gassed out the whole club!' And because she was only wearing a leotard she didn't even have anywhere to hide the CS gas thing, so she was stood there sort of hiding it behind her back. I kept looking over at her thinking, Jen looks even naughtier than usual tonight, and getting quite horny off it – not realising she had actually been a Very Naughty Girl. So that gave us a fucking excuse to have a good spanking session a bit later!

Delicious at Boulevard closed at 4 a.m. and then we'd all go down the road to this late night coffee shop. We'd picked up a few more potential 'bleachers' by then and got a proper little ravey posse on the go. We'd give it an hour in the caff, necking coffees, whizz milkshakes and polishing off the odd tasty Danish – that was Helga, the waitress. Then back out again and back up the road to the Boulevard.

It only shut for an hour after Delicious to give the cleaners time to go round sweeping up bodies and pile them in the wheelie bin round the back. Then the Boulevard would reopen at 5 a.m. as another club called, would you believe it, Insomnia. Insomnia full of insomaniacs. That place was mental.

FRIDAY

It was morning by the time we left Insomnia, which would go on till about 10 a.m. Then we'd go up to Shepherd's Bush for about 11 o'clock to the Loft Club and a do called 'Still Buzzin'. You can really tell from the names of these clubs that they're run by people who've been there and done it, can't you? Still buzzin' . . .

But it *was* just a total buzz – going out at nightime with the car system booming out tunes, pulling up outside the club and walking straight in past the queue cos we know everyone there, going in and seeing hundreds of people bouncing around and loads of them shouting hello or coming up for a chat and a dance; getting a wave from the DJs; me getting off on Jenny doing her horny dancing and MCing or even getting off on watching everyone else get off on it; running into mates you hadn't seen for months or might've just seen in another club a few hours ago: whizzing through the whole night until you burst out into the street the next day and it's a race between who's coming up the best – you or the sun.

That's what it was like coming out of Delicious early Friday morning and shooting up to 'Still Buzzin'. It was about 11 a.m. and we were driving through ordinary daytime London, past cabs and buses of nine to fivers. We'd have a three- or four-car convoy by now with the windows down, music playing, people getting undressed and changed on the back seats. We looked like a cross between the Love Parade and the fucking Wacky Races.

One time, I just couldn't resist it. Driving through the West End in the afternoon I pulled over to the curb and called these two geezers over. We're sat there in the Rolls all sparkly eyed and in the glammed-up clobber with some anthem blaring out. When they reached the window I pointed inside and said, 'Do we look the bollocks, or *WHAT*?!' and drove off. Well, I didn't need an answer for fuck's sake. And those were the two most puzzled Japanese tourists I've ever seen in my life.

We'd leave 'Still Buzzin' still buzzin' in the afternoon and go across town to the Buzz Club Charing Cross Road. Brendan would pop up again there after going missing in the last place. The ladies' toilets in any club are like the Bermuda Triangle for Brendan: if he gets anywhere near them he disappears. Usually inside to bonk some bird in a cubicle.

One of the best Brendan stories (and there are many) was when he was at it in the ladies' bogs with this girl and he lost his footing and fell through the door, right out onto his back on the floor with a hard-on and his strides round his ankles. He looked up and saw these women doing their make-up in the mirror all looking down at him. He just went, 'Erm . . . excuse me, ladies,' got up and went back to finish the bird off in the cubicle. I think that's what they call grace under pressure. Or maybe she weren't called Grace . . . I don't know.

Late Friday night, after the Buzz Club, we'd go over to Paradise, Park Street, Islington.

SATURDAY

By morning then, we'd leave Paradise and suddenly remember that thing called food. So we'd go for something to eat at School Dinners. You must've heard of School Dinners. It's this mad little restaurant that actually does serve school fucking dinners! Sticky puddings and custard, the lot. And the waitresses are all dressed up as sexy little schoolgirls, which is a bit of a bonus. Especially when one had to bend over and chastise me for not eating all my sprouts. Serves me right for ordering three bowls.

Needless to say this is one of Brendan's favourite eating spots and he often pops in for a little pork.

Saturday afternoon we'd go to Babushka's in Elephant and Castle, which is a wine bar-type chill-out place for resting ravers, like a pit-stop for you to refuel and get a retread. We'd stay there during the afternoon and early evening. During summer we'd take over every table outside and sit there watching the world go by, trying to catch us up. We were like a little circus come to town. You could see passers-by looking around for cameras cos they thought a film was being made.

Saturday night was the big one. That's when we done a tour of all the clubs – the Ministry of Sound, the Gass, the Astoria, Heaven, the Aquarium. The Aquarium's run by my mates Lou and Timmy Ram Jam, Paul and Tony (who also own the Temple and Grace). It is the only club in London with a swimming pool inside, which is the absolute bollocks if you suddenly fancy an underwater shag. Funny as well, like when I saw this geezer off his head belly-flop in fully clothed. Then he remembered he couldn't swim and came up shouting. Only he was so out of it, the div, he didn't realise he was in the shallow end.

If we came out last out of the Astoria (after Jen had done another club gig) there was this café bang opposite the club. I remember the first time we walked in. It was still an ordinary sandwich bar-type place run by this oldish little geezer. It was a quiet place. Then we walked in and things were never the same again. There was a gang of us all still buzzing from the club and we just took the place over.

They were playing Bryan Adams, or something stupid, on the stereo so I asked the bloke if I could put one of my tapes on. I got this tape from the car of all the big dance tunes of the moment and put that on. Everyone started bouncing around and coming over to listen. The place got really crammed. But I said to everyone, 'Don't just sit there, buy something!' So the owner loved that cos his takings went through the fucking roof.

And to this day they play dance music in there and it's a really popular little spot with clubby people, and a right good little spot to go in between clubs. Oh, da power of da *tune*!

SUNDAY
Sunday morning gave you the choice of the Yacht Club, Arches, Locations or 'Mums The Word' at the Frog and

Nightgown. Or just Sunday mass at your local church. (Actually there was a club called 'Sunday Mass', so you could say you were going there and make yourself sound like a real good boy. Or a prick, depending on your view.)

Being devoutly religious myself, of course, and by that time having a fucking awful lot to confess, we'd pop down to the nearest Catholic church, break some bread, nick some wine, goose a nun and burn a priest's ears off in the confession box – 'Forgive me, Father for I have sinned. It has been thirty years since my last confession. And ever since then I've got "Not guilties". I thank you!' Then the priest just gives you ten Bloody Marys and ten how's your fathers and you're absolved. Wicked.

The Yacht Club was on Temple Pier and it was a club on, surprise surprise, a yacht. A big one and a half million pound yacht. It was run by a fella called Dobs and I used to have a rave there on Sunday mornings and afternoons. It was at the Yacht that I did one of the best exits I've ever done.

I had this mate Colin who also had his own million pound yacht, and one day I asked him to come and pick me up in it. So everyone's there on the Yacht Club, dancing away, and alongside pulls this big, gleaming white cunt of a ship – even more impressive than the one they were partying on – with music blaring and champagne on ice. Everyone's looking at it. The hooter sounded and someone on the boat said, 'Is Dave there?' I looked up and, dead casual, said, 'Yeah . . . I'll be with you in a minute.' Then I pulled on my jacket, said a few goodbyes, jumped from one yacht to the other and got the flashiest lift home I'd ever had in my life! Also with me that day doing the yacht-hopping was Jenny, Nigel Benn and Caroline, Big John and Sandy, Charlie Dixon, Joyce and Dave, Colin Butts and Dave Hurst.

The Yacht Club was also where I saw someone drown at a Sunday night do called 'Roast', held by two very good friends of mine, Everton and Kingsey. This geezer must have been out of his head raving and fell in. I just saw him shoot by in the water, shouting for help. That must've been some fucking wake-up call?: you're partying one minute then *Bang*!, in freezing cold water the next going 20 mph. I later heard he did actually die.

Sunday afternoon was the best because everyone went to the Park Club on Kensington High Street. Now you just can't park anywhere on Kenny High St, it's real posh-people country up there. Up that end of town even the pigeons wipe their arse after they've shat on you. And anything that don't move for more than a minute gets a double-yellow painted around it, then towed away. Even ambulances aren't safe. Paradise for car clampers. Or 'cunts', as we call them.

But . . . did we let that bother us. Ever so slightly NOT, I think you'll find. Because by this time we're rolling off the back of four-and-a-half days' solid clubbing, mate! And at this stage it didn't even matter if you ran out of petrol cos you kept going on adrenalin and willpower. Our own personal Loved-up Parade was up to about a dozen cars long by now and when we got to the Park Club there was forty or fifty more cars just parked everyfuckingwhere.

The clampers and tow-truck boys used to turn up, take a few cars and then just give up cos they couldn't cope with the workload. And it's always nice to get a result over those clamping cunts, ain't it?

One of the best times I remember was when we were going towards the Park one Sunday morning. There was me, Jennifer, my mates Big Jim and Birmingham John and his missus, Sandy, all driving along in this massive fuck-off Mitsubishi Shogun of John's alongside Kensington Park.

Sandy and Jen are stripping off in the back getting changed into new outfits and I'm sat up front with Big John, skinning up (see we're not that different from ordinary people – just as most of the country's preparing their Sunday joint, so are we).

I normally change in the car as well, between clubs. I've got it down to such a fine art that I can even do it when I'm driving (although we don't really talk about the polo neck/zebra crossing incident). Once when we were between clubs, and I was mid-outfit change, Jen said she fancied a cup of tea. What a fucking good idea, I thought. Then she saw a McDonald's and said, 'There! There!' I stamped on the brake and said, 'OK, babe!' and jumped out. Like Batman on a mission. I walked into McDonald's in the state I got out the car – No trousers on, just boxer shorts, shirts undone and open, one foot bare and one foot with a sock and boot on. And this was at half nine in the morning so the place was packed. But cos I've got a bit of a naughty look about me no one starts laughing or taking the piss, which is fucking funny in itself.

So I asked for some teas. The guy asked how many. I said, 'A baker's dozen'. He went, 'I know that – thirteen!' I said, 'No, eleven – divvy baker!'

Anyway, back to the story. Picture this: the sun's just coming up and the sky over the park's going all silvery-grey and orange, really putting on a good show for us. I'm sat there with one of my best mates, sharing a joint with him, our ladies are half-naked in this morning light and then, to top it all off, the tape rolls round and starts blasting out one of our favourite songs – 'Oh the love, the love I lost, was the *sweetayyst*!!' Remember that one?

I thought, Oh it just don't get any better than this. I went, 'Stop the car! *Stop*. The car!' It was one of those must-share moments again. The lucky punter this time was this old geezer shuffling by the park railings. We pulled over and I shouted to him, 'Is this a *tune* or what, mate?!' And he nodded, bless him. Then, as we were at the curb anyway, Jen and Sandy jumped out on the pavement and carried on changing and dancing. The old guy can't believe it. One minute he's out strolling along minding his own business. Next minute there's a big bald geezer shouting *Pop Quiz* questions at him, and this horny black chick in a thong and her big-titted mate in her knickers dancing on the pavement. What a touch for the old bloke, though! I bet he walked past that same spot at that same time every fucking Sunday morning for the next year.

Yeah, so Big John. You probably remember him from *Stop the Ride I Want to Get Off* (Virgin, all good bookshops). John's the only bloke I know who offered to buy his wife's tits for cash. Get this. John, cos he's a wealthy businessman in his own right as well as being a right tasty geezer in a row, took his missus Sandy to some top-notch Harley Street surgeon to have a boob job. So they're in the surgery having a consultation and the doctor says it can go ahead and the fee will be £3,000. John, being a business-minded Brummie, immediately pipes up, 'Erm . . . 'ow much would that be for cash, like?' The doctor said, 'I must say that's certainly the first time I've ever been asked!' Knowing John, I'm surprised he didn't ask if it was 'buy one, get one free'.

But, yeah ... the sun coming up over the park just as we were coming up in the Shogun, and that tune playing; that was a wicked, wicked time. I tell you, I nearly came over all hippyfied and kissed a fucking flower. Bit worrying, actually. So I whipped out my knuckleduster and whacked a low flying pigeon, just to check. (I've still got its head, stuffed on a little plaque above the fire.)

That early morning, coming-out-of-a-rave time can be a bloody funny time anyway. We went to Renaissance one New Year and we came out to go on somewhere else – fuck knows where on a New Year's day, I can't think, but I'm sure we would've found somewhere. So out we come from Renaissance and as usual I'd been sweating like a pig on a spit. It was a really nice day, the sun was just coming up, so I got some clothes from the car and started getting changed in the street. It weren't till I was half naked, just down to my undies, that I realised the 'wall' behind me was actually a massive window. It belonged to a cafe and it had completely steamed up, but someone inside had seen me and wiped a little circle to look through. Then everyone else in there followed and wiped a little circle, so I was looking at about thirty pairs of eyes looking out at me!

Which is why you should always listen to your mum and wear clean undies when you go out; just in case you're in an accident, or end up stripping off in the street in front of a cafe full of people. Funny one though that, innit, the old clean undie/accident thing? I can't imagine a doctor putting the same importance on it, somehow. Like he'd say to the parents, 'I'm so sorry. Little Johnny's broke his back, he'll never walk again, and he's also brain damaged. But worst of all ... his underpants were an absolutely bloody disgrace!'

Another time, coming out of a rave, I was really sweaty again and started to get changed. I took my shirt off cos it was wringing wet and this bloke with us lent me his leather jacket. The police pulled up because they saw me dressed like that and asked if I minded being searched. I said I didn't and they found nine quids' worth of puff in one of the pockets. And once the Old Bill checked my name they wouldn't have it that the jacket wasn't mine!

They took me to court and even though there was the guy who owned the jacket saying it was his, backed up by three other people who were there as witnesses saying the same thing, they still convicted me of it. And that was only because it was a magistrate's court. Magistrates are ordinary people, like the greengrocer or something, who volunteer to do the service once a week. They're not proper legal people really and they are ruled by the police, not by juries. The police would only have to say to them behind the scenes, 'This is Dave Courtney here, this is what he's done in the past so we'd like a conviction for this one.'

So, anyway, back to us – me, Jen, John, Sandy and Jim. We bumped the Shogun up on the pavement, bang outside the club, and left a note in the window, 'Doctor on call'. And leaving a stethoscope on the dash works fucking wonders, mate, believe me.

The Park was an interesting club for reasons beyond what it was actually like. It was more to do with where it was and what it represented. And the fact that a travelling circus like ours of spliffy, bugged-out, eeed-up, in bits, off-their-tits, up-for-it, naughty, sparkly, freaky-deaky, happy blissed-out raving lunatics could *infiltrate* the out-of-bounds posh West London and – and this was the best bit – actually take over!

Because the Park was actually a very classy joint and somewhere that would've been very much off-limits to most of our set. It was very white, upper middle to upper class, OK-yah type of set-up. But what was actually happening was that raving was evolving and acquiring a class of its own. First it had come from barns and cellars and warehouses and now it was in Kensington High Street. That was the natural progression as it went more mainstream and clubs had to roll over and play the stuff to get people through the doors, cos that's what they wanted.

It had moved on from raves like mine at the Arches, which was really a glorified car park, to the actual Park Club in Kensington.

So we just used to really, really buzz off that one. Everyone used to think they were right having it in that club cos they knew that they wouldn't have normally got within a mile radius of this place on a Saturday night without a police helicopter being mobilised and the fucking Prime Minister got out of bed. *BUT* we was in there, in the same place as them on a Sunday.

People felt accepted as well, which was a big thing. Because people now forget how shat-on and criticised and just generally kicked-about the first ravers actually were by everyone. So being there, to the geezer who's been right there from the beginning in warehouses and tents, was a big thing.

Because ravers always looked at themselves as the underdogs. Them against The Rest Of The World. Like all cults first feel (no, *cults* . . .). The rest of the world had been going, 'Just Say NO!' And the raver was frowned upon. As the doorman was when I started. Same feeling. As soon as you said 'doorman' they thought 'thug', and as soon as you said 'raver' they thought 'drugs'. Which weren't too far wrong, as it happens, but not in the negative way that it was meant by everyone else.

Everybody part of the scene just knew it was the absolute bollocks so when you were being attacked for it made you feel closer to your mates as a result. Like the siege mentality you get if you're under attack. It's just a natural defence mechanism.

And the fashion for clothes in raving developed so rich and poor looked alike. Or more accurate to say, the rich started dressing down to look like the poorer kids. Imagine that. The street kids were leading the way. You couldn't tell which was the rich kid and which was the council estate kid. So those kinds of barriers went as well.

So to go from muddy tents in fields, sewers in Slough and clubs in railway arches with very dicky toilets, to go from that right up to a swish club in the West, made you feel you were accepted – you and yours. You and your people. Best of all though, you hadn't given in or knuckled under. You had the same clobber on, same mates, same dance, same music, same drugs as you always did but in better and better places. You were winning. Or winning them over. That was the other way of looking at it: They were succumbing to Us. That's how it felt. That's how it went.

So you just picture *that* – the Park Club in Kensington and all its classy surroundings filled with us lot all dancing and bouncing around: over there's my old mate Seymour, rolling one and slowly shaking his locks; in front of Seymour a bunch of proper, old-school, baggy ravers really having it; next to them some black geezers and their ladies; at the back a clump of proper naughty lumps who are too chilled-out to do anything but smile; all around them loads of young working-class kids who are really going for it next to some older been-there/done-it boys who are still going there and still doing it; some geezer dancing and whizzing away the last of his giro money next to some glammed-up babe escaping the nine to five; Brendan with his eyes breakdancing cos there's just too much skirt to take in at once; me dancing with my Jenny dancing in front of me; Big John stood next to me, beaming like the biggest, naughtiest-looking nice guy you've ever seen while his lady, Sandy, is out on the floor shaking every penny's-worth of those three grand boobs of hers. And all this on a Sunday afternoon.

And you wonder why I never, EVER saw an episode of *The Antiques Roadshow* or *Songs of Praise*. I was *busy*, mate!

It ain't over yet. Oh, no. Not by a long chalk (whatever the fuck that means). We've still got Sunday night to do, and Sunday night was always 'the Gass' at the Koo Club, Leicester Square. Appropriately for a Sunday night, 'the Gass' became like the church, the temple of clubs.

You see, on this long long weekend you did drift in and out of company but it was the same company; familiar faces popping up and then disappearing somewhere. Saturday day there was only one or two clubs going so, if you didn't want to go home, you'd see most people there at these clubs. All the other dirty stop-outs. Then there'd be a hundred clubs Saturday night so everyone would get split up. Sunday morning there was only one or two places to go, Sunday afternoon maybe six or seven clubs, and then, Sunday night, the big one.

Because loads of different things happened on Sunday day, and there was loads of different places to go, or some people even went home to get changed, come Sunday night everyone that had split up over the weekend all converged on one place. And that was The Gass. It was time to pay homage at the great altar of The Tune in the Temple of Beats! Amen.

The Gass went on till 6 a.m. and, let me tell you, you had really been through it by that time. Through the mill and out the other side, flattened or in bits. You'd had your pills and your whizz and an awful lot of natural high just getting off on it all. You felt as energetic as you did on Wednesday or Thursday but your body had been through it. Your body was saying, 'Hang on a minute! Am I missing something here or should I have been put to bed about four fucking days ago?!' But the stuff in your veins – that little amount of blood left in your drugstream – was singing and dancing round your body, waiting for the next big chorus.

The clever ones, the bleaching regulars, the Volunteers, they brought out a few changes of clothing, a toothbrush, a bottle of scent, pen and paper to write home to their families, that kinda thing. The other ones, the Conscripts, they still had on the same fucking clobber from Thursday; wrinkly clothes from them getting wet and drying out a dozen times, hair slapped flatter than a ferret's tit, their jaw doing a go-go dance and their eyes trying to cut in. Not a pretty sight but if anyone asked you, 'Do I look all right?' you couldn't help but say, 'Yeah, mate, you look fucking top!'

It was really only the hardcore out now who went to the Gass. 'Hardcore – you know the score!' All the professionals or weekend people had got to go home cos they had work the next morning. There's the odd few, well quite a lot actually, who blast right on through and go straight to work. And you've got to admire them for that. Who said the youth of today were lazy? That's proper hard work that is, going straight from a club to clock on! Mind you, who knows how many millions have been accidentally wiped off the stock exchange, or heart attack victims left in the hospital service elevator because of some fucked-up leftover of a raver walking round on auto-pilot. Remember Chernobyl, the nuclear power plant that blew up? That was caused by one of our lot. I remember the geezer saying he had to get back to work. And the NASA space shuttle that exploded. One of ours. She fell asleep at the wheel. And don't even get me started on why they had so much trouble finishing the Millennium Dome on time . . .

If you were still with us by this time, late-on Sunday night, then you were a different kind of professional. You'd now entered the weird and wonderful world of the professional nightpeople. *Not often seen during the day, a nocturnal, nighttime creature that shuns normal society, forages for food in nearby kebab joints, drinks at some shady watering hole and often mates with the female on the fire escape steps or in a toilet cubicle.* See . . . David Attenborough? I could do that. Piece of piss.

The doorteam on the Gass were my old mates Lance, Neil, Dave Dunn, Jay Dennis, Locks, Windows, Manny and Elliot. The club was run by Dominic 'Spreadlove' (and ain't that a name you'd love having on your passport!) and a geezer called Andy Swallow.

The Gass was the place I was coming home from once, back to Woolwich, and it was about 6 o'clock in the morning. I had a car full of the usual nutters and we looked fucking monstrous. We'd been out since about September and we looked like we'd proper been through it – red-eyed, sweat running down us and steam coming off us. I pulled up at the lights next to this bloke waiting there and I saw him look over and then look away. Gotcha!

I jumped out the Roller, ran round to his car, jumped in his passenger seat and slammed the door. He looked at me like I'd just thrown his granny's head in his lap. I think he set an acceleration record for shitting yourself. I said, 'I'm coming with you! I'm not getting back in there with them!'

'You can't come with me,' he said, 'I'm going to work . . .'

'Well I ain't getting back in there with them. Just look at them!' He looked around and saw Big John, Wolfie, Funny Glen, Danny and Jacket all staring back, steaming and grinning like escaped loons. The lights had gone red and green twice by now. He said he couldn't take me to work because there was security guards there! So I said OK, thanks, and jumped out.

But that was a rare occasion when we actually came home after the Gass. It stayed open until about 6 a.m. Monday morning, which just did us fine, thank you very much. Because that just about set us up for going straight on to 'Crazy Mondays' at Futures. Oh, *listen*! 'Crazy Mondays'. I've got so much to tell ya. In fact, this five-day weekender of ours is so fucking long, I'm actually going to need another chapter . . .

9 Back to Futures: Crazy Mondays – Bleaching part II

MONDAY . . . *Hello again. Nice to see you. Glad you could make it. What? No, you look fine, mate – no, really, you look fucking top. Nice shirt as well, cheesecloth is it? Oh . . . sorry. Anyway. What do you do? Yeah – really? No, I wouldn't worry about missing work tomorrow, mate. No, don't worry. I'm sure Sellafield Nuclear Plant can manage without its Safety Manager for one day. This place? . . . it closes about . . . March, I think. Something like that. Yeah. And I love you too, matey . . .*

So many of those conversations you'd have, wouldn't you? You'd just have so many of them. All the same and all different, though. At this stage of the proceedings most people don't really know who they are, let alone where they are. And isn't it great when you're in a club full of people in exactly the same fucking state?

Which brings us to the very last club of the extended weekend, the place where it all ended, the last resort, the only place to be, the Cup Final of clubbing; ladies and gentlemen, the one and only 'Crazy Mondays'! I thank you.

'Crazy Mondays', at Futures on Deptford Broadway, became quite an infamous little gaff, as it happens, for reasons you'll soon realise. You might have read a bit about it before but I'll give you the full picture now.

Although Futures was my event, I ran it in a club owned by a geezer called Harry Hayward. Harry is a real character and is, in fact, a big face in his own right. Him and his brother Billy ran JR's down in Catford where the big shoot-out with Frankie Fraser took place. He owned half of Deptford once, did Harry – all the cab offices, nightclubs, restaurants.

Harry was famous for doing one-handed press-ups. He is a real gentleman and, in his time, was a real Robin Hood. He did a lot for the community. He could've been a multimillionaire if he'd got into some of the naughtiness that was going around, and also if he weren't so fucking generous. Cos he's got a million friends, has Harry.

There was a programme on him on telly a few years ago, *Harry's Out* or *Flash Harry* it was called; a sort of gangster documentary about him coming out of prison. He's a big joker as well. Once during the London Marathon he came out stark bollock naked and jumped on Jimmy Savile. He just launched himself through the air and Jimmy Savile saw this big, naked geezer flying towards him. He ended up rolling on the floor shouting 'Rape! Rape!', with all the crowds watching on. It was really funny. Harry definitely fixed it for Jimmy!

'Crazy Mondays' at Futures was my favourite, my fucking favourite. It ran from 6 a.m. Monday morning till about 2 p.m. in the afternoon. Remember now that we've been out since last Wednesday night, so anyone that's still along for the ride is either fucked, really fucked, completely fucked, or just about ready to leave their body to science. Science fiction, that is.

Futures was just about as fucking mental as you could get, and the fact that it was all happening on a Monday morning when most everyone else was getting up for work or taking the kids to school meant it was even more mental.

Every raving gangster in London going was there on a Monday morning. It was just packed out with what I called 'the naughtiest of the naughty'. The World Cup of Naughtiness, if you like. And all the other punters were proper, professional night people. Well, who else is going to go to a club on a Monday morning?

So there was villains, hardcore ravers, pimps, prostitutes, drug dealers, lap dancers, strippers, drag queens, club owners, club promoters, club dancers, celebrities, sports stars (Nigel Benn and Gary Mason were there), doormen, bar staff, waitresses, croupiers, gamblers, cab drivers, sex club people – basically, mostly everyone that had worked over the weekend in the nightclub trade watching other people having a good time, all came down to mine to have their own. These people weren't just colourful, they were fucking psychedelic!

Just my doorman mate Ricky walking in was enough to flip-out any 'Crazy Monday' first-timers who happened to be there. See, Ricky had a hook instead of a hand. He lost it in a car crash cos he had it out the window on the roof when the car flipped over. First he had this plastic hand but it just looked too much like what is was – a plazzy fucking hand. And like a handicap. So he had it replaced with this big hook, this big pirate's hook. It transformed him: he looked proper evil and it didn't look like a handicap any more *at all*. It actualy gave him a licence to stand there with something on the end of his arm that we would've got a couple of years for carrying. And if we ever needed a bottle opener . . .

Just the car park alone at Futures was wicked, I mean the cars out there. Professional clubbers are quite flash. They like showing out. And flash is more than acceptable. So there was rows of Bentleys, Lexus', BMWs and Mercs with alloys and dark windows. Even the motors looked naughty. The car alarms didn't scream – they just growled at you.

And everyone had their money – the workers with their wages, the drug dealers with their wedges, gamblers with their winnings, etc. And everyone was completely *fucking* cake-holed, mate! Completely. It really was the absolute bollocks.

One of the maddest bits of it was how you got into the club. Futures was a massive club but 'Crazy Mondays' was held in this VIP part at the back. So to get to it you'd walk across the floor of the main club, which was completely empty, and get to this door at the back. When you opened this door that went down into the basement it was *just* like a scene from a film! Totally silence outside . . . open the door . . . then WHAM! you got punched in the face by the heat and the noise and the smell of it. *Whack!* just like a smack in the face. The racket and the lights came up out of the cellar and punched you.

And trumpets. Yeah, truly, fucking trumpets. This black geezer whose name, believe it or not, was Lester Piggot, used to bounce around blowing on this bleedin' trumpet all night long.

When people opened the door you could tell if it was their first time cos they'd just stand at the top of the stairs going *Wowwww!* And when you walked down into it it was like walking into hell: low ceilings, really hot, everything deep deep red and brass, blood red flock wallpaper, red carpet and these four red leather Chesterfield sofas. What I did was push them all back to back in the middle to make a space for the DJ to play in. Then there was this hole at the end for a bar.

It was like something straight out of a film. This ridiculously hot, dark, noisy little nuthouse full of the sparkiest cunts going; so there'd be this black geezer blowing a trumpet over there, thick-necked clumps over here, out-of-it ravers going fucking barmy, drag queens coming out of the ladies' bogs, sexy babes talking to scarred, scary-faced hardnuts. If you'd tried, really tried to make something look the most illegal and naughty thing in the world, Futures is what you'd model it on. It was Base Camp One for sparkly people.

Actually, it was the closest thing I'd seen to what you imagine those American speakeasys of the 1920s they used to have in New York and Chicago during Prohibition. Y'know, those little secret-knock-on-the-door places in basements. As close to that as you'd get in real life. But with dance music instead of jazz.

It was the only club with no doormen. Well, I weren't gonna pay my own boys to work my own place, was I? All the doormen from all the other clubs came down. And all the other club promoters as well, cos you couldn't really enjoy their own nights cos they were working. You never enjoy doing your own, really. Timmy 'Ram Jam' and Lou from Aquarium came down, amongst many others; all the people from the Chocolate Candy Box, and all the naughty girls from School Dinners in the West End and Jan.

Anyway, we didn't really get much aggro, funnily enough. There was odd bits. Like one time I saw this row brewing so I told them to take any fighting outside. I asked what the problem was. These people said this bloke had been robbing handbags, but he said he hadn't. I asked him to empty his pockets and he did and there was nothing there so I told the others to fuck off.

He was a big French geezer, he was. A right big bodybuilding cunt in just a leather waistcoat, leather trousers and black Raybans. Yeah, I know, I should've known just from how the geezer was dressed. So, then he's dancing away and smiling over at me like everything's OK. Anyway, bit later on I'm up in reception and the same people that had been arguing with him downstairs come up to the door with bits of wood. I said, 'Where are you going with them?' And they said they were going downstairs to do the French geezer. They'd just smashed his car windows in and found all these stolen purses and bags inside. They showed me the stuff.

I said to them, 'Hold it. No one hits any cunt in my club unless I've hit him first.' I thought, That cheeky cheeky bastard. He'd put me in a position of actually defending him when he was in the wrong. I could not believe he'd taken the piss out of me like that.

So I goes back downstairs and he's dancing away, still smiling at me cos I saved him earlier. I thought, Wait a minute, I ain't done the old Whispering Trick for ages. So I push through to him where he is on the edge of the dancefloor bit, motioned to him as if I wanted to whisper to him, and when he turned his ear towards me . . . *Smack!* First Class delivery from Knuckleduster Inc. Knocked him spark out. They took him upstairs. Later on in the week, by the way, I saw him out in a mate's club and gave him a clump there as well, for good measure.

Mostly, though, it was just funny stuff. Lester Piggot, for instance, the black trumpet player, our own little resident Louis Armstrong, he was a fucking funny fucker. He was such a sticky-fingered little bleeder that, after a club, if you went back to someone's house to chill-out, Lester would always nick stuff. Then he'd give it away to you, like he was being really generous! So next time you were out someone would come up to you and say, 'Dave, don't get me wrong, that waistcoat suits you and you can keep it now, *but* it does happen to be mine, mate. Lester nicked it from my wardrobe!'

He really didn't give a fuck, old Lester. One time he had these really fucked-up, moody fifty pound notes. I said I didn't want anyone taking fifties in the club cos I knew I'd get some of these dodgy ones. Harry Hayward was generous with friends but in business he was so tight that even though he was making three grand from the club – *and* on a fucking Monday morning when everyone else was shut! – even then, if he found a dud note in the count he'd say that I owed him fifty quid! Eh? Get that! I *know*, it was fucking ridiculous.

So Lester ends up giving one of these duff fifties to Tucker, Ian Tucker. Now that's not a very smart move, and Lester must've known he'd get beaten up for it. But he didn't care. He just lived for the moment. He didn't even think of the 30 seconds ahead of that moment: which is about all the time it took for Tucker to notice that on his fifty the Queen had a beard and a mohican haircut. Tucker couldn't get his head round it, that this cheeky geezer had tried to so blatantly skank him with a fake fifty. In the meantime the black Lester Piggot had gone off like the white one on a horse with its arse on fire – he'd fucking bolted, mate.

Another time a bad fifty figured in it. I didn't have drugs in there but if it happened, it happened, y'know what I mean. Anyway, this woman came up to me and asked me if it was my club, so I said yeah. Then she went, 'Well, I've been selling Es in here and look . . . someone's given me a fake fifty pound!' I just stood there genuinely gobsmacked, which ain't like me. I thought she was winding me up but she was serious. She was genuinely outraged. I thought, *What!* That fucking takes the biscuit though, don't it? A drug dealer making a formal complaint to 'de management'. That's how mental that place could be. You just didn't get that kinda fucking nuttiness elsewhere.

What was really funny was when someone booked a strippergram dressed up as a policeman and the second he walked in the door he just got jumped on and beaten up. No one even thought for a second it was a stripper. He just walked in, opened his mouth to start singing his little ditty and WHACK!

The music was underground house and garage. That's how much things had changed since when I first went clubbing, just in the names of things. I remember when underground house meant a gaff with subsidence, and garage was a lock-up where you kept nicked gear.

The DJs at Futures were Dean Lambert, Dominic Spreadlove, Creed, Carl 'Tuff Enuff' Cox, Nigel Benn, Carl Brown, Brandon Block, Ian Jay, Norris d'Boss Windross, Daniella Montana, Bob Andrews, Steve Flighty, Ray Hurley and Boris. All blinding DJs, but I couldn't help watching them and thinking, I could do that.

So one time when the DJ put on a record and went to the toilet and while he was there it started jumping, I thought, I've always fancied this DJing lark, it can't be that hard. So I just got up and put another record on (I didn't even know what record I'd picked out), wedged the headphones against my ear, queued up another disc, spun it and practically threw the needle on. I actually managed to do a perfect mix and everyone just started cheering. I thought, Touch! Give me some more of *that* (applause junkie? What . . . me?). So the DJ come back and me, old cocky bollocks, said, 'No – I'm doing it now.' And then in the next minute I really cocked it up and proper mugged myself off.

Another time, right in the middle of it all, music playing, everyone dancing and all that, I got up on the DJ stage bit, stopped the music and got out these two, big soup ladles. I said, 'This is my club and if you don't clap you can fuck off.' Then I played 'Slave To The Vibe' on spoons. The full routine, on my head and on my knees, for two minutes. That went down like a two-bob tart on roller skates. But they *did* clap, bless 'em.

You can see that people from all walks of life went to Futures, but everyone was pedalling at the same speed, if you know what I mean. Professional night people all of them. From cab drivers to gangsters. And it had the most unified, clubby, Them and Us feeling about it. That feeling that you always loved the most when you got it. You felt honoured to be part of it. It was one of those that felt like a second home for you. Probably first home for some of them. We even had big rubber plants in there, for fuck's sake!

And Harry, old Harry Hayward, he used to sit there in the corner of the club watching all these lunatics. He could *not* get his head around it. He has this really deep voice as well, does Harry, and he leant over to me one time and said, 'I've never seen so many ugly birds in my life,' then he pointed at one and said, 'That's mutton dressed as pork, that is.' Oh, get that! I really *love* that line – Mutton dressed as pork! I didn't have the heart to tell him it was a drag queen.

No, Harry just couldn't get to grips with it. But the tills were going ker-ching! ker-ching! He used to sell shit champagne, though. See, Harry, in business, was so tight he'd actually water down *water*. And one weekend he went, 'Dave? End of every night I keep finding forty empty Moët champagne bottles everywhere, and I don't even sell Moët!' I said, 'Well, take the hint, Harry. Sell Moët and nothing but Moët!'

He'd just sit there looking at it for hours, shaking his head, for eight hours on end. It was mental, though. He had plenty to look at. Also, because it was a basement – low ceiling and no windows or ventilation – you really did get stoned just from breathing in. You didn't even have to do anything. I sometimes wondered if Harry stayed on that seat in the corner all night just because he was fucked from passive smoking.

And he could not believe how much I sweated. Cos when I have a little dance it really leaks out of me, it pours out of me. Harry couldn't believe that one geezer, me, would go out and bring six shirts with him. Which I did because I'd get soaking wet, wringing wet.

So what with all the mutton dressed as pork, me sweating more than Tom Jones in a sauna and knocking out French bodybuilders, dealers complaining about moody money, mysterious bottles of Moët kicking around, dancing doormen, chilling Rastas, hand-waving ravers, Lester Piggot on trumpet, Brendan on any bird, me on spoons, and everyone else on anything they could get their little hands on . . . Harry had a *proper* little window on the best wildlife show this side of an African safari park.

So the, for Futures, we even hit on the idea of promoting it with novelty flyers – funny flyers. It didn't need promoting at all, really, but I just wanted the excuse to do something stupid. But then people started looking forward to these flyers coming out so we had to keep it up. They looked something like this:

BACK TO THE FUTURES
AND ABOUT FUCKING TIME AS WELL
FROM THIS SUNDAY 14TH JANUARY
6 a.m. till 1 p.m.
£4 ON DOOR OR £10 WITH THIS FLYER
DJ's – Ain't made my mind up yet
PAs by my Bird.

THE FIRST 7,000 GET A FREE OUT-OF-DATE KINDER EGG.

THIS TIME ROUND WE WILL BE TAKING <u>NO MOODY</u>
<u>MONEY</u> BEHIND BAR
(So Sorry Lester)
STRICT DOOR SEARCH – ANYONE FOUND WITH EITHER
ILLEGAL SUBSTANCES OR AT LEAST ONE WEAPON WILL
BE FUCKED RIGHT OUT OF IT.
ALL FIREARMS, HAND-GRENADES AND CROSSBOWS
MUST BE LEFT AT THE DOOR – HAND TO HAND
COMBAT WEAPONS ARE OK.

ANYBODY TAKING OFFENCE TO ANY PART OF THIS
FLYER FUCK OFF AND DON'T COME

<u>STRICT DRESS CODE</u>: ALL MEN IN GREEN WADERS, RED
THONG AND LONG BLONDE WIG. ALL WOMEN MUST
WEAR A BROWNIE OR CUB UNIFORM – OK

ABSOLUTELY EVERYONE IS INVITED . . .
except people I don't like.

PLEASE BRING YOUR OWN RIZLAS AND STOP
ASKING ME!
THE MANAGEMENT RESERVE THE RIGHT TO KICK
EVERYONE'S HEAD IN IF THEY WANT JUST FOR FUCK
ALL . . . THANK YOU
ADVANCE TICKETS – CALL SCOTLAND YARD OR ANY
LOCAL POLICE STATION

You get the idea? The other side had a photo of me posing artistically with my knuckleduster. I actually got took to court over one flyer and they fined me £1,000 under the Obscene Publications Act, just because it said 'cunt' a couple of times. That's five hundred quid per cunt! Cunts.

The Old Bill knew very well what kind of place it was but, as one of them said to me, 'We don't know what you're doing in there, Mr Courtney, but it's really nice for us to know you're all under one roof.' Well, it obviously weren't a local Tupperware party, know what I mean? Sorry, Dhalia (a dealer I know).

The police finally decided to shut us down after four independent drug squads, which were all from different forces and all following different people, all converged on the Futures car park at the same time! I think that was a bit of a sign. I just liked the thought that four different sets of undercover Bill ended up sat out there in the car park checking each other out, looking at each other and thinking, Who the fuck are they?

The biggest crime committed over 'Crazy Mondays' at Futures was that it got closed down at all.

Boris was a mate and I'd done Futures with him and a mate called Nashers. He was a blinding geezer but as mad as a boiled fish. And talking about 'boiled', that was Boris's racket. Boilers, that is.

Listen to this. If Boris needed money quick he used to go and nick boilers. Yeah, boilers. Not cars or stereos or jewellery or TVs or garden fucking gnomes: nothing easy to carry and sell. He knew this geezer that'd give him four hundred quid on the spot for a boiler. And when Boris wanted money now, Boris wanted money NOW. He wanted it that minute. So if Boris ran out of cash halfway through the weekend, he'd run out the club, find an empty house, rip its boiler out, sell it, and be back in the club buying drinks a few hours later. I swear to God that's what he did. How fucking *nuts* is that? And how much did old Boris love raving that he'd go out on a fucking Boiler Mission just to stay out?

This is how much Boris loved raving – when it ended at Futures he took over the 'Crazy Mondays' name and started having it at his house. I mean, get *that*. Fucking hell, that's what it meant to people. And Boris missed it so much, and everyone couldn't bear it not being there any more, that he started doing it in his *own house* for fuck's sake! Every Monday morning. He ended up making so much money from it that he actually gave up work. He was making thousands just from doing 'Crazy Mondays' at Boris's gaff one day a week. Check that out for enterprise. He should've got a fucking government grant for services to the community.

Mind you, the neighbours didn't think so because there weren't no closing time. And come Monday morning when they were all going to work or taking the kids to school, Boris's place was still jumping, music playing, people sat along the front wall still buzzing, fifty geezers in the front garden, half-dressed tarts and fully cut ravers all dancing about, cars bumped up on pavements everywhere. We even put a three-piece suite out on the curb and sat out on that in the sunshine. It was almost as mental as the Futures version.

The neighbours would rush by shielding their kids' eyes and trying not to look themselves. It weren't built to last, really, and it didn't. Cos someone burnt poor old Boris's house down, as it happens. The local Neighbourhood Watch were strangely quiet on that one as well. Funny that.

Sometimes the best bit of the night is just chilling at home with your mates. Some nights I'd go out just so that I could come home. True. I'd go out an hour before the night ended just to find a good group of people to bring back my house. I do enjoy sitting around in a room after a night out.

I used to have a flat in Docklands, and straight out of my window was the only man-made beach on the Thames. Granted it was only a little strip where they set the canoes off from, but it was still a fucking beach in my book. Especially when me and my mate Warwick stuck a couple of sun loungers and a big sun umbrella out there. That made a few canoeists flip a few Eskimo rolls I can tell you! And it was a fucking good place to sit in a morning after a club.

But the whole going back to the house thing, after a club, was the modern equivalent of the slow last dance that they had at the end of the night when I first started clubbing. In them days the last dance was when everyone began to wind down. Now, though, it's the absolute opposite of that – the last song in a club is probably the banging one of the night! Everyone's going mad, arms in the air, and then STOP, just like that. Lights on. Everyone's shouting More! One more, they say.

So the wind down, last dance, chill-out part of today's clubbing became going back to some geezer's house and crashing on a bean bag. Then the chill-out became such a major part of clubbing that they incorporated it into the club: the chill-out room. That's something that weren't there at the begining of raving. And now there's even after-club clubs. Chill-out clubs. Little after-hours dens where people can crash out for a smoke.

Afterwards it could be so funny, just so funny, watching the after effects of being stoned on people around you. It's always better in the right company as well, ain't it? About a dozen mates all in the one room brings out the humour in it all. That was just a wicked, wicked time.

Also, back home in the chill-out room is where you'd get the really good gurners. You get good ones in clubs under the strobe lights, y'know, where it looks like a geezer's face is having a fight with itself! or a girl looks like she's trying to turn her jaw into a shower cap. But it looks even better and more freaky outside of a club and under normal conditions. Like when someone's sat on a sofa opposite you, you can get a proper uninterrupted view of their face arguing with itself – jaw going south, eyes up north, tongue heading west, then they all change and go the opposite ways!

We'd usually end up crashed out at my place, cars filling the drive and up on pavements. The curtains drawn to block out the day cos you wanted the night to go on. I'd be in an armchair with a joint on the go and Jen probably sat on the floor between my legs or in my lap; Seymour nodding his locks to some mellow music, Jack beside him; Brendan on the sofa gurning for England with a girl either side of him – one monged-out, one merry, both in trouble cos he's gonna shag them; DJ Daniella still moving to the music in her head; Wolfie and Danny Do and me swopping stories; a few nameless babes scattered about for visual effect; Johnny Jacket fishing into his pockets for . . . whatever: and everybody still buzzing but in that quieter, after-club come-down way that just feels like the absolute bollocks. Just pure entertainment.

And that, ladies and gentlemen, is the finale to the Wonderful and Weird World Of Bleaching. Mental, though, wasn't it? All done on nothing more than a few strong coffees. He said. And even after all that – out and about five days solid – I still made it in first thing Tuesday morning to help out at the local Help The Aged shop without fail. Yes I did.

In fact, I think I might open up my own chain of little charity shops to dispense care and biscuits to those unfortunate members of the nightclubbing community who sometimes need a bit of shelter after the weekend. What d'ya think? I'll call it, 'Help The Ravaged'.

10 Let's Have a Whip Round!

I've had some raves and club nights in some fucking funny places, come to think of it. And I don't just mean Peckham.

How about 10,000 feet in the air? That was the idea anyway. I was gonna have a rave on a plane and call it 'Cloud 9'. Hold it in an army tank carrier type plane. Capital Gold were going to sell tickets for it. They would be £500 each and the capacity was 180 without the staff. And once you're over a certain height in the air there's no drinking laws or stuff like that. Which ain't very reassuring if you've got a pilot who's into drink driving, but there you go. They keep telling us that more people die in cars than planes, don't they? And don't they always forget to mention how many people survive car crashes and how few walk away from plane smashes? I've had loads of car crashes and I'm still here. But when you crash in a plane you fucking *crash*, mate, don't ya? You know that.

Anyway, fuck all that, I thought, if there's no ordinary laws up there I can make myself King for the day! And the first law I'd pass is that it is compulsory for all beautiful women to sleep with the King Of Cloud 9. And pay for the privilege.

In trying to organise this rave I had to buy air space to get a test flight done. This was to see whether the music and everyone dancing at the same time might affect the plane too much. So the aviation authority got those part-time army blokes to go up in the plane and drill march in mid-air!

Fucking hell, what a thought, army-organised raves! You'd have to be out of bed by 6 a.m. with your clubbing gear all laid out on your bed for kit inspection – clothes, change of shirt, fags, Rizlas, puff, pills, chewing gum and Ribena. You can just see the sergeant major shouting at everyone, 'Put your arms in the air you 'orrible little ravers! Wait for it, wait for it ... right, *DANCE!!*'

I spunked three-and-a-half grand on setting up 'Cloud 9'. On paying for air space, hiring the plane and blokes and buying fuel. Three-and-a-half grand ain't much when you're looking at a return of 90, but it's a fucking lot of money when your return is fuck all. And the return was fuck all cos the flight tests that day came back saying it couldn't go ahead. Too much wing-wobble or something like that. As if anyone on that plane during one of my raves would've even cared if the wings fell off the plane, or even *felt* anything if it hit the ground.

So I organised to have a do on a train instead. And just hoped a plane didn't crash on it.

It was the Brighton Belle, from London to Brighton. You can hire the Belle for private parties but not for a club night. So I just didn't tell them. Then once it was under way it was too late to stop us. I mean they weren't gonna slam the brakes on and back up were they?

That was a really good one. It was like a long, skinny club! – people dancing up and down the aisles, one carriage was taken over as a chill-out zone, on board bar, ready-made-shagging-cubicles (sorry, toilets); they even supplied these little red toffee hammers on the walls behind glass! Nice touch. A lot of people got sick though, and blamed it on bad pills, but it was just the rocking of the train that fucked them up. There was half a dozen ordinary British rail staff on duty and trying to keep things in order, and clean up the sick. You just had to dance in time to the train, that's all!

The plane didn't get off the ground, the train rocked, the Rolls was too small to have much of a party in, so that only left a boat for me to try out. So I had a few raves and fetish dos on ferries, the Ostend ferry. As well as natural rave sickness we also had wave sickness. E-legs and sealegs all 'round then. On the way back we could have all been on the *Titanic* for all we cared.

Then I had about twenty more little fetish nights on the hire boats going up and down the Thames. They were really horny little nights. But way before then, when I'd first heard of the fetish scene, I thought it was full of a bunch of freaks, to be honest.

First time I worked security at a fetish do was Sunday afternoon at the Limelight. Working there with me was a big geezer called Scotty, Chris, Terry and Tony from Croydon and Phil. At the time, cos I didn't know the scene, I thought it was a fetish do but actually it was more of an S&M thing, which is different. (Even more different is an M&S do – that's where everyone wears clothes from Marks & Spencer. Yeah, I know – ain't that sick!)

It was weird old music they were playing as well. Hard, disturbing stuff, not dance music cos they weren't there for dancing. They were there for the hardcore whip action! They really wanted to be bashed around and smacked. Yeah, proper hardcore smack heads.

In the S&M world there's fewer grey areas (not counting some old birds' pubes). You can't be just half into it, you've got to go all the way. And there's less spectating as well. It's too fucking hardcore and not at all erotic, to me anyway. Each to their own. I'd get no pleasure from nailing Jen's tit to the wall. I'm sure she wouldn't either.

But at fetish nights there's loads of people jumping around raving in sexy clothes, y'know, the dancing and having a laugh is half of it. But this S&M thing was purely for the pain of it, the whole play-acting-fantasy bit. I stood there watching it and I got it all wrong because I thought fetish nights were all the same. And I thought, Well having my bollocks nailed to a piece of wood and a satsuma shoved up my arse just ain't my idea of fun, y'know what I mean? It weren't like I was a Tory MP or anything. So someone doing tug-o-war on my nipples with wooden clothes pegs, beating me with the ironing board, sucking my knob with the Hoover and whipping me with the washing line is not what I'd call a good night out. (Actually, that sounds more like a night *in* . . .)

This was all on a Sunday afternoon as well, which made it seem stranger somehow. While people were outside going about their everyday business, there were people in the dark in there hitting each other so fucking hard they were bleeding, and then rubbing witch hazel in the wound. When I did debt collecting I didn't treat people half as bad as that, even when they owed millions!

That would've been an idea though, wouldn't it? Using one of these S&M geezers on a debt collection. Pull up outside the bloke's house and if he hasn't got the money just give a signal and out of the back of your car climbs the Gimp from *Pulp Fiction*! How fucking freaky would that've looked?! A geezer in a full black leather suit, leather hood and studded collar stood in your front room whimpering behind a face mask. Fucking mental. Pay by next week or we put a pool ball in your mouth and set the Gimp on you.

I mean I haven't led a sheltered life by any means but some of those sights at the Limelight opened my eyes. Maybe it's cos I'd never seen a women tied to a cross with her fanny lips clamped in the teeth of a geezer down on his knees and wearing just a thong. Or a half-naked, sixteen stone woman in her fifties with a shaved head and nipple rings, wanking-off a young black guy over her tits. And a fat geezer in biker boots and shorts being paddled on the arse by a young bird. I mean, call me old-fashioned. But that ain't exactly *Songs Of Praise* is it? Thongs Of Pain, maybe.

Then after I worked security on the other kind of fetish parties it started to intrigue me. The first I'd heard about it was from some really good friends of mine who were proper respectable. You wouldn't call her a tart or him bisexual. I got talking to them one day and they explained about these places they go where they jump around having an orgy. And I'd been thinking it was some other geezer rubbing up against you with no clothes on, and I wouldn't want that whether I was shagging his missus or not.

So I got to see that it was just really horny, sexy people with no hang-ups and into having a fucking good time. I thought, sounds like my kinda scene – cancel my library card I'm going fetishing! They didn't have any hang-ups about jealousy either, these people, and that was the key to it. But I guess if you're fucking some bird over the sofa you're in no position to complain about your wife getting banged on the pool table. Probably in no position to see it either.

The first one I went to was in this castle in Tunbridge Wells. It was mental. Really good and very, very horny. The place was massive so there was loads of playrooms with different things going on. Very S&M in some parts, so if you wanted that you just followed the sounds of someone having an egg whisk spun up their backside. And parts of it were orgy-like.

Or you could just borrow someone else's missus and go off with your missus. I'm lucky because Jen is bisexual. She likes a bird as much as I do. Her philosophy is: why go and shag one bird when I can take her home and have two! I'm a very lucky fella.

So we started going regular. There were different levels according to what kind of parties they were. There was one called the 'Toucan Club' at Bootleggers, and they were milder compared to the S&M ones. These were the kind of clubs where you could join in and get a foothold, so to speak, and a little control. I found it exciting anyway, and cos Jen is such a star she started doing her shows at these places. Stark naked rapping shows. It was mental.

It was easy for me to get right proper involved in it cos I'd walked in first as a voyeur. On top of that I had the sexiest dancer on the firm, my Jen. And with my Jen as an added attraction to get another bird. It was like having the top conker – a real 74-upper! I could grab anyone in there. We played more along the lines of attracting other ladies for us, rather than couples with a bloke for Jen cos that's not her thing.

Doing security at these places and going there for pleasure as well gave me a Filofax full of nice, high-ranking, well-connected perverts. As high up the ladder as you can think in the legal trade, lots of professional people. I met a lot of police in there, as it happens, and actually took a couple along myself. I took one copper to one of these dos and Jen ended up banging his missus. Now you never saw that on *Dixon Of Dock Green* or the fucking *Bill*, did you?

Most people, if they do see a copper they recognise, get frightened that the copper's gonna recognise them. The punters are too hung up on that – 'Oh God, he's seen me, what if he tells the school?' – that they don't think about what they might have on the copper. But ain't that obvious? He's only seen you there because he's there. And let him try and pass off having a baby-oiled broomstick stuck up his arse as undercover work. Fucking deep undercover that one. Above and beyond the call of duty I'd say, officer.

But I looked at that particular discovery in a different way.

You'd be surprised at the people that go there. You really would. I'm not saying the Queen Mum goes there or anything, and you wouldn't want her to, would you? Just the thought of her bent over getting her wrinkly arse caned and grinning with those teeth of hers like a row of dirty peanuts. Urgh. And wanting to see something like that ain't no fetish, mate, that's either mental illness or proper short-sightedness.

Actually, there is a porno fetish for old birds. Out of morbid curiosity I once watched this video a mate brought back from America. *Cock Gobblin' Grannies*, it was called. Sixty and seventy-year-olds sucking and fucking these twenty-year-old geezers. Oh dear, it was *fucking* repellant. I was nearly watching it from behind a cushion. I lit a cigar just to get rid of the smell it made you imagine. And I never thought I'd be able to eat another chicken or turkey as long as I lived.

But the Queen Mum aside, you did meet all the kinds you read about in the papers being there but never thought would be – police, lawyers, judges, bank managers, school teachers, politicians, doctors, TV weathermen. Fuck knows how that last one got in! TV weathermen? Oh yeah, that was cos one night I saw . . . well, I can't tell can I? All I can say is there was a very warm front moving in down south on that person. And the TV presenter I saw there once? Let's just say when he asked someone if they wanted a suck of a ginger nut he weren't talking biscuits.

I didn't really have to go too out of my way to be all fetishy. I'm usually all blacked-up, clothes-wise, and a shaven headed geezer in black looks like some people's fetish anyway, know what I mean? So if me and Jen were there, me looking like I do and Jen looking and dancing like she does, we'd get people coming up to us all the time. Men and women. The men we gave a polite refusal to, the women we asked to form an orderly queue. And no pushing at the back – we will get through you all!

And doing the raves and especially the fetish things I learned that you have to be gay-friendly to be successful in certain businesses cos a lot of people in that world, and music and entertainment, are gay or bi. And they do spend their money when they go out as well. Not drink-nursing cunts like some ravers are.

Anyway, so a lot of these geezers on the scene actually liked me and Jen cos they saw us talking to everyone, so they'd approach us. I'm the skinhead in black and they like that look. And they'd say stuff to Jennifer like, 'When you've done with him, I'll have him!'

I once nearly cut a geezer in half with a whip, though. This geezer come dancing up to me in a cowboy hat, two little guns, and wearing leather cowboy chaps, no trousers, bollocks hanging out and carrying a whip. I wouldn't say he was exactly *Butch* Cassidy, more like the Bumdance Kid. Anyway, he danced right into the middle of us and without saying a word he put the whip in my hand, turned around and faced the wall. I turned to Jen and just smiled, like 'He can't say he didn't ask for it . . .'

You're supposed to just go tap, tap, tap and all that, gradually building up to however hard the person wants it. I thought, This geezer looks like a glutton for punishment to me so let's not mess about. Start as you mean to go on, as my nan used to say. I unfurled the whip and did a proper Indiana Jones swirl round the head and then whip-crack-*away*! – SMACK!! He jumped forward so hard that even above the music we heard his bollocks splat against the wall. He went, 'No more! No more!' Good call. His arse swelled up redder than a baboon's.

Some people just go a little bit too far though, don't they? There's always one. This one geezer, for instance, was dancing around wearing just Caterpillar boots and bright pink Speedo shorts with Australia written across the bum. Not exactly your typical Aussie bloke and definitely someone you wouldn't want to see down under.

Anyway, this geezer kept dancing up to me and shaking his arse at me and all that stuff, and I just smiled and let him go on with it. No harm. I put up with it for ages but he just persisted so fucking much that I could barely even talk to someone without him getting in the way! It was getting downright fucking rude, to be honest. Then he'd turn to me and say, 'Oh, making you embarrassed am I?'

So I took my cigar and blew the end till it *glowed* and touched the tip to the map of Australia on the back of his little wiggling pink Speedos. I torched him right on Sydney! He shot off like Linford Christie on crack. What a dance he did then, it was like a cross between the Twist and the Black Bottom.

Another time one of them big trannies got me. He was about seven foot fucking tall this geezer, you know how big they are in their heels, and this one was a proper man-size cunt in a dress and wig. He went, 'Oo look at you, ya big skinhead!' and grabbed my face and squashed it like a cushion! I'm there, with my face all squidged up! And if he'd just pecked me I wouldn't have done anything – unlike most of the chaps I know who would've broken his wrists, for starters – but I can handle that kind of stupid stuff more than most. BUT, and this is the thing, this cunt actually *licked* me across my mouth. I just went, Arrgh! and did the old cigar trick on his arse.

He did a bloody good impression of Linford Christie as well. Maybe I should be there behind our guy in the starting blocks at the next Olympics. You can just hear the commentary can't you? – 'The German trains fanatically, the American is a natural, the Italian is hungry for success, and the British guy is about to get a lit cigar stubbed out on his arse.'

That was bang out of order and disgusting though, wasn't it, what that tranny did? I don't even want my own tongue in my mouth sometimes cos I know where it's been! So I'm fucking sure I don't want some bleedin' drag queen's. Anyway, the cigar solved it because, to be honest, I just did *not* want to get dragged into it.

It is easy to misread people though. This guy once started dancing behind Jenny when she was dancing in front of me. Fellas often do that to my Jen, she brings that bit of sexy boogie right out in them and it's good to watch. Especially if the bloke's a crap dancer. But this particular geezer just wouldn't stop and he got closer and closer and kept making these funny sounds. I said to him, 'All right, mate, enough's enough'; but he wouldn't stop. He was nearly up her arse now and still making these odd noises, so I chinned him to get him away.

Anyway, later Jen goes out to the foyer to get something and she sees this bloke with a bust lip trying to explain to one of the doormen what happened. And it was then that she realised he was a deaf and dumb geezer! If I'd known that I wouldn't have had to fat-lip him, I could've just given him the 'wanker' hand signal and then stuck two fingers up. Well, that's sign language, ain't it?

Then there was this girl tied spreadeagled on a cross with a gag in her mouth and blindfolded. I thought, I hope that ain't the cloakroom attendant cos we're going in an hour! There was a bloke stood nearby watching people watch her and I figured out it must be her fella. So I had a little chat with him, all friendly, and found out the name of his missus on the cross. I went back a while later, no, it was about an hour later, come to think of it, cos we got distracted, and she was still fucking there.

I put my mouth up to her ear and said, 'Hello there. It's Angela ain't it? . . .' Her head turned to me but she couldn't see or say anything cos of the blindfold and the gag. I went, 'Thought so. I used to go to school with you, babe. I'm here with another girl from the same year who remembers you. If I'd known this then I could've knocked you up a cross in woodwork!'

I said I'd meet her behind the bikesheds afterwards and fuck me if she didn't look excited by the prospect! You just can't fucking shock anyone in those places.

What a lot of the fetish clubs actually are are places to meet new stock to take back to your house for private parties. That's what a lot of them are used for. Like a big, horny persons Job Centre. And I just got *right* into that, the recruitment centre bit. Putting people with people is what I'm best at and known for doing. Hence *The Yellow Pages* of Crime nickname I got. And that's where meeting some of the professional people in there came in really handy. Especially in the legal trade and the police.

The fetish club scene ain't really a jack-the-lad type thing. Although they like to think it is, a lot of young blokes, with what they imagine goes on there. But in reality it's all too open for them. They'd freak out. 'That bird wanted to put her fingers up my arse!', that's what they'd say. A lot of geezers back down when they meet upfront women. Me? I usually just *lay* down. (Start as you mean to go on.)

So it attracts a different crowd. Not older really, cos there's loads of young people there, but different. And a lot of wealthy people. It's a common fact, I think, that the rich have the more bizarre sex lives. People think the word 'slut' goes down to council estate level, or whatever, but the more bourgeois the people the more decadent they are. It comes with money: the freedom to be able to indulge in all that.

As well as playing on the fetish scene I was also working it. I started my own night called 'Hot and Spunky'. We had that all over the place. In hotel suites, Limelights, Futures, Lakeside, Cherry Tree at Stoneyford Lodge in Nottingham, one in the restaurant of the Post Office Tower (which was hired out for private functions). All over. We literally fucked all over London. The Thames is really just a big wet patch.

In the Post Office Tower one we had people getting fucked up against the glass as the restaurant span round. They got a proper good view of London as they also got properly poked. You'll not hear one of those people moan about service from the Post Office.

There used to be a club called the House in Forest Gate. It had a big swimming pool and was a really top venue. I'd had a couple of blues and I was proper on it. I had a hard-on like a baby's frozen arm. Jen got out the jacuzzi and lay on the tiled bit so she still had one leg in the jacuzzi. I had one leg in the water and was half-standing up for a bit of leverage. Now that's a proper power-fuck, ain't it? Y'know, when you can really get a foothold. We banged away for a couple of hours, with everyone else doing it around us. It was quite mental.

That was the same night that Jen nearly swallowed half the swimming pool. She was sat on the edge watching me swim about. Then I ended up treading water by her but she thought I was standing there. I didn't realise that so when I pulled her in she didn't prepare with a breath and sank right to the bottom of the deep bit with no air. That was an interesting next twenty seconds. We stayed on dry land for a bit after that.

They had this stag do once at the House. These three strippers got these blokes on stage, stripped them off and handcuffed them to the chairs. Now I cannot believe that these blokes got up on stage for *that*, but if you watch strippers work a crowd they don't half make it hard for blokes to refuse. The girls rip the guys' shirts off and get the crowds cheering. So then, after a bloke's been dragged out of the audience and on stage in front of his mates, been cuffed to a chair and had a sweaty pit pushed in his face, the last thing he's thinking about is getting a hard-on. And all three of these geezers on stage couldn't get it up.

I was stood there watching and because I'd had a couple of blues again, I thought, I could really do something here. No point in wasting this. At this point the strippers were leaning over the geezers, bending over the chairs with their arses in the air. I went, Right, here I go! and jumped on stage. I did them all from behind and got massive cheers from the crowd. I felt like a fucking warrior! I could've put myself out to stud, y'know, shagging ponies, but I've never liked it whenever I've felt a little horse.

I was quite proud of that little triple stripper bonk. I felt like rushing home and putting it on the fucking Teletext.

We also went to this club called the Mansion which was actually in a mansion. We went through that party like a dose of salts, I can tell you. It was run by this really posh couple called Phil and Christina who we met through going to the air hostesses' parties. She's a Thai wife. She was really funny as well. One time she was telling me about her husband Phil. She said, 'Him sick! Him sick in head. I come in kitchen other day and him lying on table fucking himself with a potato peeler!' I thought fuck me, hold the chips.

Then there was the Dungeon. Guess what that was. One night about an hour before the people were due to be let in, the guy who ran it let me and Jen go in first. It's a proper dungeon with all this fancy fucking apparatus – chains with pulleys from beams, hammocks, wrist clasps, leg manacles, stocks, fucking-chairs, and a mop and bucket in the corner (well it's only polite to clean up after yourself). I said 'Come on babe, get in this . . .'

There was this contraption there that was like a hammock but with all hooks and straps and leg stirrups for the women. So you can position her and then change it, lower, higher, whatever. And the art of a good shag is 'comfortable', ain't it? By that I mean that little search by the man to get *just* the right position, a good bit of purchase, the best hand hold and foot rest. Like when you're having a bonk in bed and you end up with one foot against the wall, one against the cupboard, and both hands on the headboard. Something like that.

Well this contraption was tailor-made for that. It was fucking mental. So I got Jen up in the air, going right at it and suddenly this strap broke holding her leg and she half fell and went all diagonal on me! We were in a real twisted position. Just then the owner only came down to check everything was OK – great timing – and found us like that! I could see him thinking, 'That thing's tailor-made to accommodate any position so how did they do *that*? He can put her in any shape he wants and he's done it in a way that breaks the fucking machine.' We fucked up the fuck machine with a fucked-up fuck.

I could also see he was thinking what is this guy gonna do next – a dick-first dive off the top of the speakers? I knew I'd gone too far when I saw a bloke who runs a fetish dungeon actually looking at me like *I* was a freak!

One time some fetishy type clobber got me into trouble. I'm coming out of this club in Swanley called Hickorys, which is now called Deja Vu, and I caught this geezer trying to nick my car. Fucking liberty. Cheeky little monkey, I thought to myself. (Or words to that effect.) I was with my mate Big Marcus from Margate at the time.

Actually, what happened was that my car drove past me. There was no mistaking it cos I had a 1960 Mark II Jaguar. I couldn't get in the front door because it was going too fast but I managed to get in the back one. I was lying on the back seat and the geezer in the passenger seat started battering me with the crook-lock. He really pasted me, but when I sat up he couldn't swing it any more cos of the roof.

I dipped into my pockets and got a duster on each hand and then smacked the cunt driving right in the head and knocked him out, then hit the other one just as we went out of control and hit a fucking wall. I was smashed up as bad as the car.

Marcus pulled up in his car. We emptied the boot of the Jag of all the gear I had in there, props from Jennifer and her sister's act the Rude Rude Courtney twins. So into the boot of the BMW we were putting peephole bras, handcuffs, crotchless knickers, chainmail undies, vibrators. The full Ann Summers Catalogue of Filth collection. And as well as that stuff Marcus already had some gear of his own in the boot. A couple of knuckledusters and a massive Bowie knife.

We were both proper off it as well. We'd had about three bottles of Bollinger each. So we set off with all this gear rolling around the boot. Driving along, Marcus took a look at me and said we'd better get to a hospital. I had proper gashes in my head, like Frankenstein before the stitches went in. I'm out of it, half-unconscious and bleeding everywhere so I'm not exactly on top map-reading form. I was in a worse state than Fred West's back garden.

Marcus not being on top form either, he went straight past the hospital and just drove for fucking miles. Up Swanley bypass, got on the A2 and went the wrong way through the Blackwell Tunnel. I woke up in Leytonstone. We stopped at these traffic lights and I was leant against the side window which was smeared with blood. I was in a pretty bad state. All I needed now was for a cop car to pull alongside. Which it did, right on cue. Cunts.

They followed us to the next lights and then pulled us over there. Marcus opened his door and just fell straight out into the road! Nothing suspicious there, then. Now the amazing thing here is that I've seen Marky absolutely lagging pissed and blow into a breathalyser and it stays green. Don't even go orange. I don't know how he does it. No, actually, I do. Here's the tip.

Swell your chest out as if doing the big inhaling bit but when you blow, only blow the air in your mouth. Make it last as long as you can and when you see the thing go orange, run out of breath and sag (which won't be hard to fake at that point). It looks like you've blown your bollocks into it but do it right and it don't go red. (Or, if you're in the cells, swallow the corner off a bar of soap and it should fuck up the piss test.) They're just a couple of tricks I've heard of, but don't quote me.

Anyway, the Old Bill searched the car and found all the gear and nicked Marcus. Well, for the knife and the duster anyway. I don't think you could class a dildo as a deadly weapon. So we go to London County Court at Tower Bridge. As I was the passenger I'm up as Marcus's witness. We did have some fun that day.

The barrister went, 'It says here, Mr Courtney, you are a writer, an actor, a doorman and a singer. How do you see yourself?'

I said, 'Normally from the side, sir.' I kept a dead straight face and he just looked at me.

Then he said, 'So, you do some acting. What kind of characters do you play?'

'Villains mostly,' I said, 'I don't know why. I've written off to *Baywatch* but they haven't replied.'

He started getting a bit bolshey then because I'm taking the piss. 'I put it to you, Mr Courtney, that the reason you were driving around with a knuckleduster in the car is because you were fully intending to use it.'

I said, 'Listen. There was also a vibrator in the boot but that don't mean I was driving around looking for someone to use that on!' That got a big laugh from the court, but not the prosecutor.

He carried on, 'Your behaviour here today makes me think that you view this whole court ceremony as a joke!'

I said, 'Correct, sir.'

He said, 'So you think of yourself as a bit of a hardman?'

'Oh, very much so,' I said.

It was fucking wicked, all of it. It was like a show off the telly. A cross between *Porridge* and Del Boy. Everyone was cracking up. The prosecutor was getting redder. When he said that I seemed very familiar with a court room I told him that I'd probably been in more than he had. And when he asked if I always went to work with a duster I asked him if he'd go to work without his wig. The jury loved us.

Little tip here – if you do get nicked for anything, say something daft to the arresting officer because he has to write it down as evidence and read it out in court. Whatever you say. ('Arrgh! Stop kicking me, officer!' is a good one.) So when our arresting copper was in the box and 'Exhibit A' was laid in front of him, a pair of handcuffs and a dildo, he had to read out exactly what he'd written down: 'Mr Courtney said, "Those are for just in case we pull a bird, mate!" . . . erm . . . your honour.'

The knuckleduster knife was a real piece of work though. A gold, oversized Bowie knife with a serrated blade, spiked knuckleduster finger bridge and bone handle. It was like something from a gladiator duel in *Spartacus*. The prosecutor asked what it was.

'That,' said Marcus, 'is an ornament.'

The weapons and stuff were actually the property of a wrestler friend of ours called Ricky Hards, or Ricky 'Too Sexy' as he was known. He was one of those American WWF wrestlers. You know the kind, those massive geezers that seem to sweat hair gel and spend one half of their life in the gym, the other half under a sunbed.

The court didn't believe us that the gear was Ricky's, which pleased me no end cos it gave us an excuse to call Ricky and ask him to dig his wrestling thong out. Of his arse, that is. He came to court to testify in the full regalia, mate. The FULL wrestling clobber. Long Tarzan hair, Red Indian feather headband and bone-tooth necklace, red satin shorts, red boots, and a red cape with tassles. Imagine *that* walking into a court room. Fuck me, it was funny. We could've sold tickets for that day's performance.

We sat in court laughing our bollocks off while a geezer who looks like Tarzan's flashy brother was in the witness box in a loin cloth giving evidence on our behalf. What a character witness that is – The King Of The Jungle.

While it was going on me and Jen snuck upstairs into the public gallery bit. It was empty but we had to bend down and crawl along so we weren't seen. I'd always wanted to do this in a court room, so I did. We had a shag. The wood's all creaking and I'm really going at it, trying to make Jen make noises. And how dare you say I have no respect for the seriousness of the court.

Anyway, Marcus got off. And, up in the gallery, so did I.

Another time, me, Marcus and some of the boys were coming back from a rave. We were all soaking wet from dancing and everyone had steam hissing off them. Marcus took his T-shirt of and then fell asleep under a coat on the back seat. All was going well until we had a puncture slap-bang in the middle of London.

It was 8 o'clock Sunday morning but there were thousands of people everywhere cos it was the day of the London Marathon. We didn't have a jack to get the car off the ground so we woke Marcus up. Big Marcus. The human jack. Now, Marky's done plenty of the old bodybuilding in his time and his arms are so fucking thick they had to do his tattoos with knitting needles. And we were only in this VW Golf GTi, so to see Marcus climb out of the back of this little car like a fucking giant stepping out of a cave was a sight and a half. People who were stood waiting for the runners starting turning round to watch. He stood up, took the jacket off, and now he's stood there stripped to the waist looking like bloody Hercules. Then he bent down with his back to the car, put his hands under the wheel arch and stood up. He lifted the car right off the ground on one side, both wheels off the ground, and went, 'Hurry up'. All the crowds were watching and going, Wow!

We got the spare on and Marcus dropped the car. Which did a nice job of checking the suspension worked. When we looked round we saw we were completely boxed in by cones and barriers and people. The runners were coming down and we couldn't get the car out. Marcus got back in the car to try to get some more kip and we decided to watch a bit of the race.

Marathons? Yeah, I've done loads. And Mars Bars, and Topics (old chocolate bar joke). I can't see the attraction myself but I suppose when you finish you do get some feeling of achievement. For not dropping dead. Like that famous American runner who helped make jogging really popular, he wrote books about it and got on TV. Then he dropped dead of a heart attack while out jogging. But having heart attacks didn't really catch on in the same way, so that was a fucking stupid career move by him, wasn't it?

The first marathon runners started coming down the road. These were those super super-fit bastards that live off satsumas and vitamin suppositories and have arms and legs like bits of rope. They always look like one good slap on the back would snap them, don't they? But they're tough little cunts, the lot of them. This African geezer zipped past in the lead. There was a motorbike in front of him with a big steaming bowl of rice tied to the back seat, which I thought was a bit unfair. Proper donkey-carrot situation there.

We were getting a bit pissed off by the time the charity runners were coming through. Y'know, guys dressed as chickens (good move, that ain't gonna be too warm is it?), disabled people in wheelchairs with racing slicks, blind runners with proper fucked-off looking labradors, someone dressed as a *bus*, loads of old geezers who were probably still trying to finish from last year (and looked like they might as well just run straight up to the cemetery and jump in a hole), Jimmy Savile, and an overweight geezer in blue shorts.

I mentioned the geezer in blue shorts for a reason. I was getting withdrawal symptoms from no 'silly cuntishness' in the last hour so I went into a nearby pub and got two triple vodkas and poured them into a plastic cup. Then I walked up to the nearest 'drinks station', where they handed out water cups to the runners, and handed this cup to the fat geezer in the blue shorts. He downed it in one while he was still running, then the vodka went 'crash-and-burn' onto his tongue and I just heard – 'Arrrrggh! You *cunt*!' He didn't stop running though, that was the best bit, and I could still hear him shouting as he ran away, 'Yoouu fucking *cunt*!'

Anyway, we ended up being there so long that we decided it was pointless going home. Well, we were only gonna come back out again! So I reversed the car out, killing a whole row of traffic cones, and drove us on to the Park Club in Kensington.

Early next morning when I got home I saw the breakfast TV news about the marathon. They were talking about an overweight runner in blue shorts who'd died of a heart attack on the course. Oh fuck. I was halfway up the stairs to pack my bags before I realised they meant another fella. Thank fuck for that. Next time I'll put a little water with it.

Plenty of nutters in that race, I can tell you. Nutters are well worth the price of admission though, ain't they? Top entertainment. And listen, I know fucking clubfuls of them! Read on.

11 Club Nutter: Funny Glen, Mad Jack & the African Exorcist

I like a nutter. I couldn't eat a whole one but I do like them. I'm one to encourage a nutter. In fact, come to think of it, I'm a bit of a fucking nutter magnet I am. What the fuck's wrong with me that they search me out, anyway! I'll tell you why. It's cos I'm sympathetic. Stop sniggering at the back, cunts.

Serious Nutter Talk now. Even in normal everyday life if a nutter comes up to me I won't go, 'Fuck off', like a lot of people would. More so if I'm out clubbing cos they're good value for money, aren't they? They are good val, though. Nutters are funny. You can't deny it – what are you, fucking nuts?

I met one guy in Paradise Club who thought he could kill people by the power of thought. He gritted his teeth together and bulged his eyes till they nearly popped out. I thought, I've got a *right* one here, mate. Top drawer stuff this. So the club was going mad around us, everyone dancing and all that, and I'm sat chatting to this wild eyed geezer who thinks he's something from *Star Wars*. You've heard of the boxer, Sugar Ray; well, this was the mind-bender, Death Ray. I knew he must've already been told to fuck off a thousand times by less nutter-friendly clubbers. I pretended to believe him and he was so happy!

'I don't believe it,' I said. 'I pay people thousands on my firm to hurt people and now I've got you! Can me and you team up together?' He went, '*Yeah!*'

I said, 'And you're like a secret weapon really cos you don't look dangerous. In fact, you actually look like a bit of a wanker but you can do *that*!'

He was right on it now. Proper carried away – and I think he should have been (in a box). He told me that on the way to the club some car had cut in front of the bus and with the power of thought alone he made this car veer off and crash. Try explaining that one to the insurance company; 'I was driving along when an invisible Mind Beam pushed me into a wall.' That's your No Claims Bonus fucked, ain't it?

I said I couldn't wait and I just had to tell everyone he was with me. I told him to wait where he was so I could let everyone know. I thought I can *not* keep this guy to myself. That would be just plain selfish. So I brought my pals and doormen over to meet Death Ray. I said, 'Listen, this geezer is now my minder. If he goes like *that*! then he'll kill you.' Then I turned to him quickly and said, 'Don't do it! Don't do it. They're friends of mine.'

I asked him what he'd been doing over here in this bit of the club. He said he'd been getting 'bad vibes'. I went, 'Yeah . . . I'm picking them up. I'll find out who the cunt is giving off these bad vibes.' He said he knew who it was already! Touch, I thought, I don't even have to pretend to look. And he pointed at this geezer at the bar in a brown jumper. I thought, not far off actually, that fucking jumper's even giving me bad vibes.

Anyway, I said I'd sort it out for him and walked off and forgot about it. I weren't really gonna do anything, of course, but it'd been a good little laugh.

So half an hour later someone fainted in the club and the medics came in to help out. I was walking around and I sees old Death Ray walking towards me. As he gets nearer these medics go past with someone flaked out on a stretcher. Death Ray clocks this, his eyes go proper saucer-size and he starts nodding over to the stretcher. I thought, Fuck me, he thinks I've done the geezer for him. Result, then.

He rushed up to me and asked me what I'd done. I told him I'd done over the bloke in the jumper for him. Stop the bad vibes, man. 'And now,' I said, 'I want you to do one for ME . . .' He ran off, eventually. I think I out-nuttered him. He would've been well handy for clearing traffic jams though, wouldn't he?

The brain can be a dangerous thing. Even more so if you haven't got one.

Another time in the Ministry I was looking at this guy moving across the dancefloor. My nutter Alert Alarm immediately went off. He must've been tripping right off his trolley cos he was spacewalking like his feet were four foot long. It was a Hallowe'en night rave as well, this night, and they kept flashing different images on the walls. Witches and moons and stuff.

Anyway, for about five seconds this massive image of a devil was projected on the wall: a laughing devil with horns and flames behind it. Now this has been up on the walls enough times for everyone to get used to it or not even notice it at all. But I saw the Spacewalker on the dance floor clock it obviously for the first time. And he thinks it's real.

He looked around to see if anyone else saw it and then looked back to see if it was still there. He's convinced now that he's the only one that's seen it. I waited until he turned towards me and let him catch my eyes. I thought, *Gotcha!* He beamed in on me and came across. He said, 'D'ya see it? Did you see it!'

I said, 'Fuck me, yes!'

'I haven't done anything wrong!' he went. 'Nothing wrong.' I said, 'Neither have I!'

I told him to calm down and not turn round. I said 'I'll get help.' I was out with my mates Danny Dolittle, Boxer, Baz, Mickey Taylor, Mickey Goldtooth, Jamie, Amon and John O'Keefe, Terry Turbo, Togs, Scully and Spud and loads more. When we got back five minutes later Spacewalker was still stood on the spot, not moving. He noticed a cig burn on my arm and asked me what it was.

'I don't know! But I only mentioned your name and look at *that*.' Then I saw this massive African-looking geezer dancing on a speaker. Sweating like a burst pipe and proper having it. I said, 'He saw it as well.' So the guy turned away from me cos he half knew I was taking the piss, but for him it was still all too serious to forget. He ran over to this bloke and started tugging at his trousers and saying, 'Did you see it!?' The big African geezer's trying to shake his leg loose and going, 'Fuck *off*!'

Then there was this fella Mad Jack, who was a mate of mine and one of the firm. Mad Jack. Now there was a perfectly named geezer. Jack's stocky, like a Staffordshire Bull. He was a blinding bloke and really, really funny but also as mad as a boiled banana. He'd just do whatever came into his head for a laugh. Cos making people laugh was Jack's thing. He loved that. And fighting.

There was this geezer once, at this club, a black geezer who'd had a full set of false teeth fitted. They didn't fit well enough though, and every time he talked they nearly fell out. Jack spent the rest of the night trying to catch him out. He'd run up and slap him on the back really hard, trying to make the falsies fly out.

One time we were doing security at this rave in Eastbourne. It was at this open air theatre, like a little arena. It was absolutely pissing it down, though, and Jack found this yellow builder's hat with NO ROADBLOCK on the front. You could alter the band inside to make it bigger to fit your head but he never did that.

We just saw him out on the dancefloor with this yellow hardhat jammed on his head, stuck up like a Martian's tit. And when Mad Jack danced you didn't know whether he was dancing or having a fight – he was ON it, mate! Proper determined wild dancing. You had to step back in amazement.

And he wore that fucking yellow hat everywhere from then on. NO ROADBLOCK!

Anything could happen when Jack was around. He had a manslaughter charge on his head years ago, but he pleaded diminished responsibility and did six years in a mental hospital. That's gotta leave its scars, y'know what I mean. If you play it long enough, you become it.

You could have some blinding laughs with Jack. Dean Lambert is a DJ and good friend of mine now but when we first met he was very eager to please. So me, Mad Jack and Big Joe, Little Joe, Matt and the Gravesend crew walked into the Gass club, where Dean was playing. It was Sunday night, the big night, when everyone gathered there from the other clubs. Everyone in the crowd's really going for it to these banging tunes.

I looked around and thought, Wouldn't it be funny if someone put on a really, really stupid record right now? And, wouldn't you know it, I just happened to have one in the car. Fancy that. It was 'Tiger Feet' by Mud.

For those of you too young to remember, 'Tiger Feet' was this big, Glam Rock-type pop song from the 70s. Stupid words to it but it's a cracking song and it went to No. 1 for weeks. But whatever it is, it is definitely *NOT* a club tune and shouldn't be within a hundred miles of any club except a 70s revival.

Which is exactly why Me and Mad Jack thought it was a brilliant idea to get it from the car. I went up to the decks and asked Dean if he had 'Tiger Feet' (or maybe he just always stood like that). He asked me if it was a new white label release! Wicked. I said, 'Yeah, sort of. Jack'll bring it over.'

I could see Dean and the other DJs, Creed and Dominic Spreadlove, looking at this record thinking, What the fuck! It was a seven-inch disc for one thing. They ain't seen a seven-inch record in their lives. They think the world began with the twelve-inch remix. And every time they looked over at me I wouldn't look back.

I sent all my pals over to ask for it. Everyone in the club was right on it, jumping up and down, shouting 'Make some noiiiise!' Even if the mixing was a bit off they went mental. Then it all suddenly stopped – BANG! – and then, 'Whoooaaah! I really lurve your tiger feet! *Awright!* Lurrve your tiger feet!' This mental pop song came on and stopped the club dead.

Three-quarters of the club were too young to know it and just thought, What the *fuck*?! And the others who could remember 'Tiger Feet' just thought they were tripping or having some freaky hallucination: 'That cannot be Mud!'

I looked over and what did I see but Jack, Mad Jack, in that yellow NO ROADBLOCK hat, fucking disco dancing in front of the DJs' booth! All these hardcore clubbers and ravers were just stood there completely fucking gobsmacked. And I was absolutely pissing myself, mate. Dean kept looking over at me, like pleading with his eyes 'Can I take it off now?' Then the crowd snapped-to from the shock and started throwing things at Dean, so he pulled it off. Fucking funny, though.

Jack was a good one to have on your side, but the thing was, you needed him on your side to help sort out whatever trouble it was he'd just fucking started! Catch 22 or what.

After the NO ROADBLOCK do in Eastbourne that time, we went to Hastings to a place called Saturdays. Jack had on his black

Blues Brothers sunglasses as usual. He couldn't see a thing, really, but he could see enough to spot this woman. She was sat down with her foot folded under her and you could see this hole in her shoe. Mad Jack saw it as well. She became aware of him looking and put her foot down but it was too late. Cos Jack was on it! Man with a mission – expose the hole!

He walked over, lifted her foot, lifted the shades into his hair and began inspecting this fucking hole. He took the shoe off and wiggled his finger through the hole. This bird's sat with her boyfriend and they didn't say a word. Jack put her shoe back on her foot and lowered it to the floor. Then he came back to the bar, crossed his arms and looked back at them like he'd discovered a big secret.

What a fucking nut, but it was really funny. The girl and her bloke didn't think it was too funny though. I was later told that he'd asked around about this little firm of ours. No one in there that night knew me or who any of us were. Which just goes to prove one thing – whatever reputation you have is worth absolutely fuck all if someone isn't aware of it. It's worthless then, ain't it?

They didn't know it was Dave Courtney and his boys so they didn't give a fuck. I was stood at the bar with Jennifer, with my back to everyone. Next thing I knew I was waking up on the floor with people fighting everywhere and Jenny next to me.

What had happened was this geezer had run up and smashed a bottle on my head from behind. I was out before I hit the deck. Fuck all I could do about it. Then he knelt on my chest and was getting set to stab me in the fucking face with the broken neck of the bottle. Jack just jumped across and grabbed this geezer and completely battered him to bits.

A massive brawl broke out all over, chairs flying, bottles smashing. A real big John Wayner, this fight was. Proper cowboy tear-up. Like I said, though, you'd want Mad Jack on your side when it kicked off. Just to help get you out the trouble he's just got you into. He was one of those who, when he got in a fight, he *really* got in a fight, know what I mean? NO half measures. He'd rip his shirt right off and scream, 'WHO WAAAANTS IT!!' and throw himself into a crowd.

Now Jack talks about how he saved my life, and I say, 'Yeah, and thanks Jack, but remember it was you that actually caused the fight for fuck's sake.' But then this was the geezer that dropped a petrol bomb in his own car. He lit it and went to throw it but it went off in the car and blew it up. Jack crawled away from it singed, mate. Well singed.

He said to me once, 'I hate my name, "Jack". All my life people have just been saying, "Jack, Jack, Jack", Just Jack-ing me off!' Wicked. Then he told me there's one thing you should learn – don't ever trust bricklayers and doctors. I said, 'Why's that then, Jack?'

He said, 'Seen that wall in my back garden, really high, really long? It's fucked up. All bent, not pointed right, higher one end than the other. And you know who built it? . . . a *doctor*!'

Point proved then. How can you argue with logic like that? He made us laugh so much. He was fucking funny. I asked him once what his second name was and he said, ' "Jack, innit. My first name's "Mad".'

In the odd quiet moments I get I sometimes think I'd like to see old Jack again. Then I realise I've only got the odd quiet moment because I *don't* see Jack. No fucking roadblock.

Only one person made me laugh more than Mad Jack and that was Glen. Or Funny Glen as we called him, surprisingly. I used to hang around Croydon a lot then with Stormin' Norman, Warren and Funny Glen. Glen would walk round a rave with his ponytail pulled round and bunched on his forehead like a horn. He'd walk around like *that*. He was like Jack in that he just loved laughing and making other people laugh.

He'd do the funniest dances you've ever seen. If you think God moves in mysterious ways you ain't seen Glen dance. And when he got out-of-it it wasn't falling on the floor out-of-it, it was talking absolute bollocks out-of-it. He'd run up to you and say, 'There's three squirrels after me and they're over there!' and then run off. You'd be left standing there thinking, What?!

At the club in Croydon he'd do a real funny one to watch. Knowing it was all 'peace' and 'love' at the raves he'd do this one on purpose – he turned the straw around on a Ribena carton so it was aiming out. Then he walked up to someone and went 'Awright?', pretended to go for the straw with his mouth, but squeezed the carton and shot them *right* in the face.

Then he'd act all sorry, apologise, and say they had to forgive him even though they were stood there, face drenched with Ribena.

Or he'd be talking to someone on the edge of the dancefloor and he'd unbuckle and drop his trousers and his pants while he was talking. The other person wouldn't know cos they were stood too close but we'd be stood back just wetting ourselves. And there's Glen nodding all seriously in conversation while he's stark bollock naked from the waist down.

Glen was a doorman alongside my mates Warren, Marky Mark, Johnny Jacket, Pit Bull, Hippodrome Ginger, Neil, Terry, Tony, Gary and Stormin' Norman. Norman went and bought this new house on a 100 per cent mortgage knowing that he weren't gonna pay a penny on it. We all got a key cut and used it as our after-club place for smoking, chilling-out, banging birds. Why get ash on the carpet and spunk on the ceiling of your own house when you can do it at someone else's?

We'd use the gas and electricity for nothing, not pay a tenner on the mortgage and then when we got evicted we'd get another beautiful, big gaff and do it again.

One of these houses was fucking wicked, with a white spiral staircase from the living room. We all rolled into it one morning after being out all night and Warren started studying the staircase. Now Warren was really, really tall. When he danced you couldn't help but watch him cos his long arms seemed to bend twice more than everyone else's. If you were stoned he looked like a fucking poplar tree having a dance.

Warren took it into his head that he could go up this spiral staircase by bending *between* the stairs, y'know, through the little gaps like a snake. He was tripping, and we can't have been far behind cos we agreed it was a good idea. So he strips off and gets all baby-oiled up and starts bending through these fucking stairs.

Surprise surprise . . . he got stuck. So he was wedged there screaming for help and we just couldn't stop laughing. The career of the Human Snake was cut tragically short.

One of these places we all got was this massive ground floor flat in Blackheath with six bedrooms, four living rooms, gardens, all fully furnished. Even the garden. We all had keys cut, about twenty-five of us, and it was our place. It was Base Camp One for after-hours shagging, drinking, spliff-smoking, telly watching, card playing, basket weaving, whatever you couldn't indulge too much in at home in front of the kids. And the neighbours loved us cos we were really nice to them. These old ladies thought it was great having twenty-five flat-nosed, suited-up geezers next door that opened doors for them and helped them carry their shopping. The younger ones loved us as well cos we could open any door for them in London's clubland. We had cases of champagne and beer around the place from whatever club we were working in, so any tradesman who called at the house like window cleaner, plumber, postman, they had a fucking good time before they left.

The window cleaner once got so pissed he forgot he'd already done the windows and staggered out and cleaned them all over again. On the first sunny day that house sparkled like a fucking diamond.

Because there was so many people with a key to the place, if the police ever raided and found a gun there (which they didn't), as long as everyone went 'no comment' they couldn't do anything. You can't nick twenty-five people for one gun. So there was loads of people there round the clock.

One Saturday a couple of the doormen went up to a fair on Mitcham Common and got a bit of a hiding from a gang of the fairground boys. The rest of us got back to the flat from work Sunday morning and found them there. So nearly thirty of us went back out to the fairground, all fully charged-up, looking for these geezers. I know that's naughty but it's also exciting – run up there, club a few blokes, avenge your mates, come back with a goldfish. Result.

When we got there the only one of these blokes we could see was working on the ghost train. So we all got on the train and went in, jumped out of the carriages inside and got this geezer. We gave him a battering and dumped him back on the train. Then we thought, Now we're in here let's have some fun because we were off the train and all walking around inside the tunnels.

We were just pissing ourselves at these luminous green devil masks and chopping axes and big spiders everywhere. Then the trains started coming back in full of punters so we hid until they came through and then tapped them on the shoulder or just touched their faces, and it scared the absolute shit out of them. They were expecting a plastic axe coming down and instead they got these twenty-stone doormen jumping out the dark screaming 'AAAARRGGGH!' Or we'd give them a little slap on the head and you could see they were thinking, fuck me, that was a bit strong for a fifty-pence ride! Fuck me it was funny. Parents were in the train with their kids and someone like Stormin' Norman would jump out with an axe he'd taken off the wall. The mum would scream and get hysterical and the kids would go, 'Wow! That was great!' Warren squeezed himself into a coffin in there, but this ball and chain part of the ride swung around and cut his head open.

So the trains were coming back out of the tunnels either empty (because us lot had all got out inside), or full of nervous wrecks. The fairground boys were onto us already. They stopped the train, switched the music off and steamed in. So now there was this big fight *inside* the ghost train ride. There was no music now but the lights were still flashing and the cars clanking around, which made it even stranger. And the monsters were still laughing (or was that us?) and you could hear fighting going on all over: the sound of a clump and someone hitting the deck. I found a big fibreglass club on the wall, like something Fred Flintstone would use, and I took it down and proper battered this fairground fella with it. What a buzz! I felt like beating my chest, calling 'WILMA!' and going for a drink with Barney Rubble!

We fucked off to another part of the fair after that. I bet loads of kids brought their mates back to the ghost ride thinking we'd still be there, and then came out saying it's shit and asking for their money back.

Old Stormin' had a go on one of them Test Your Strength machines with the big wood hammer. Thing is with that though, it's all in the way you just drop the hammer from high up, that's the trick really, not sheer strength. It's like when I used to work on the dust. A dustman could pick a heavy bin up cos he had the knack but someone else who's just as strong couldn't do it.

Anyway, Norman don't know this so he's fucking pounding away like an Irish navvy and we're all rolling around on the grass laughing. He couldn't get his head around why a big geezer like him couldn't ding the bell. He kept taking longer and longer run ups, which meant fuck all cos he'd run up from thirty feet away and then still stop before he swung the bloody hammer! So he went to take this last massive run up. We were watching him walk away and he got further and futher and we thought, Fucking hell, he's gonna be fucked by the time he runs back. Then he disappeared into the dark and didn't come back! He just walked right off with the big wooden hammer. We were sat there waiting and he just fucked off. Wicked. Now all Norman needs is some two-foot nails.

Stormin' Norman was a sight and a half when he got going, though. Norman's the doorman that used to dance on the speakers of my place the Arches. Shirt ripped open and gushing like a loose tap. Mad sight that was, used to freak quite a few people out. And those were people he *knew*!

One thing that freaked me out was when me and Norm were at this big 5,000 crowd open-air rave. And ain't that the best thing, raving outside? I don't wanna get all cosmic-hippy-trippy-tree-fucker about it but there is something extra wicked about dancing outside. I think it comes from the fact you're doing something so basic and primitive as dancing in the place where we used to do it – outside – when we were all living in caves.

Anyway, me and Norm went to this funfair bit they'd set up. We shot a few teddies, threw a dart through a goldfish, knocked down cans with a knuckleduster, jumped on the Speak Your Weight machine and after it told us both to 'Fuck Off!' we went for a ride on the dodgems. And we didn't dodge *at all*, as it happens. I remember when they were called Bumper Cars so we fucking bumped, mate!

Unfortunately I was inhaling a bit from a bottle of poppers when I had one really big bump. I hit something at such speed that the front of the dodgem actually fucking lifted up and made me tip a whole bottle of amyl up my fucking nose. All at once. It set my nose alight. I rolled out of the car in absolute agony. It felt like I had napalm snot.

Talk about stop the ride I wanna get off! I had to go to bloody hospital with that. Terminal nostril burn! Fuck me, it got hot up there.

Outdoor raves really are the nuts, though, aren't they? You *know* that. And an outdoor shag just cannot be beat. Primitive man again, that. We all went to a big top rave once. A big circus tent with about 10,000 people in it. And what happens at them is that cos it's about twenty-five grand to hire the tent and then ten grand extra to have a floor, most promoters don't pay for the flooring. But after a few hours of dancing, and spilt beer and sweat, you're knee high in shit.

Everyone was doing their best to dance but leaving their shoes behind in little mud holes. Every above ground surface like speakers and boxes and tables was taken over by people dancing on them.

The hot dog sellers were the big, smart earners there, believe it or not. Hardly any costs or overheads, he just turns up at a rave gig, hands over hot dogs and says, 'two quid, two quid' all day and night. He earns about three grand a day, twice a week. That's 300 grand a year. I used to have my boys escort the fucking hot dog man home.

Anyway, I was with Stormin' Norman again and we were trying to find somewhere to sit down. Then we found this big box of large hot dog sausages that the hot dog man had left. We started chucking them about. If you threw them hard enough they just opened up midair and went splat! like a pancake. Then I spotted this fire door. It was bright yellow with a big red circle on it, and the bit in front of the door was cordoned off with red hose to keep people out.

It looked like a little stage to me. Well, it would do wouldn't it, me being a flash cunt. I've only got to open the fridge and see the light go on to burst into song. Anyroad, I positioned myself flat against the door, in the red circle, and Norm started throwing sausages at me like a knife thrower. Splat! Splat! One hit me in the eye, another one on the forehead. Everyone was watching and laughing and cheering. I ended up completely covered in that crap. I was proper sausaged-off.

Stormin' Norman, the daredevil sausage thrower! I took all the risks though, don't forget that. He could've had my eye out. We didn't know it at the time but someone videoed the whole thing. A year later they used the film in the advert for that year's rave. They said that the Unknown Sausage Throwers would be back by popular demand.

Anyway, back to Funny Glenn. Where did he go? Down to Clink Street with me that's where. We went to the Clink club – the old converted prison. We were there with Divvy Dave. As I've said, Dave sometimes worked as a stripper, and from time to time he'd get so carried away in a club he'd forget he wasn't at a stag do and rip his clothes off.

This night I had to leave the Clink earlier than normal because my daughter Chelsea was getting christened the next day. This is going back a fair few years, by the way. Anyway, I was more than a little bit stoned, to be honest. Glen was going somewhere else but some mates would go, 'Don't drive in that state, Dave. I'll take you.' Glen didn't. Not cos he didn't care cos he did, but because he just thought everything was funny. And me driving home stoned would be, to him, very funny.

So I set off and ended up going down the Old Kent Road. The driving was so fucking easy, or seemed it, because everything looked so BIG. The steering wheel was like a bus's. I was in a red BMW 6 series. This was the time when I had the BMW spares place with Herbie and this car I was in was a ringer. What I didn't know was that Glen was behind me, following on and watching for the sport of it.

I wanted to play a tape but I couldn't see anything inside and the dash was black. I switched on the interior light and as I bent down to look for a tape I completely lost track of time. And because I bent to the left, my hand on the wheel dropped right a bit and started pulling the car over to the right.

Afterwards, Glen said he couldn't believe it. He saw the light go on, then me bend down, then I didn't come up and I didn't come up. And I still didn't come up.

I was still bent down there looking for a fucking tape! I was going through lights, overtaking people. I must have gone three, four hundred yards at 60 mph without looking up. I completely lost track of time. I was still looking down, getting the tape I wanted – Yes! That's the one, 'Showaddywaddy's Greatest Hit' – when suddenly *BANG!* and the car lifted.

What had happened is the car had wandered from the inside lane to the outside. And right down the middle of the road was a massive stack of those yellow plastic pipes they run underground cables through, a big triangular pile of these tubes all tied together and stacked like a long pyramid. I hit this stack side-on, really fast, and it acted like a ramp and shot the BM right up into the fucking air. We have lift off! I hit them at sixty and went skyward.

I snapped upright and the first thing I saw, the *only* thing I saw, was a windscreen full of stars! Black night and white stars! So for a few seconds when the car was frozen in mid-air before the drop I thought, Wow! *Fucking* hell I'm in Heaven! I didn't even know I knew the way there. I'm proper tripping now. *Fuck* me – stars. What do I do now – go left at Mars or what? (I was gonna go left at Uranus but I didn't want to come anywhere near your arse.)

And you never have the phone number of NASA handy when you want it, have you noticed that?

Then it was 'Huston, we have a problem!' The stars flipped away, I saw buildings, then road, then SMASH! I landed on the other side of the Old Kent Road. I hit the kerb, straightened the cunt up and I was now heading the wrong way into traffic. Cars were swerving me and blasting their horns. I pulled over and stopped the car.

I thought, Bit fucking lucky there, mate. I mean, even Chitty Chitty Bang Bang had wings to help it stay up. I hadn't even opened the doors.

I could hear some shouting so I got out and there's Glen on the other side of the Old Kent Road. He's stood on the bonnet of his car so he can see over the pipe stack and he's wetting himself laughing. He started shouting, 'You ARE the bollocks, Dave! The fucking bollocks, mate! D'you know how far you went without looking up!?' I thought, Yeah. Jupiter.

We got back to my house and by now Glen's forgot this bird he's arranged to meet and he just wants to talk about the flying car thing. He thinks it's the best thing he's ever seen. I'm feeling rougher than a Mexican tart's mattress but the Moon Shot in the car has woken me up a fair bit. That's a proper wake-up call I can tell you, playing space hoppers in a BMW. And I've still got a christening to go to.

I drive off to the church making sure I made full use of that big fucking piece of glass in front of the steering wheel this time. Meanwhile, back at my house, Glen has had a little

pick-me-up and is whizzing off his tits while making sandwiches for everyone. And is he making sandwiches or is he
making *sandwiches*? He's chopping up cheese, salad and
chicken like a machine. He's cut off three fingers and thrown
them in as well. He don't give a fuck. There's sarnies piled to
the ceiling like a big, bread skyscraper. Not only that but he's
whizzed them all up, put speed in them all. And these are for
my relatives!

Spiking people with trips was a favourite little trick of
Glen's. I'd seen him roll up a trip and push it down a Ribena
straw. If you went to his house for dinner he'd put one in the
baked potatoes. One time when I'd cut my arse open after
really bad constipation he even put a trip in one of my
suppositories. I put it in the next day and properly tripped my
arse off.

So he'd whizzed up all the sandwiches, bless him. Cunt. And
then he found a video camera that one of my uncles had left
at the house. He thought, I'll have some fun with that. He
balanced it on the toilet and switched it on. Now he really is
out of his fucking head, is Glen. Steam's coming off his skull,
he's got eyes like boiled eggs and sweat leaking out of him. He
looks into the camera and goes, 'Hi! I'm Glen. As you can see
I'm *right off my face*! I'll show you something that's really
funny . . .' then he switched it off, turned the camera upside
down so it was filming him the wrong way, switched it back
on and said, '. . . I am now upside down, hanging from the
lightbulb by my feet! Thank you.'

We didn't know this till later when my uncle picked his
camera back up and played the tape! What I also didn't know
is that when the club finished at nine in the morning everyone
decided to come back to my place. And Glen's there to let them
in and give them whizzed-up sarnies.

So I get back to my house with my mum, my dad, my family
(Tracey and the kids and the new baby) and my in-laws, and I
find thirty geezers in the house and back garden. It was like a
welcoming committee from Rampton Ravers' Society! And in
my back garden is a big roundabout that I'd nicked from a
local park.

Listen! I'm there with all the families and uncles and aunts
in their best suits and hats, new little baby in her christening

outfit and the house and garden is overrun with over thirty marauding, wasted nutters bouncing round in the sunshine. Big doormen and ravers everywhere.

In the back garden they were 'shooting' cans of lager. That's when you bang a hole in the can, shake it and then shoot it all out at once into your mouth. They were all doing that, then taking it in turns to jump on the roundabout, spin round loads of times, get off and take a pull on a joint, and they try to run back up to the house. So there's geezers collapsed in flowerbeds and staggering at an angle up the garden.

My poor mum-in-law just burst into tears. In one morning she'd gone from quiet prayers in church to being an extra on the set of *Invasion Of The Brain Donors*. My Uncle Frank was looking round and saying to me, who's that dancing on the chair? 'Oh, that's just Stormin' Norman.' And that one in the rose bushes? 'Er ... that's Divvy Dave.' 'And the big naked orange boy?' 'Oh, that's Dean the Tango Man, Frank.'

I just thanked fuck Mad Jack weren't there. Trying to explain a geezer walking round wearing a yellow hardhat with NO ROADBLOCK on it would have been a real tester.

It could've been something to do with the special spread that Glen had laid on but all the relatives started really getting into it. Well, they were whizzing off their tits is what they were doing – let's be fucking up front about it. Before I knew it, Auntie Beryl was being spun on the roundabout by a Rasta and Uncle Frank was dancing with a twenty-year-old in a mini skirt. And what that young geezer was doing wearing a mini skirt I'll never know.

They were all nice nutters though, my nutters.

That was the same house, at Linell Road, where I had an eight-foot flagpole stuck out the window with a black skull and crossbones flag on it. We adopted the same formality as royalty. When I was in the flag was out and when I was out the flag was in. Not that I had any delusions of grandeur or anything.

Linell Road was also where I had the bodybuilders' dance. My missus Tracey had got the right fucking hump, for some very very good reason I'm sure (I'll say that cos we're still good friends and I want it to stay so!), and she'd gone out with the kids. But the skull and bones was still out cos I was *in*. Also in were half a dozen bodybuilder mates of mine. All proper big cunts, each one looking like a condom full of walnuts, as someone once described Arnold Scharzenegger. Did you know he only went into bodybuilding to develop a chest big enough to get his name across on a T-shirt?

Any road, it was a really sunny day that day so we thought we'd give the neighbours a treat. Now most bodybuilders have no fucking shame whatsoever cos they're so used to stripping off. So these geezers stripped off down to their thongs and got out on the roof above my bay window at the front of the house. Now there's these naked musclemen ten feet in the air all striking poses to music! This old girl going by in her electric-powered wheelchair nearly had a fatal crash.

Tracey was just coming back up the road – still getting over the last silly thing I'd done – and she saw this display going on in front of the house and just turned round and went off again with the kids! So it worked. Result. (Joke, babe.)

Come to think of it, that club Saturdays in Hastings, where I got bottled, was the scene of a few things with the 7-Up Boys. The 7-Up Boys were a little gang made up of me, Jonathan Evans and five of his college and public school mates (including Danny Dyke). I was never public school material but I did brilliantly at school. On both the days I went.

Jonathan Evans you'll remember from my autobiography, or Posh John as I called him. He is posh, is old Jon – his dad's a baron, and both his parents, Val and John, are lovely people – but he's also a very very handy geezer with a strong naughty streak. If he hadn't been born to go to Eton he would've made a fucking good baddie, would Jon. And if I'd not been born into my life I would've been a good businessman. He would've been me in my world and I would've been him in his. Which is why, when we met, we got on so well.

Jon's a big strong geezer (we first met when we boxed together) but many a man's misjudged old Posh Jon. Especially when we were out clubbing. One night we were leaving a place called Zens and Jon said to me, 'You call a cab and I'll get the coats.' One of the doormen in the foyer overheard him and started mocking Jon's accent, putting on this lah-di-dah voice. I thought, Oh dear, mate – you have made a proper *proper* mistake here in thinking that Jon's a wanker.

So we ended up outside the club having a big row in the street with the doormen. Jon grabbed this bloke by the neck with one hand, and by the bollocks with the other, and *lifted* him in the air! – the fighting sort of froze for a second cos everyone couldn't believe it – and then Jon threw this fucker into the road. I bit someone's ear off. Eventually we jumped in a cab, bleeding everywhere, and went back to Jonathan's parents' house.

The police traced where we'd gone by the taxi driver. So, me and Jonathan are sat in his parents' house, which is this big beautiful house in its own grounds, and the Old Bill come and raided the place at four in the morning and nicked me and Jon. When we were in the cells they brought us some dinner and as they were handing me mine through the hatch I knocked it by accident and it flew out over the floor. Jonathan, in the cell next door, heard this and took his own plate and threw it right over the screw! He was stood there dripping in beans. It was really funny. Afterwards I asked Jon what the fuck he did that for, and he said when he'd heard my plate hit the floor he'd thought I was doing a protest!

So, yeah, Posh Jon's mates were all really posh as well. I was the sort of anti-posh. The thing about posh people, money people, is that they can have different kinds of laughs to us. They can afford to finance bigger practical jokes or indulge in whatever their little whims are. Which is wicked. Which is exactly what we'd all do if we could, wouldn't we? I don't think I'm just speaking for myself there.

Me and Jon once drove a car off the end of Hastings pier just for the laugh and to fuck up the local fishermen that sat on the pier and always tutted at us for breathing too loudly. So driving a car down the pier and off the end gave them something to fucking tut about. I think the ripples reached France.

When Jon wanted to go deerstalking he just bought his own fucking forest in Eastbourne. Now deerstalking is all about the stalking not the killing. The creeping-up bit is the art. And they give you such a small area on the deer's body where it's legal to shoot it. So that fucked me for using the sawn-off.

So the plan is to get up close to be sure of killing it so it don't crawl away somewhere to die, or call Crimestoppers and shop you to Nick Ross. And cos they live on their wits, you don't half have to be clever to creep up on a deer. It might look like it's eating but it hears a bee fart 200 yards away and its head snaps up, all bug-eyed. And they can smell for miles.

I only learned all this about the deer's super sensitive senses after Jon invited me to go deerstalking. And by that time I'd already turned up slapped in aftershave (I was proper Armani-ed up, mate), wearing gold jewellery and shades with gold bits on that all glinted in the sun. And in white jeans, white trainers and carrying a gold-plated Colt .45!

Jon looked at me like I'd just pissed in the grand piano and said, 'Dave? . . .' and that's all he could manage. Jon and his mates started rubbing dirt all over their faces like GI Joe commandos. I said, 'I ain't doing that! I wanted to stalk deer not go to fucking Vietnam!' If I'd known I was in the army I'd have gone AWOL the week before.

Anyway, we had a blinding time. And so did the deer, when my gold caught the sun and the reflection blinded it – *Bang!*

Jon also got one of them vehicles they use to fix streetlamps that have an elevating bit and used it to put a dirty great big sofa up a tree! They put a big plank across the tree and nailed the bleedin' sofa on it. So Posh Jon in his tweeds can sit on an old green leather sofa halfway up a tree in Eastbourne and shoot deer with a long-nosed Magnum .44 when they walk below. Never mind that though, where do people get this idea from that the English are eccentric? Fucked if I know. We could ask Jon I suppose, but he's busy right now, sat halfway up a fucking tree!

Yeah, but Jon has got a licence for that Magnum. Even *I* don't know anyone who's got that. He has the authority for it because he's the one responsible for putting down any injured deer. He has to have a licence to get a gun for that. What a *touch*! And Jon went and got a long-nosed Smith and Wesson Magnum .44. That's my boy! Dirty Harry the deer killer. Go ahead, Bambi, make my fucking day!

Anyway, back to where we were, down clubbing in Hastings. We were having a night out at Saturday's club. One of the 7-Up blokes had this long mole on the side of his neck, about half an inch long, and when you talked to him he'd touch it. You couldn't stop looking at this fucking thing. I thought why the fuck don't he cut that off? When I asked him he said no, no – cut off a mole and you bleed to death. I said don't be daft, people get run over and lose legs and survive. It's only a bleedin' mole.

He said to me he didn't like it, so I told him that by the time we went home tonight that mole would be gone, and whatever happened he would thank me. So two hours later he's forgotten what I've said and I saw him sat with his back to me, talking to these people. I crept up behind him, made my thumb and forefinger into a pincer, and pounced.

The plan was this – I grab, I pull and *snap*!, followed by a little blood and 'sorry'. What actually happened was I grabbed, I pulled and *rrrrip*! The mole pulled off but so did a vein connected to it, and that came away and tore a flap of skin off his jawline! Fuck me, it was disgusting. He went, 'Aaarrgghh!' and jumped up; I went, 'Urrrgh!' and jumped back. Blood spurted everywhere. I'd made a real fountain out of a molehill. And to think I'd told him it wouldn't bleed. Talk about being embarrassed.

He was walking around clutching his neck as if he'd just been bitten, like Hastings' first ever vampire victim. So he was taken to hospital and they had to stitch him.

So now he had a big scar, which is good for him cos it makes him look a proper tool. And the truth is that, he tried to be a hardnut but people knew he wasn't. Now he's got a fuck-off looking scar when before he had a wobbly fucking wart! Even though it hadn't gone to plan I'd actually done him a favour, but he just thought I was to blame. Honestly, some people have no gratitude.

It can happen that a scar can be the making of someone, or at least make people think that a geezer isn't a wanker when really he is.

There was this young bloke in the Scrubs when I was there for the Chinese sword-fight thing. He was a long, lanky streak of piss that geezer, and a proper wanker to boot. Now, in the workshop there one of the tasks was winding this copper wire around a little drum. It was strong stuff, almost like a spring, and you had to bend it. One day this bloke lost grip of it and the end of the wire whipped around and split his face open from cheek to forehead. So he ended up with this long, James

Bond villain scar which made him look the nuts. To anyone who didn't know him.

Once before, when we were planning another 7-Up Boys night out, we went into a Cancer Research Shop – and they weren't doing any cancer research at all, they were just selling second-hand clothes: no wonder they can't find a cure! – and we got kitted out in the most ridiculous clobber we could find. Flared trousers, wing collar shirts, kipper ties, tanktops and long leather coats. I had a green 70s suit on and the pants were so fucking tight on the crotch it looked like my bollocks were coming up for air. I also had a yellow and orange tie that made it look like I'd just vomited down my shirt front. Jon had a brown tartan sports jacket and a long brown leather overcoat. We looked like really poor pimps on an away-day.

So we went to this club and the doorman looked us up and down and I thought, uh-oh, but he just said, 'Looking smart tonight, boys!' And he fucking meant it! That was the best bit. I thought what sort of place *is* Hastings, where you can go out dressed like Shaft and get a compliment, y'know what I mean? Welcome to The Land That Style Forgot, and beam me up Scotty.

We strutted into that club, mate, like the Huggy Bear Seven. And we were giving it some on the dancefloor, spinning and doing the full disco dancing bit. That club didn't know what had hit them.

So cos we were all wearing this cheap, naff clobber, the idea was to rip it off each other as we were talking. So I'm stood there talking to this bird – 'So, babe, what do you do? Oh yeah, hairdresser? Well my knob's wet, any chance of a blow dry?' – and one of our gang walked up to me, put his hand in my jacket pocket and just ripped it right off. And walked off. I carried on talking to this bird, real casual, like nothing's happened.

We spent the next hour just walking up to each other and doing that. At the bar, on the dancefloor, in the bogs. Danny was chatting up this cracking-looking bird at the bar and I just walked up, grabbed the cuff of his shirt and tugged it until the arm tore right off. He didn't even look at me, just carried on talking to her. Then I got Posh John on the dancefloor, grabbed the tails of this long leather coat he was wearing and pulled the two halves. It split up the vent in the back, right up to his neck so the two halves were only held together by the collar. You could see that the whole club was thinking, oh dear, this Care In The Community idea just *is* not working.

Best bit, though, was that there was this bloke in the club wearing a yellow Fred Perry shirt, green tonic jacket, white Sta-pressed trousers and white Fred Perry flat cap. I started laughing. I thought that's one of ours! We must've missed him. I knew he was one of our mob. I didn't recognise him but, as well as the original 7-Up Boys, there was some of John's other mates along for the ride as well. So this mate of John's is there on the dance floor, mooching away dead serious and looking like a right prick. He was even keeping a straight face dancing with this girl. I thought, nice one, good effort! Really getting into the spirit of it there, mate.

So I walked up, grabbed his jacket at the back and *rrrrip!*, tore it in two. I proper pulled it apart as well, and the two halves slid down his arms and hit the floor. I could tell then, from the second I done it – and from the way his jaw hit the floor just after his sleeves – that he wasn't one of ours after all. He actually was just some prick who dressed like that. I thought, Well I'm definitely in the wrong here. But I wasn't gonna get dragged into it.

So I apologised, or tried to, but it ain't easy when you look like Robinson fucking Crusoe. I'm stood there in a suit that had one trouser leg cut off at the knee, the other leg split up to my bollocks, a jacket with no arms or pockets and a tie with the knot pulled so tight I'd have to cut it off. I looked like I'd just been washed up off the *Titanic*.

I was trying to keep a straight face and apologise but this geezer just ain't having it at all. He went, 'What do you think you're doing? Look, I'm an upstanding member of the community!' Well that little line did it for me. I said, 'No, you are now a wanker. I was sorry before, but not after that little outburst.'

I mean, *upstanding member of the community*? How the fuck can anyone say that about themselves and keep a straight face? And any cunt who wears a white flat cap probably ain't wanted by the community. I thought, What fucking community is he talking about, La La Land on the *Teletubbies*?

Yeah, Danny Dyke, one of Posh Jon's mates, was one of the 7-Up Boys. That's the Danny I've talked about before, lovely kid who got mixed up with the wrong people, got involved in a drugs deal, and got killed for it. So we became the 6-Up Boys.

Now Jon and his mates were all nice geezers who enjoyed their money, and good luck to them. Early on in life I realised you never had any real power unless you had money. That's how it works. You get money first, then power. Then the ladies. And while I find that very wrong in society, I truly do, that if you ain't got a few quid you won't be listened to, that is how it actually is. Even in what was my world, you might be a gutless sod but if you could afford 15 grand to have someone shot then you're a scary cunt.

One thing you couldn't do, though, was buy yourself into being a hardnut or one of the chaps. Because there will come a time when you've got to be what you're supposed to be and they'll just gobble you up. Sometimes money soils the view and natural leading ability gets overlooked. But long-term, class will shine through.

Oh, listen to this! Fucking hell! This thing that happened at a club once was, without doubt, one of the scariest, strangest things I've ever seen in my life. And I include seeing Dean and the Tango Man in his underpants in that list.

It was at The Gass Club on a Sunday night and me and Jen were there with Tucker, the usual suspects and also my mate Ian and this African girl he'd brought. She was a tall, black-black girl who talked in a proper strong African accent. She'd bought herself nice Versace pants and top, cowboy hat and put her hair in weave cane so she looked the part. But when you talked to her you could tell she was young and sort of naive, like she'd just come over from Africa. Which she probably had.

Everyone was dancing around having a good time. This girl had had an E and after a few hours was starting to look a bit the worse for wear. Which happens. But when you've had an E there's a certain amount of fluid you've got to have. She had this Lucozade bottle but Jen noticed she'd only drunk an inch of it in four hours. Jen does get concerned for other girls she sees if she don't think they look too healthy. She's great that way. Whereas other people might not care, or be too embarrassed to say anything, Jen will be straight in. She can be a good club mum.

Anyway, Jen got her a pint of orange and handed it to her. She was jigging up and down all the time but it looked like she was dancing. We didn't know it was the first tremors building up. She took the orange pint, still jigging, lifted it to her mouth and then the tremors moved up a gear and she just exploded. That was what it was like, like a bomb went off in her. She flung the pint glass over her shoulder. It smashed on someone. Then she flung her head and body back, her back arched right over like a bow, and the top of her head hit the floor, bang! So now her heels were on the floor, digging in, her spine's bent like a rainbow and frozen solid, and her head's upside down and propping her up! Then she started shaking and growling.

We all just moved *right* back, mate. You couldn't help but do that instinctively. Onlookers were just fucking freaking right out. Girls crying. Then the girl started trembling and making these godawful chattering and clicking noises. She was still bent over backwards on her heels and head. Her jaw muscles started flexing and then grinding her teeth together and pushing her jaw out so violently all her front teeth started breaking off and dropping out. Her lips started splitting open. I thought, this is the fucking *Exorcist* this! When's her head gonna spin!? Either that or it was the freakiest fucking breakdancing I've ever ever seen.

People were screaming now and shouting for someone to do something. Everyone was going, I ain't touching *that*. Two doormen got down and tried to straighten her out but couldn't do it. Couldn't shift her. She weren't having it. She was rock solid. Then Tucker just grabbed her round the waist, picked her up and ran out carrying her frozen in that shape she was in. She left behind a puddle of blood, piss, spit and teeth, and one fucked up, freaked-out crowd of people, I can tell you. I know cos I was one of them.

Now I've been in the game long enough to know a fit when I see one. I'll show you a million different ways to be out of it and collapse. I've had people die on me; I've been to some black people's churches and seen people in proper trances; I've seen drug-induced seizures; I've seen people have heart attacks: but that was nothing like anything I'd ever seen. It was like all the above, times ten. Fucking unnatural.

That girl had just come from a country where getting into a trance to music, and ritual and emotion being heightened by that whole ceremony thing is a way of life. And she slipped right back into it and more. That wasn't a fit and it wasn't out of it on drugs; it was like a possession. I've run it through my head a million times since then because I know I saw something supernatural. She looked fucking demonic. I don't know what was buried in her waiting to come out but it woke up in a pretty fucked-out mood. She slipped back into something primitive.

We took her to hospital and she ended up in a bad way on life support machines. They found half a slice of toast in her stomach. That's all she'd had to eat that day. At the hospital they were asking loads of questions, so we just said we'd brought her.

John said that her car was parked outside his house. So, like a prick, I went to move it. It was still dark when I got there cos it was only two in the morning. When I was driving the car away I thought what if her head suddenly flops on to the windscreen, as if she's laid on the roof of the car, spitting teeth and rolling her eyes! And when I'd put that little image in my head I could hardly look out the fucking windscreen. I was driving side-on. Then I imagined her head popping up in the rear view mirror, all grinning with blood round her mouth. Fuck me, I was properly shitting myself.

That was the kind of night you just wanted to be over in a hurry. When I got back home Jen and some people from The Gass were sat all round the table having an inquest into what happened. There weren't a spare chair. I threw half a dozen dice into the middle of the table. Or they thought they were dice, at first, until they stopped rolling. Then they saw they were the girl's teeth. I'd collected them. That cleared the table sharpish and meant I could actually sit down. Thank fuck for that! What a night.

A funny one that also happened at The Gass was when we were getting ready to leave. It was about seven in the morning. I've got this cloth with me and it's soaking wet from wiping sweat off my head. We saw this geezer sat asleep in a corner. He wouldn't wake up so I threw the cloth at him. Bullseye! right in the mush, but he didn't wake up. I started doing all these silly, elaborate throws – over my shoulder, between my legs and running up like I'm bowling and throwing the cloth smack right in his face. Everybody's stood around laughing at this geezer so spark out he must be dead.

My final delivery was a corker; a reverse twist overarm lob with topspin that whacked him on the cheek with a wet *smack*! The geezer woke up, jumped up, barely noticed we were there, and then went on to auto-pilot and started unloading this bag at his feet. He started getting tools out. We thought, Who the fuck is this cunt?

Turned out he was a builder doing some work at The Gass who'd turned up for work early. When he'd found the club still going he'd settled down in a corner and fallen asleep! Mental or what? And what a fucking alarm call, ay? A sweaty wet rag in the mush. The thought of that would get me up ten minutes early every bleedin' day.

Yeah, that builder fella definitely looked like he needed a holiday. But if he'd come away with us he'd have got even less rest. Because when we go away, we go away to party.

12 Fuck the Suntan . . .

Have gear will travel was our motto when we went off somewhere overseas. Our little Outward Bound clubbing-abroad bashes were a proper riot (the police thought so as well cos they got the water cannons out). The film version would've been *Carry On Caning It*. And anyone back home who held their breath waiting for a postcard turned a pretty shade of blue.

People actually began travelling the world raving. What about *that*! Going to other countries and uniting at some rave in another land! Fucking wicked. At one time it was a big deal just to cross the Thames to go out. Then raving changed that. Then it made people travel all over Britain. Then when Britain got too small everyone went on a world invasion. Fuck me, it was like the start of a ravey British Empire.

I went to a mental little do in Germany. Well, I say 'little' . . .

Jennifer had been in a play called *The Silent Twins* up in a theatre in Glasgow for six weeks and the bloke that produced the play was called Angus Farquar. It was all staged in the old Partick police station where they filmed *Taggart*. Angus was also involved in putting on one of the biggest raves in Europe; and he wanted me to open the British part of the rave. So we got a VIP invite to that.

It was in Germany at this airport in Hamburg. The planes that were there were all parked up down one end, and each country involved had its own aircraft hangar playing their own dance music. You could waft along the runway in and out of all these different raves – England's, Italy's, France's. It was mental. A whole world of raving in one massive place.

In the hangar for the British rave they had these steps on wheels that they use for getting on and off the planes – big white things about forty feet high. Anyway, the hangar doors were shut and everyone's waiting outside, and in the hangar they wheeled these steps right up against the inside of the doors. And who should be on top of those steps waiting to open the event? Only yours truly dressed as the fucking Pope! Oh yes.

Straight up, I was stood there looking like I was taking the Persil Challenge in the bright white Pope-smock, gold necklace, black Raybans, cigar and freshly shaved head. And stood next to me was Jen, all dressed up as a really sexy little nun. Blasphemous? What, us?

I needed the Raybans to disguise the fact that, at that point, I was a little worse for wear. It had happened during the day. The event was sponsored by Becks and, I'm telling you, about the place there was just mountains of beer. Mountains of crates as big as houses and as long as a lorry, all dumped over this airport. You just got what you wanted. And they had schnapps there too, which is deadly, mate. You just knock them back not realising what you're doing.

Now a combination of that and whatever else I'd had meant I got proper fucking off my cake, I did. Right off my head. Almost embarrassingly so. I thought, I'll leave the company I'm in cos I don't want to behave too badly. You know when you get to that point where you just *know* you've got to be alone for a bit? You DO know that feeling, you cheeky monkey.

I just wanted somewhere to lie down and I'm walking around really fucked up, right off it. So I walked out and it was so big, and so many people milling out that you just went where the crowd took you. I was bobbing along like a fucking cork.

Then I got lost, surprise su-fucking-prise, in some nearby woods. I remember some people telling me to tuck my gold chains away because of the gypsies about. It was cold in there as well, and when you're in a bit of a state your vision gets shorter, don't it? The world shrinks in on you. So I'm there in the woods, totally boxed. It was like an early version of the fucking *Blair Witch Project* – the Caned Courtney Project. Then I saw this fire and went towards it.

Giving it massive with the missus

It's a Jungle out there. Me with drum 'n' bass star Goldie

Top: 'And then I smacked this geezer . . .' Me at the Talk of London

Below: The only man who's seen more violence than me – Jerry Springer

Top: Celeb pal time. With *EastEnders* star Michael Greco . . .

Below: . . . and a less-than-bonny Prince Charlie

Top: If you want to get a head . . . Nick Reynolds adds me to his rogues' gallery

Below: I'm a Union man. Addressing the students at Oxford post *Stop the Ride I Want to Get Off*

Top: Largin' it in Tenerife . . . me and the boys: south
London's answer to *Reservoir Dogs*

Above: The shoeshine man was somewhat unorthodox

Livingstone, Norris, Dobson, Kramer . . . or Courtney?

Top: Jester minute – clowning at the High Court

Below: Courtney Love . . . me and the missus

Now, get this, what I didn't know is that this is the gypsies' bit of wood where they live. Their little clearing and their little fire. They're all sat around it but cos of the heat they're all sat well back, so I think no one's there. Then picture this, I stumble out the woods into the clearing like Frankenstein's fucking monster, saying 'Fire good! Fire keep Dave warm!' They've all stopped what they're doing, strumming their guitars or whatever, and are sat round the edge watching it all! Then I saw the hammock.

Never get between a tired man in a wood and a hammock. Now getting in a hammock is fucking hard work at the best of times, but imagine what it's like when you're fucked. I think I deserved a round of applause for doing it whilst hammered, thank you very much.

I rolled out twelve times. I didn't even know I had an audience for all this: a forest full of these gypsy fuckers watching this silly English cunt wrestling with a floppy bed! Anyway, I finally got in it and just died, just collapsed and went spark out. I slept like a baby – yeah, I cried for an hour and then shat myself.

Because the event organisers had made a bit of a fuss about me going out there, some of these geezers in the wood recognised who I was, 'That English bloke who's supposed to be naughty' and all that kinda bollocks. So they went and found Jennifer to get me out. She told me later that this geezer approached her and they had a conversation she never would've thought she'd ever have – a German gypsy trying to explain to her that his woodland hammock had been commandeered by her husband. He said, 'Dave.'

She went, 'Yeah?'

He said, 'Dave? . . .'

Jen said, 'He's gone for a walk, mate.'

The guy went, 'No. He is in . . . my bed!'

Jen said, 'Sorry?'

And the geezer said, 'Do not be sorry. Just come . . .'

She came back with them and this gypsy geezer is saying, 'I live here. That is my hammock. That is my bed!' Now you can't always tell when a foreigner finds something funny but you can be pretty fucking sure when they don't, can't you? And there I am, beached out like something dead with my shoes still on in this cunt's bed, snoring away like a Volkswagen Beetle! So he was a pretty fair few miles to the left of being happy this geezer. All he'd been doing was sitting in the woods having a sing-song with his mates when this happened. Talk about if you go down to the woods today you're in for a big surprise . . .

Which is why, a few hours later (after Jenny had woke me), I found myself in an aircraft hangar on top of these airplane stairs dressed as the Pope with a head as sore as a rabbit's knob, and wearing shades to hide the pickled eggs I had for eyes. So I'm there in the God clobber, Jen right next to me dressed as a nun with some very dirty habits and behind me there's these deep red lights all pointing upwards, smoke machines going ten to the dozen filling up the hangar and music blaring out the speakers to announce the start. Outside there's forty thousand maniacs screaming for the doors to open.

I wiped my head, lit the cigar, paused, and then stretched my arms out. The electric doors began to slide back and when everyone got a load of the lights, the smoke, the music, and this cigar-smoking Pope forty feet in the air they just went mental. Fuck knows what the ones already on acid made of it. It was a living trip to begin with.

I had to say, 'Welcome, come, come in . . .' and I was right off my head I can tell you. I leaned into the mic and said, 'Come, come, come inside! . . .' and then turned away and went, 'Yeah, come in you cunts . . .' but only Jenny could hear me. It was really funny. And everyone went absolutely mad in there. It's not every rave that gets a papal blessing.

I've done raves in Belfast. This was as it was then, before the ceasefire, still in the middle of the bombing and shootings. You'd see people crying in these raves, actually crying because they knew that this room was the only place they could talk, drink and dance with these other people – tomorrow they'd be expected to shoot them.

The Protestant–Catholic thing went straight right out the window when they'd had an E or smoked some puff. No one knew, or cared, what religion you were because everyone was just dancing to the same beat. It was the first time, for some of these kids, that they'd ever shared the same experiences with people who were supposed to be the enemy. And it drummed home to them that they were actually more alike than different, and that it wasn't right what was happening over there.

Out of that club, they knew the next day they'd go back to the world of the proper raving lunatics, bombing each other to bits. The very next day. But they couldn't turn around to people, y'know, their parents or politicians and say, 'But we've found out it ain't like that.' Because they'd just answer by saying, 'Don't tell me what you've found out while you were on drugs! That's not real life!'

So, these ravers couldn't tell anyone what they'd found which made the nights over there even more fucking special. And that was their other community. And it actually broke down barriers over there that a million armies in a million years could never have done. You ask any DJ that's played Northern Ireland, or did during those days, and they'll say the same thing – the people there are the absolute bollocks. Because if you're surrounded by death and someone gives you a chance to show you've got some life in you, then you grab it with both hands and you fucking *show* it!

One time I even turned Irish. No, I know that sounds like I'm about to tell some bad joke – as if I would – but I ain't. I was in an Irish club called Circus Circus and I was stood at the bar when I felt everyone's eyes on me. I thought, can't be my flies are down cos I'm facing the bar. But what it was was me being a 30ish bloke, English and a skinhead; to them I'm obviously a squaddie, ain't I? So anyway, I said 'Two pints of lager please,' and every head went SNAP! and turned back to me, so I ploughed straight on, this time in an Irish accent, '. . . and two fuckin' packets of crisps an a couple a brandies!'

Anyway, my Mum's Irish so at least they might have felt a bit guilty if they'd shot me!

Yeah, but the raves were wicked. What I was also doing was this, during promoting the raves I was also promoting Jenny and her sister's act, the Rude Rude Courtney Twins. I realised how much money there is in the music game. You only need one hit record and you can really crack it off. When their record 'They Took The Rap' came out I was taking the act all over the country and Europe: Tenerife, Ibiza, Germany, France, even the Mayfest in Glasgow.

I did the whole Ibiza thing many times. Put on events over there. I used to go out to Ibiza two or three times a year for about five years. Sometimes just for long weekends, sometimes for holidays.

I did events with a Lou of the Aquarium, Colin Butt, Terry Turbo and Manumission. The Ibiza dos were the Lou and Terry 'Ram Jam', who used to own another club called the Arches, like mine, but his was in Southwark Bridge Road behind Ministry Of Sound. I also went out there with Brandon Block, Fabio & Grooverider and Dean Lambert.

I ran a couple of my own things out there, 'Splash' and 'Hot & Spunky'. 'Hot & Spunky' was the fetishy club I did in London in the basement at the Limelight, but it went down a storm out in Ibiza cos they're up for anything out there. I did them as one-offs and cos there was loads of my friends out there the nights were bound to be packed.

Everyone's up for getting laid, getting pissed, getting stoned, getting completely off it, whatever. It's very gay-friendly as well so there's all that and all that comes with it – wild clubs and street parades, transvestites on stilts, bondage midgets on bodybuilders' shoulders. Blackpool it ain't, mate. And the fetish club thing took off out there in that atmosphere. Club Manumission was a much smaller concern then but now it's absolutely massive. Mind you, one of the promoters regularly having sex with his girlfriend on stage in the middle of the club can't have hurt ticket sales, can it? Then the live sex show became a regular thing.

It was at one of those that I first saw Nick Reynolds, son of Bruce Reynolds, the Great Train Robbery mastermind. Nick's an artist, just like his old man. He's a sculptor. He's the one that did the casts of me for his exhibition this year, *Cons to Icons*. But when I first saw him in Ibiza he was up on stage in a club doing plaster casts of blokes' dicks and birds' fannies, or a cast of some geezer shagging his missus! Call that work? Well I would, given half the chance. And I'd volunteer for overtime.

My mate Tank came with us to one of the gay-friendly clubs out there. Tank is a massive black guy. Very frightening-looking fella. To a normal geezer he'd be scary, so you'd think he'd be even more so to a drag queen in high heels, wouldn't you? But oh no, these Spanish ones went for Tank in a big way. Big mistake. I mean, he's called 'Tank' for fuck's sake!

I've never seen so many drag queens knocked on their bums by so many right-handers in one night as I did that holiday.

One would totter up to Tank and go, 'Ooh, big fella. Are you as ferocious as you look, darlin'?' – *Smack!* On her arse. Another one, 'Did you just hit my mate?' –*Smack!* Two down. Third one ran up, 'There's no need for th–' *Smack!* And another one bites the dust.

It ended up with this massive, scowling black geezer, Tank, knee deep in feather boas, broken high heels and unconscious bodies.

I imported a limo out there. It was an old fifties American Lincoln limo. Two-tone cream and white with big fuck-off fins and white leather. Cost me six grand at auction and I took it out to Ibiza to cruise around in like a flash cunt. Thing was though, it was so fucking big you couldn't bend it round those dinky little Spanish streets. You couldn't get anywhere in it! So it ended up as a static caravan.

But more sex went on in the back of that motor than most hotel bedrooms. You could get pregnant just by sitting on the carpet. If you pressed the horn it didn't honk, it moaned. And if cars could talk, that Lincoln would've been one dirty-mouthed fucker, mate.

But Ibiza is just the maddest place, ain't it? You *know* that. More so than any holiday place because it's built around clubbing. Fuck the suntan, let's dance! Even on a normal holiday people turn into real tarts and do the full sea, sea and sex bit, but because Ibiza is actually known for all those things than it just attracts those people. People abuse themselves more there cos it's common knowledge what goes on there. The partying is widely known and the parties are known to be wild.

Put it this way. If your bird was going on holiday with her mates and said she was going to Ibiza . . . you'd definitely prefer it if she said Margate. But anyone, male or female, who's a tart on holiday can still come home and be a librarian.

Fucking top, though. Clubbing all day and night and then chilling out on the beach.

And there's always loads of geezers coming home from Ibiza with cuts on their knobs. Banging away on the sand does it every time. Everyone's off their heads and wanting to shag on the beach but little grains of sand ain't really knob-friendly, know what I mean? So drilling away on the beach at night don't do your piping the world of good.

I tell you, it was hard enough finding somewhere to park your towel during the day, but just as difficult to find somewhere to shag at night. You'd be walking along in the dark and tripping up over legs everywhere. You'd just see these heads pop up, like those fucking beach turtles that hide in sand you see on wildlife programmes. How many 'excuse mes' did you go through before you'd find a spare bit of beach? And one without a wet patch.

Funny thing is, we'd bump into the same people out there as back home. It was a proper clubbers' home from home. So some blokes and birds I'd see down at the Gass or the Buzz in London, I'd walk into the Ku club in Ibiza and see the same cunts heavin' on the dancefloor there! It was mental. I could've gone out on my own and still seen loads of mates there. (Seeing my Mum dancing on top of a speaker one year was a bit of a shocker, though. Fuck me, I didn't even know she did Es!)

I'd go out with the usual mad crowd. Some of the people I went with were Big Marky, Mad Jack, Blonde Simon, Billy and Billy The Car, Big Larry, Brett, Denis Firman, Little Legs and Big Terry Webb, Paul, Amon, Dukey, Costas, Marco, all the boys from Bobby's, Leopard Lounge, Linnekars, Boobs and Ministry, Happy Days and the rest of the Tenerife Crew, Reema and Tony, Frank and Sheila, Faz and family, Big Mel, Dave Parks, the Mapp brothers, Docherty, Danny Dolittle and Steve, Steve Low, Creed and Wish. We even had fun on the plane out.

One time I bought this Spiderman outfit from a fancy dress shop, all velcro down the back, you just stepped into it. It was so thin you could roll it up like a stocking. But when anyone got into it with a normal physique – not some superhero's body – it didn't look the same as the comic. With your pot belly stuck out you looked more like Spider*cunt*.

Anyway, I went into my dressing room, or the plane bog, as it was called. I was with Amon Ash and all the boys from the door, Johnny and Trevor, Ned Rawlings and loads more. I jumped out the toilet in the full outfit and started climbing around singing the Spiderman theme. Proper Spidermanning it about, big time (I was the first Spiderman to carry a knuckle-duster). One kid on the plane started freaking out though. He didn't think it was funny at all. All the six-foot flat-nosed geezers with me are laughing but the kids are going mental.

Now when one kid cries another kid can tell from the pitch if that's a child's cry of hunger, loneliness or distress. In this case it was fucking distress. So all the kids went off like car alarms in a high wind. They must've all been part of the same union because they all came out in unison – one cries! we all cry!

It's all gone wrong now and the stewardesses were saying they were gonna land the plane and all that bollocks. I was trying to tell them it was a joke. As if I had to. Standing there in my red- and blue-webbed stocking feet and with big cut-out eyeholes, trying to be really serious about it being a joke. Honestly, I got *fuck all* respect from those people . . .

I said, 'What d'you think I'm going to do? Hijack the plane and demand you fly me to Gotham City to see my mate Batman!?'

That Spiderman outfit was a cunt, actually, and it nearly fucking killed me later on on the same holiday. It was the first day. The complex we were staying in had all these balconies that curved around the pool. I was on the second balcony – about the same height as a high diving pool, I thought. (Bit of a clue there.) So I put on the old Spidey outfit, lined up the eyeholes and the breathing hole. I made sure there was a gap in the bathers below and then jumped off the fucking balcony, two stories up, doing a 'Banzaaaiii!!!'

I hit the deep end like a bomb. The force plunged me right to the bottom and twisted the head bit of the outfit right round. The eyeholes were at the back of my head, the nosehole was over my ear and I had a mouth full of nylon and water. Now I was in trouble. I couldn't fucking see or breathe and I was proper drowning.

Everyone topside around the pool either thought I was joking or they were throwing chairs and sun mattresses at me in the water! I started thrashing about like an epileptic on a hot plate. A beach ball bounced on my head and I went back under. Cheers! I finally got back up and ripped the head of the outfit off me. I got out the pool gasping like a cunt.

What a shit way to go that would've been, eh? And what a crappy headline: 'Dave Courtney Dies In Spiderman Suit Bombing Kids! – pictures inside'. I mean, what would've they buried me in? A fucking cocoon?!

But after my good times in Ibiza my luck with the Spanish ain't been all good. Have I told you about my holiday in Spain and the Jeep crash? Oh, fucking hell, have I got a story for you!

What happened was, I was taking Jenny, Beau, Jenson and Drew to stay at my friends' yacht in Spain. I'd just got out of the A-Cat wing in Belmarsh, y'know, when I was in for The Big One (I got off, obviously, I hadn't fucking escaped). Anyway, so after being cooped up in a cell for a year on remand I wanted to get off to somewhere where the sky's a bit bigger than in England. And a lot more fucking blue as well.

So we went to see my really good friends Les and Jo. Their boat's moored off Gerona, this real rich people's yacht place. Five quid coffees and dustmen that salute, that kinda thing. We'd only been there four hours and we'd already unpacked and gone to hire a car. We got this big 4 × 4 Jeep. Everyone piled in the back and we set off up the mountains.

I'm having a right good skid around in it when I see this field full of ten-foot-high corn. I could see it was completely untouched and got that naughty little urge I was talking about before when you see fresh cement. Seeing this untouched corn was like seeing all that virgin snow at Glen's house. I thought, That'll be wicked driving through that, like in a movie. Big blue sky, yellow corn, wind in the hair (of the nostrils), beautiful missus and kids. Walt fucking Disney.

Now, driving through you can't see where you're going, just corn thrashing down in front of you. It's like a rollercoaster ride and the kids were in the back screaming and loving it. And I'm driving round trying to write 'DAVE' in the corn big enough to see from a plane. So I get to the end of the 'E', jump the Jeep off a bump, do the full stop, and drive into the next field.

I got out with Jen and Drew and let the boys drive, Beau and Jenson. Beau's fourteen and been driving already anyway. They're roaring around doing wheelspins and having the time of their lives, loving it, like you would, cos you just can't drive that mad in the middle of fucking London. Unless you're a black cab, obviously.

So they're spinning around, Jenson's holding on to the roll bar and shouting, Beau's driving it. Middle of a deserted field in Spain, what could possibly go wrong? Apart from, say . . . Beau flattening this corn and suddenly finding a big shed wall there. Well, Beau flattened this wall and suddenly . . . the Jeep smashed straight into the wall and knocked a big hole through. I ran over and jumped in the driver's seat to reverse it out.

Just as the dust's settling and I'm trying to find reverse, twenty or more screaming Spanish gypsies suddenly leap out of the hole in this building! From nowhere. It looked deserted but it was their fucking house and they thought we'd tried to kill them.

I can't even get it in reverse before they're all over the bonnet and grabbing for the keys, all jabbering and screaming. It was like Dawn Of The Living Gyp. So I went smack, smack, smack and belted a few and they went even more mental. Beau came over to help me and one gypo tried to whack him; Jenson, my little Jenson who was only nine at the time, picked up a pitchfork, bless him, and tried to stab the geezer swinging the shovel at my head. Someone hit little Drew, Jennifer's screaming, and all the gypsy women are picking up rocks and hitting me! It was a proper, proper nightmare.

In a split second I analysed the situation and thought, well, the gypsies' kids are no trouble, and the ones 50 plus should be no trouble. So that leaves the younger, stronger ones. They all jumped on me over the top of the car, kicking, punching and scratching. I just wanted to get the main ones out of there but there was just too many.

So picture this. The Jeep's hit the wall and knocked it in, maybe killed someone cos they're acting that way, all screaming and trying to smash my brains out with rocks. I can't drive the car cos it's fucked. My kids and missus are there, and Jen's pregnant, so there's no option but to fight and it's a fight *I cannot afford to lose*. There's too much at stake. I can't have a straightner cos there's too many of them. If they do beat me, fuck knows what will happen then. They're already trying to hit my kid with a fucking spade! It was a fight I had to win. And I'd only been in the country *four fucking hours*.

The plan was this, I draw them away by running from the Jeep. Then I'd stop dead, turn around and whoever was fastest would catch me up first; then I'd hold out my hands as if giving up, or offering money, they'd drop their guard a bit and I'd drop them – wham! – and then leg it. Number of times this worked was unbelievable. I'd stop and say, 'Money? Money?', then *smack*! Then run, stop and start to offer my rings, then *smack*!

By now the fight had gone on for maybe ten minutes. I've knocked out about half a dozen and the rest are still chasing and catching me now. I've got scars and blood on my back cos they're stabbing me with scissors and knives, there's scars all round my neck from having this big gold chain of mine ripped off (and it did take some ripping). I've got black eyes, bumps, bruises, the lot, mate. And it's a boiling hot day, there's dust kicked up everywhere and it's sticking to all the fresh blood patches. I looked like a big piece of battered sandpaper. I thought, I don't remember booking an Extreme Sports holiday. It was like Club Med meets *Gladiator*.

I can see Beau and Jenson in the background, by the Jeep, keeping some other gypos at bay, and a trail of battered ones from there to where I was. Eventually they caught me. I decked the first geezer, a young bloke, and then butted the cunt that followed in after him, who was older. Looked like his fucking dad, in fact. But they all overwhelmed me and dragged me down, laying into me.

There's maybe ten people now all over me like a rash, holding and kicking me. But, when I fell over, because there's all these fingers over my face scratching me and trying to jab my eyes and stuff like that, I'd just opened my mouth and bit. Now we're on the floor and they're kicking me in the nuts and stamping on me, I look to the left and there's this guy laid next to me screaming like a woman. Because I've got his first two fingers clamped between my teeth.

I looked up a bit and through these gypsies' legs kicking me I could see Jen and the kids by the Jeep. I'm laid there, face down in the dust, arms and legs being pulled and this gypsy geezer's fingers leaking blood into my mouth and I'm thinking two things – 1) I am *not* letting go of these fingers, come what may! and 2) Thank fuck I'm not a vegetarian.

And this is how it happened next, this is *exactly* how it went – these mental gypsies are all pulling me one way and pulling their mate the opposite way and the combined forces made us both rise in the air, like a big wishbone. Five of them with my legs and arms and the other lot with his. My teeth were clamped down on his two fingers, just above the middle knuckle, joining us together. He's screaming and crying. They're all screaming and crying. It was like a really, really violent version of the bumps!

They all started building up to one big pull – One! Two! Three! – then *HEAVE!* His teeth started to leave my mouth and I bit down even harder. My teeth bumped over the two knuckles and then I took the whole of the flesh of his fingers off, inside my mouth, like unpeeling a glove. I had all the lot of his finger muscle and skin in my mouth. It just felt like sausage meat. All could see was his two boney skeleton fingers, like two red twigs. I thought, You won't play the piano again, mate.

I spat the meat out. The geezer fainted. There was a second's pause when everyone couldn't believe it. Then they freaked out again and went berserk. I didn't feel any of the kicks and punches cos by now I'm completely fucking past it. I've been kicked, punched, stabbed, pulled and stamped. And that was just by the women.

Then the Spanish Old Bill turned up and I've never before been glad to see a copper. Trouble is, this ain't holiday-maker Spain we're in here so they don't speak English. I'm just about crawling out of a pile of bodies I'm under when it kicks off again and the Spanish coppers turn around, join in and start beating me up! It was like being back at Carter Street police station in the bad old days in south London all over again. But with sunshine. So nice of them to make me feel at home, don'tcha think?

Not that I'm one to expect anything from any Old Bill, Spanish or not, but I couldn't believe it. I thought, What is this – some kind of charity sponsored Beat-Up-Dave-Day or what? Then I heard a few words said in English and I realised they thought I was a football hooligan. I suppose a big skinhead covered in blood is gonna look like a right nutter to anyone, let alone Spanish Old Bill.

I made out the words 'Manchester United'. I thought, Fucking cheek, I'm Arsenal me!

So now I was being held by the coppers. Then this crazy woman gypsy ran forward and hit little Drew! I broke away and slapped her. She spun off like a bent firework and there was a moment's silence. Then INSTANT MAYHEM! This woman's geezer jumped on me and the fucking coppers joined in, whacking me with the nightsticks.

My kids started crying then. They hadn't done before in the fight but afterwards I suppose it was a kind of release.

I got taken away by the police but they wouldn't let Jen and the kids come with us. But cos I was the one who'd driven up Jen hadn't really paid much attention to directions so now they're lost up some Spanish bleeding mountain. While the fight had been going on all our bags had been nicked by the gypsies, all the shopping, wallets, money, jewellery, everything. The whole lot.

As I was being taken away I looked back. The field, which had been so untouched before, just pure yellow corn, was now like a fucking battlefield – smashed Jeep smoking away, wrecked house, bodies everywhere, walking wounded limping back, crying women, blood on the grass. You could see big flattened patches where I'd stopped and fought with them. It was like an aerial view of Dunkirk.

You just couldn't get your head around it.

Down at the station I thought it'd be a simple case of explaining the accident and that the gypsies had gone mental and mugged us. But the Spanish police didn't give a fuck about that. They still thought I was a drunk English football hooligan. So they handcuffed me to a radiator to the station and started beating me up again! Round two!

Every time these Spanish cunts walked past me they'd say, 'You football pig!', and they'd kick me or pour cups of hot coffee on me. I couldn't even get out the way.

They left me there all night. Nothing to eat or drink. I was just one big black bruise, aching all over, and half unconscious. I was covered in clotted blood. I even had to wet myself. And I was still chained to this radiator like a fucking animal.

Now, I don't know about you, but this is the kind of thing that can completely put the dampers on a holiday for me.

I wanted to get to hospital but I couldn't. It took Jen a day to find out where I was. All the gypos had been to hospital already, apparently, with broken jaws and bitten off fingers. And this had all been on the first day of our holiday. It was mental. When they did get me to hospital all the mad mountain gypsies were still there. They saw I was handcuffed and started attacking me again. Round three!

Jen had to ring my Spanish mate Frank, and Frank talked to the police. Then they put my name in the computer and it started pinging like a fruit machine on jackpot. 'Dave Courtney' had come up like three fucking lemons! Now they were saying, 'Ah, you are on Interpol!', and they took me to high category prison in Figerola. And that journey took all fucking day, bouncing around in the back of a dirty police van being driven by some cunt with a fetish for potholes. Wanker.

Next morning I woke up and realised I'd now gone nearly three days without hearing any English apart from 'football', 'pig' and 'Manchester United'. (And it's gotta be an abuse of human rights to be called a Manchester United fan.)

Les with the yacht helped Jennifer get in touch with this English bloke called Vince. He did a karaoke thing out there called That Man Vince. Les said to ring Vince and he found me and looked after us. Came to prison every day. He is a top geezer (although I do know that I still owe him £300. So get in touch).

Finally, this bloke comes into the prison and asks for me. I said, 'Please tell me you can understand English . . .' and then told him the whole tale of the accident, World War Three with the gypsies, the police, the whole bollocks. This geezer listened to it all and then said fine, but he couldn't apply to the judge until he sat and that wasn't until tomorrow. I had to spend another night in prison just to wait for a judge to say it had all been a mistake.

Next day in the courthouse the judge apologised for me being beaten up and banged up, which was a bit of a first for me (the apology, I mean). See, there's two types of police out there: the local police, who are like inbred, low-forehead throwbacks in Mickey Mouse uniforms, i.e., the cunts that had first come on the scene. And then there's Gardia, who are the proper fucking deal with the sharp little hats and machine guns.

It was the Gardia that raided the gypsies' house and found all our nicked gear and loads of other stuff nicked from tourists. So I got a written apology from the court and the police started being double-nice to me. Which is as bad a case of 'bolting the stable door' as I've ever fucking heard.

Coming out the court, though, I did a naughty little thing. But you got to remember I was tired, hungry, thirsty, black and blue and aching all over, covered in cuts and stab wounds, burnt, broke, and stood in an old T-shirt and shorts on the courthouse steps squinting in the boiling heat (I didn't even have any sunglasses). And *before* Jen could even open her mouth to say anything to me one of them annoying timeshare selling geezers bounced right up to me and went, 'HI! Welcome to *Spain*!'

So I clumped him.

Sorry. Shouldn't have done it, I know, but that geezer had worse timing than a bust watch. And like they say, even a stopped clock is right twice a day. Well, that moment on the courthouse steps just weren't the right time.

Back on the yacht with everyone I couldn't do fuck all cos my body's just gone into recovery mode and all seized up. All I could do was lay on deck. I made Christopher Reeve look epileptic. And cos I couldn't move I got sunburnt. I had sunburnt fucking bruises! How about *that*?

Me and Jen went out clubbing a few days later, y'know, trying to recover a bit of fun from the holiday, but I still couldn't move even to have a little boogie. I just stood there like a lemon. And one that couldn't even be squeezed because it hurt.

Going back to the timeshare geezer with the bad timing, ain't it funny how you sometimes react instinctively in certain situations? And different people do react in different ways. Especially when they think they're under attack. Some people instinctively shit themselves, for instance. Me, I sort of, instinctively throw a good right hander. Which I think is a better reaction, less messy and don't smell as much.

Years ago when I lived at my house in Sylvester Road, East Dulwich, I was sat indoors one day watching breakfast telly, i.e., *News At One* (well I got up late) and I heard a knock at the door. Now there used to be this guy who peddled around collecting for Littlewoods Pools. He was big dopey ginger geezer, over six foot odd and eighteen stone. How his little pushbike took the weight of him is a miracle of modern fucking science. I think it must've been made from space-age carbon developed at NASA.

So I was sat there and I heard this knock at the door. I went to open it and no one was there. I thought, That's funny, but it might be just kids. I sat down and it happened again. Knock on the door, I went and opened it and no one there. Fuck me, I thought, that was quick. They didn't even have time to get away. I looked down as well just to check I weren't being paid a visit by a mute midget who was on the step thinking me rude for slamming the door in his face.

Third time I waited by the door and when I heard the knock I opened it right quick. Still no one. What I didn't know is that because it was raining heavy this dopey Littlewoods Pools guy was knocking and then diving into the dustbin cupboard for shelter, the silly cunt! So I didn't see him. But this time he was waiting to jump out. He was ready for me.

And I was for him because the fourth time I pulled the door open all of a sudden this big ginger nutter leapt out shouting something ('POOLS!', as it happens). I was so surprised I just sent a right hander out as the advance party. Instinctively. Even though I was in my pants and holding a bacon sarnie I was like a coiled spring, mate. Ha! So Big Ginger fell into the garden and I thought fuck it, and closed the door.

Which also reminds me of when this official looking fella called around and asked for my missus, saying he was from Littlewoods. I said, 'Great. How much have we won?' He went, 'Nothing, I'm arresting her for non-payment.' He was only from Littlewoods catalogue, wasn't he? What a let down. I paid her bail, though.

But despite that massive Spanish row I have actually won a few in Spain, y'know. One time I was out there debt-collecting for Joey Pyle trying to recover 75 grand. It wasn't a mug I was going out to see, either, no mug at all. But sometimes just turning up is enough, especially when they've gone miles away and think they're safe. So I said that they better make sure they paid by the time I went home or something would happen to them.

When I was saying it to the bloke Freddie Foreman had walked in and was stood behind me. Whether they thought I was with Fred or maybe saying it on his behalf, I don't know, but it certainly don't harm your cause to be associated with Fred.

Anyway, the geezer paid within two days. I hadn't told him when I was going back so he got it together quick.

Sometimes the easiest place to go to do a job is abroad. That's why loads of hitmen come over here from Spain and Jamaica, kill someone here and then go home. They book a two week holiday like all the other holiday-makers, do their business, and by the time the police are involved they've left the country.

At the time of that little debt collecting thing in Spain I wasn't well known. I was just a skinhead with a cigar and a knuckleduster. But by getting well known I made myself redundant. Being on telly and in the papers don't exactly help on the old keeping anonymous front, does it? Now wherever I go abroad the only thing I take with me is loads of promotional stuff for my books or records or Jen's CDs and give them out to put in bars. Then someone from Britain goes away and goes, fuck me, I've seen a Dave Courtney poster in Australia! Which is true. Someone did see that. And some geezer's only got to flip his surfboard up on Bondi and the whole beach gets a flash of a Dave Courtney flyer!

Which reminds me of my own little surfing exhibition. What do you mean you didn't have me down as a surfer-type? When I look in the mirror I see a long-haired, bronzed Adonis, god of the beach. Then I tell him to get the fuck out of the way so I can see myself. Silly cunt.

Anyway, so I was down in Newquay on holiday. This was back in the days when I was with my missus Tracey. And at the time there just happened to be the World Surfboard Championship on. I thought, *Touch!* What a stroke of luck – what with me being the top High-Wave Surfing Champion 1974, Peckham Baths. Yeah, we'd wait until a fat bird came off the top board and then ride the wave on a skinny kid.

It was a big event this thing in Torquay. Capital Radio Roadshow there, and it was a beautiful day so the beach was packed. Trouble was there'd been an airtraffic controllers' strike so a lot of the overseas surfers didn't make it. Probably all stuck in foreign departure lounges hugging their surfboards and saying, 'Let me take it as hand luggage, please!'

Anyway, they made an announcement over the speakers asking for people to volunteer to enter. Just to make up the numbers, really. I didn't think they were expecting any new world champs to be discovered.

Now I'm not really a 'just making the numbers up' kind of bloke. As you may have gathered. The only time I'm up for getting lost in a crowd is when it would make it difficult for the police to ID me. But when I saw these surfer geezers with long blond hair posing around in their wetsuits I thought, I'll have some of that old surfing lark then. So I entered.

I thought I had a chance. Of getting killed. Actually I am half man/half dolphin. Everything I do is on porpoise. No, you can laugh (in fact, I wish you would) *but* I've always felt an affinity with our finned, aquatic cousins. Especially with chips and gravy on a Friday night.

So how it worked was this: we all paddled out to sea on our boards and turned round. Then the geezer up the scaffolding tower on the beach is on Wave Watch. When he saw one brewing he'd announce it and that was your time to get upright and ride. My old mate Ray was there and the rest of the boys cheering me on. Tracey was there wondering why she hadn't married one of them shy, retiring fellas.

I got up and was horizontal for about a second before I slipped. My feet shot out and I smacked sideways on the board. Then the wave flipped me – *WIPE OUT!* – flung me off the board and threw me up on the beach like a dead seal. I waited for ages for Pamela Anderson to bounce over and give me the kiss of life, or at least lend me her silicon bags for armbands, but no joy.

But you know how some people suddenly discover they have a natural talent for something, and the first time they might fuck it up but the second time it all just comes together? You know how that can happen sometimes. Well, I'm not one of those lucky cunts and on the second ride I got completely destroyed as well.

By now I felt proper fucked. Let me tell you, it really takes it out of you, being crap on a surfboard. It was less like surfing and more like a public exhibition of near-drowning! But I was having a wicked time and everyone thought it was really funny. On the last go I decided to make a real meal of the fall and jumped off clutching my chest like I'd been shot.

Afterwards I somehow forgot to take the surfboard back and found myself in the car park with it under my arm. So we strapped it to the roof of the Mercedes I was in and set off, with Ray and the other cars behind me and Tracey. So we're driving back and in the mirror I can see Ray flashing his lights at me. I was only doing 110 mph so I thought, it can't be that I'm going too fast. Anyway, Ray starts sounding the horn.

I lowered the window and looked back and I saw the surfboard about fifteen feet in the air. I'd tied it on with those elastic-type ropes with hooks on, but one had come loose and now the surfboard had taken flight. It was still hooked to the Merc but flying like a fucking kite. Without thinking of the consequences I hit the brakes. The surfboard dropped but carried on flying forward and smashed right through the Merc's back window! WIPE OUT!

Me and Tracey had a bit of a drafty journey after that, but not for long cos then the engine blew up not long after. Talk about adding insult to a fucking surfboard through your back window! I called the AA out and the journey back took so long that I actually got to know the AA guy really well.

Later on, when I knew him better, he told me about a little scam he did – well, quite a big scam actually – when he'd arrange for a car full of whatever contraband to break down abroad. Then he'd relay it back. Before Customs got wise to that he got out of it and with the money he'd made bought himself a classic 350SL Mercedes Gullwing. They're worth over a hundred grand now.

And he don't work for the AA no more.

I tried to join the AA myself but without knowing it I called the wrong number and enlisted in Alcoholics Anonymous. First time the car broke down I asked for call-out assistance and they sent a geezer with a bottle of fresh orange to tell me to 'carry on being strong!' And, anyway, if Alcoholics Anonymous is so fucking anonymous why is it that the first thing you do is stand up and tell everyone your name?

Just a thought.

13 Clubbed to Death

I only look for people I'm looking for for so long. Then I stop looking. Life's too short and London's too small for me not to bump into you again if it's you I'm looking for. I've found people in Austalia so someone from Peckham, for instance, can definitely be found. All depends how you look at it, I guess. Like they say, small world, but I wouldn't want to paint it.

There was this geezer owed me money and I'd see him everywhere, every time I went out to a club I'd see him. He always seemed to have a bottle of champagne in his hand as well. Now is that adding insult to fucking injury or what? This prat owes me money and he's out spunking it on expensive pop. The way I looked at it was that that was my money he was pouring down his silly little neck. I thought, This has got to be some kind of joke, and I weren't laughing so it was a bad one.

I saw him again at Tasco's Warehouse which was a big venue down Nathan Way in Woolwich. Tasco's would have big promotions and DJs that had started out with me at my Arches played there – Fabio & Grooverider, Brandon Block, Ratpack, Rob Andrews. On this night the promotion was 'Telepathy', but that was one skill this geezer obviously didn't have otherwise he would've read my mind and fucked off.

I saw him at the bar. 'Look,' I said, 'I'm not gonna spoil your little buzz tonight when you're out with your mates but the bottom line is this – Tonight it's OK. But if you haven't paid me anything, even a tenner a week, by the next time I see you and the next time I see you you've got fifty quids' worth of champagne in your hand, I'm gonna batter you. Don't do this again without paying me.'

Which I thought was more than reasonable, given the circumstances. I know fellas who would've sparked him out cold the first time they saw him. But I do like to exhaust all the nicer, easier possibilities before I stamp my little size 9s. Me and this geezer had some mutual friends as well, so I cut him a bit of slack because of it.

Sometimes you just get no respect for trying to be nice, though, do you? Ask Gandhi. The world's most famous pacifist and he got *shot*. At least wear a bulletproof vest for fuck's sake, all you pacifists out there. I used to be friends with Gandhi's brother, Goosey Goosey. Nice kid, but how he got those webbed feet into his sandals I just do not know.

Anyway, I saw nothing of this geezer. No money either. So I figure the cunt's buying champagne from the offy and drinking it at home. One night I walked into the Arches club (not my Arches, Steve Gordon and Fulvia's behind the Ministry). So I goes into the place. And for whatever fucking reason, that night I had something a bit naughty in the boot of the car.

Inside the club I saw this geezer again and he was with some good friends of mine, Blackwood, Ford and Lester. He ain't drinking champagne this time but he ain't on tap water either, and being out in any club costs you. Well this night it cost him more than the entrance fee cos I knocked him spark out. Some of the people with him carried him out and that was that. I figured that one right hander worked off about ten per cent of the debt so he still had another nine to go.

So I carried on regardless and boogied the night away. The door there was run by a really good friend of mine, Cecil, and also Roy Carr, Errol, Chrissie, Hugh-Roy Curry, Dennis, Locks and Boogie. Anyway, Cecil comes over to me on the dancefloor looking all serious so I know he's not come over to try and cut in! He bent down to my ear, 'Dave, there's that bloke downstairs you took out earlier. He's at the door with a gun and asking for you.' Now ain't it nice to be wanted?

Apparently this geezer had come back and said to get me outside or he'd come in and shoot me on the dancefloor. Fucking difficult to moonwalk away from a bullet as well. Even Michael Jackson would be fucked there. But then I doubt Michael Jackson's been fucked anywhere.

I asked Cecil if there was anyone near my car and he said there wasn't. I can see that him and the doorstaff think I'm asking that so I can get to the car safely and drive off. But I ain't. I'm not going anywhere but I am also not asking them to fight my battle for me. But I can do both things with one move. You know me, I keep it calm, I keep it casual. But that don't mean something ain't gonna happen. Know what I mean?

So I walked out to the car with half a dozen doormen behind me as we crossed the car park. Oh, and the Rolls just looked fucking wicked in the early morning light. It really did. I couldn't help but think that even in this situation. I got to the back of it and stood by the boot. The fellas all stood in a semi-circle around me. I popped the boot open and there she was. An Uzi. Blue-black, fully automatic, 600 rounds a minute, leather shoulder strap. And fuck knows what it was doing in my Rolls. I was sure I'd left it in the Mondeo.

I picked it up, picked up a magazine, slipped the clip in and banged it. I pulled the lever to arm it – *chik-chack!*

Now I definitely don't want to shoot this geezer and, like I said, I don't wanna start asking people to fight my battles either. So, a little overkill can work to stop something happening at all.

I didn't look up once during all this but the blokes behind me are freaking out and going mental. Cecil said the police hearing the sound of one shot being fired – him shooting at me – could screw the club, but if there was the sound of me returning continuous automatic machine gun fire . . . then the club would definitely be fucked! I thought that was a wicked way of putting it myself. Top marks Cecil.

Everyone said don't do it, we'll deal with it. And they did. They went back and kicked absolute fuck out of the geezer.

And listen to this, the twist to the story here is that the handgun they took off the geezer, the one he was threatening to shoot me with, was originally my own gun that I'd given to someone else! Oh, larf? Listen, I nearly didn't start.

I'd originally given this gun to a guy and then he'd told me he'd lost it. So he still owed me £200 for it. But he hadn't lost it, he'd lent to to the brother of the bird he was seeing. Then him and the bird split up so he never saw her brother to get the gun back. And her brother was the Champagne Charlie who owed me money. Got it? This is worse than a fucking *EastEnders* plotline. Only thing missing is underage sex and a divorce.

The guy I'd first given the gun to told me the full story when I rang him. He was so embarrassed and shamed that I'd found out he'd been lying that he made me promise to stay at home until he got there. Ten minutes later there was a knock on the door. The first thing he said to me was, 'I can't say how sorry I am, so I'm gonna show you instead.'

We got in his car and he drove to the hospital where the bloke was recovering after the doormen had battered him. He asked me to wait in the car then he went in, found the bloke on the ward and battered him again, right there and then. Right there in the hospital. Which is a bit of good luck for the bloke really, innit? Admit. If you are going to get a kicking, what better place for you to get a kicking in than the hospital. As my nan used to say. Wise old bird that she was.

It weren't always all peace and love and smiley faces in clubland, unfortunately. Most of the time it was, and far more good than bad happened, but clubland can be a fucking funny place at the best of times. Funny ha-ha but also funny-peculiar.

Tony Smith was a mate of mine. He used to be my next door neighbour when I lived on Shifford Park Road, where I grew up. He got shot twice in the face at point-blank range in the VIP room of the Emporium. Point-blank. That put blood on the ceiling. And there's Sol, who just got shot the other day. Bald-headed Bill, he got shot three years ago. Then there was the Tucker–Tate killings.

An awful lot of people do miss, though. The amount of times that guns have gone off is a lot more than the number of people actually hit. But today getting shot at is definitely part of your job if you're a doorman.

A doorman got shot dead at the Rex, for example. Some geezer let off five shots at the door, killed one and tried to hit the rest. Scouse Jamie got murdered at the End Club. He was shot in the chest and died in his girl's arms. I shouldn't imagine it was a planned thing, just an argument in a club that blew up.

Most of these guys get away, from the police anyway. Only in eleven per cent of murders do they catch the person. And nightclubs are naturally more likely to be full of people who don't tell when they witness something. Chances are that it will be resolved before the police get to them. It's only the geezer's mum or wife who actually wants the shooter to get caught by the police. Everyone else involved wants to get him themselves and deal out their own sentence. And once your name becomes known as the one who did it the chances of getting away for ever are slim.

At one point the violence around clubs got so bad people were being murdered. Shot at and shot dead. My mate Francis was shot in the back outside the club Grace while I walked beside him down the Old Kent Road. Even old Frankie Fraser got shot in the face outside Turnmills in Clerkenwell. Though not many men would describe being shot in the head in the way that Frankie did, 'It was fun, good action, it makes a good night's drink after all.' Which is one good reason to go teetotal.

I must have seen guns pulled on doormen maybe fifty times, which is a lot. And nine times out of ten when someone pulls a gun, the person who ends up getting shot is fuck all to do with it. Nearly always. Someone on the edge will say stop, or jump in and try to calm things down. Then they get shot because they don't seem to know how easy it is just to pull your trigger finger back a couple of inches.

The territorial wars between the drug dealers that the club scene attracted have died down now. In time it sort of sorted itself out. Or people sorted each other out and that put a lid on it.

Trouble was, if you were up against a drug dealer then most probably he was on his own stuff and not in a rational state of mind, and a lot of heavy drug-orientated criminals were in that state. In that case you have to meet force with even more force. In that situation my thing was this – I would much rather use overkill to prevent something kicking off, that is, have a few really really naughty, handy people working for me as a deterrent. I always hired more blokes than necessary, and paid for the best, to make it a really silly move for anyone to do anything.

The other way is to try save a few quid and not hire enough geezers but hire a few nutters to try and cure it when a battle did kick off. In that case you might win the fight but you're left with bodies on your hands and the threat of comebacks and all that grief. But if you made sure that in your company there was about fifteen out of your forty blokes who were well known faces from the old violent world, y'know, proper go-all-the-way geezers, then that would be a blinding deterrent. You'd have to be a complete and utter fucking idiot to look at some of my mates – like Mad Pete, Brooklyn John, Big Marcus, Warrior or Wish – and *still* think it wasn't total suicide to have a go. You'd have to be pretty hard of thinking.

Warrior, for instance, is way out there where normal man fears to tread. He's this 35-year-old Zulu warrior, according to him. The only Zulu from south London I know, but he looks the part. He's big with short locks and he's very, *very* black. So black he's blue. Anyone who thought it was a good idea to have a go at Warrior would have to be pretty fucking tired of life. He'd walk around a rave with two swords on his back like the geezer from *Highlander* – 'There shall be only one!' – and when a row was brewing Warrior would draw these two long blades out! Why people felt intimidated by him I just do not know.

Even his house is worrying. Above the bed there's a lifesize Tutankhamen Egyptian mummy. The bedroom walls are like a prisoner's cell with hundreds of cut-out dirty pictures stuck everywhere – arses, cunts, tits, cocks in mouths. Good place to take a woman back to. Providing it's Rose West.

There's a massive, black fourteen-inch dildo nailed to the front door and also hundreds of flickering candles outside. It's the only gaff I know that's given a wide berth by Mormons and completely swerved by door-to-door salesmen. The postman stays by the gate and fires Warrior's mail up the path with a catapult.

He speaks in philosophical passages. He talks about 'the power within'. And he says his body is a temple. Which is why he leaves his shoes on the outside. He runs everywhere as well. I swear he does. You'll see him shooting up the street and you know he's not in a hurry, he just runs *everywhere*. Why? Because he's a warrior, of course. A man on a mission. I took him out on the Harley Davidson once, which he called my 'iron horse'. But because he only ever got anywhere by running he said he'd only go on the bike if he could wear no helmet and let the wind 'run' through his hair!

He said to me, 'Dave. You have been here before because you are a Zulu warrior in the white skin!' I fucking agreed with him like a shot, mate. What am I gonna do, argue with that?

So you definitely, *definitely* wanted Warrior on your side. Better for you than against you. He was employed because he was one of the baddest geezers out there. He'd go into the nastiest situations with ease. He was the advance party. And if anyone was lucky enough to be left standing after Warrior had steamed in we'd just go up to them and advise them to call the Samaritans for counselling.

Warrior was one of my main security people at the 'One Nation' events. This promoter once refused to pay my mate Terry Turno so we got Warrior to have a word with him. Warrior went up to him and said, 'Hey punk, I'm a dark brother. You better get that money. You won't walk out here alive. I'll come to your funeral and shoot it up! I'll open your coffin, crush up your bones and smoke you in a spliff!' That's not the wording I would have used, but the geezer paid.

He could walk into a place, a club, and straight away spot the bad fellas or know where they would be. If a situation started brewing he'd spread his arms and actually do a fucking war cry to the sky, like he was drawing his power from God! Scary.

So, yeah, prevention is better than cure, as my nan used to say. I quote my nan a lot, don't I? Come to think of it, my old nan would've made a fucking good gangster. Or Big Nan, as the chaps used to call her. Anyone with machine guns in their wheelchair and a concealed sword in their walking stick is a handy one to have on any firm. And she could chuck her false teeth like a fucking kung-fu star, mate.

I went for prevention every time but still, on numerous occasions, things happened. Because, as my school teachers used to say, there's always one, ain't there, who has to spoil it for the rest! I've had doormen come and try take over my clubs. Or teams of doormen come back at me after they've been sacked by a club for selling drugs and unofficially running the place. The smaller underground clubs, especially in the early days, didn't really give a fuck. They were set up for the moment and everyone was fucking on one. But then when raving went commercial and mainstream, as it did, and the big clubs and leisure organisations moved in, they sacked whole firms on the spot if they found anything dodgy going on.

So then that door firm would lose not only their wages but also the revenue they were making off the drugs in the club. And that was maybe a couple of grand a week each. So there was a lot of very vexed people out there, y'know what I mean? Losing all that money per week meant them losing the new house and the big flash car.

That's when they'd come round and try to take out the new doormen. One particular time, at this place I was working on the outskirts of London, eight shots were fired over the night from three different guns. How fucking naughty is that? If just one geezer pulls a gun it's bad. Two do it and it's oh, fucking hell. But *three* shooters! Having to face that is well beyond the call of duty for any doorman who's stood there armed with just a knuckleduster and a few wise sayings from his nan!

The change over in clubs came when out of necessity there had to be more security round the clubs. That was a telling time, and it showed up the problems. The police got more involved.

Promoters tried to do raves that finished at three but it didn't really happen. By then the bad guys had actually seen how much fucking money you could earn through the drugs. People were making new-car money in a couple of weeks. So now raves were popping up all over just to sell the drugs. These people didn't give a fuck what they made behind the bar or on the door cos they made so much money out of selling pills that they would've let the punters in for nothing. And if the punters knew that there were deals in there then they would go in.

That's when clubs started to become money-printing machines. So the owners of some places started throwing out any drug dealers but their own. Eliminating the competition. And if the pills were OK the punters didn't give a fuck who they were buying them off. So if you had 1,000 people in your club for nine hours and they took an average of two pills each (some more, some less) at fifteen quid each, that's £30,000 per night on pills alone. Then the bar and the door money. That's about one to two million pounds per year! A fuckload of money.

So then you got your established dealers. It was then worth fighting to have the rights to sell the drugs in certain places.

The venues were hired out for one night to do a rave in there on, say, a Friday or Saturday. Most likely the geezer who's hired it is selling on average 2,000 pills in there, so he don't really care whether anyone's really paying on the door cos he knows he's gonna sell 2,000 fifteen-quids.

That made it worth starting wars over. A lot of treading on other people's toes came into it. And another thing happened, it made dealers out of more people.

Porkpie Martin was one guy. So called cos he wore a red leather porkpie hat. He was about forty-five-years old, a real tall skinny geezer. I thought he should've been called Swan Vesta cos with him being so thin and with his red hat on he looked more like a match.

One night he left a club on Southwark Bridge and went back to his car. In the car he had five hundred Es and he started bagging some up. As he was doing it there was a tap on the window and he looked up and saw two policemen. In that situation the first impulse for a drug dealer is this – if you can, eat it. That's their motto if they get nicked with anything. Eat it. The Old Bill cannot nick you for a turd! Imagine them trying to produce that in court as Exhibit A. They couldn't tie a label on it, for one thing.

So Porkpie banged all the door buttons down and started shovelling Es into his mouth. All of them. The coppers smashed in the window and got him. They nicked him, then realised what a state he was soon gonna be in and took him straight to hospital. He slipped into a coma and died three days later. Five hundred Es. At least he died happy.

And it's those instant decisions made in times of stress – under pressure, that very second – that make or break you. So whatever the circumstances may be, what you've got to do is this: forsee all the problems that might happen to you, work out what to do for each one, log it, remember it, then if it does actually happen you don't have to make a snap decision in one second. You've already made the decision two years ago, or whatever, when you first thought of it.

That applies to any walk of life. Rehearse something in the cold light of day and you'll never get caught out.

Yeah, the becoming-the-dealer thing was one that sometimes sneaked up on people. These weren't all necessarily bad or nasty people, remember, much as some people would like you to believe. Even though he was doing something unacceptable, the dealer became an acceptable part of the whole club scene. Almost respected. The punters looked at him as the one who was risking getting the twenty years' bird so they could buy a pill and have a nice time; and he was the one who meant you yourself didn't have to risk driving around to buy one, then try sneak it through the door: he'd be waiting inside for you.

And the dealer became very influential. He had money, his name on the door list, his own supply, hundreds of women around him and always seemed popular. The poor cunt of a dealer ended up thinking he was popular because of him, not because of what he was selling.

Most dealers start off as users. The usual scenario was this – a guy will go to a club and if he liked, say, Charlie, he'd buy a gramme, then take half but end up giving half away to the mates he's with. This goes on regular. Now he's on first name terms with the dealer. After a while the geezer starts thinking, Well, if I bought three grammes and cut it up a bit I could sell two grammes and get one for nothing. And he doesn't actually *think* that that is being a dealer cos he's just getting one for free. So it's started already, the mind con.

When he's done that a couple of times he realises he's made half his weekly wage in one night. And cos people have started to notice him running around trying to sell his two grammes, they start asking him for stuff. Then he thinks, fucking hell, sold the lot and there's still ten people saying 'Have you got any?' He starts thinking, 'I could have made fortunes here'. That's his mind prepping him for the next level. So he buys, say, seven grammes. Keeps two and sells five. Now the geezer's on his way.

Suddenly he's got blokes hanging round him, birds spinning on his cock, new car, invites to parties and champagne on ice. And all because he's selling Charlie. At the begining he drove around with three grammes in the car so it don't feel much different to him to have twenty in there. He forgets that he's actually breaking the law.

Whatever his everyday job was before – waiter, office worker, police officer – gets pushed into being the 'pastime' and what was the pastime before, the drugs, now becomes his job. The drug industry very quickly seduces people financially, and then your mind won't let you work in a petrol station for £150 a week when you can earn twice that in one night in one club. That only goes on for two or three weeks and he fucks off the day job.

Now he is a professional criminal cos it is his sole source of income. But because it's happened gradually he doesn't feel like the big, bad drug dealer, and he keeps thinking that way until Old Bill bangs a hand down on his shoulder to arrest him. That's ten years' bird. He might say, 'But I'm not a drug dealer!' but he is. In one pocket he's got eleven hundred quid, in the other pocket loads of half-ounce wraps. Ten years' bird, and he might never have been in trouble in his life!

Then when he goes to prison all those people who were hanging around him are now hanging around whoever else is now selling the gear. The BMW's been impounded and his bird's now got some other dealer's cock in her mouth.

And that little scenario was done on a large scale with individuals and done on a group scale with firms. The actual ravers, though, did not give one flying fuck about the policies or where the gear came from as long as they were in there and on one.

Sometimes what you don't do is as important as what you do. And remember this, do remember this: *A man is only as strong as the thing he can RESIST.*

Because at one time I employed so many people it was impossible not to say that everyone wasn't involved in drugs. When my firm went from being fifty blokes I knew well to being five hundred geezers who were friends of friends or acquaintances, it was fucking difficult to keep an eye on everyone. I'm not against dabbling on occasion, but drugs screw up people's professionalism when they're working. I mean look at the Pope. That geezer can't even get off a plane without collapsing on the tarmac: and asking women if they'd like to kiss his ring in public, I ask you! He's lost it. Proper fucked, mate.

One way of justifying the use of drugs is if you use the right one for the right purpose, and in the right way, then that in my book is acceptable. And this *is* my book so I'll say what the fuck I want, thank you very much! If smoking puff makes you go all mellow and chilled and you do it indoors (and, like it says on the packet, don't operate heavy machinery) then there's nothing wrong with that. If you're a night-jobber like a cab driver, a dancer, a doorman or a DJ and some whizz does nothing more to you than help you stay awake then *that*'s great. And if you can't dance and you want to get involved in it all and there's this little something called an E that helps you lose your inhibitions and do it on the dancefloor, then that's OK for that.

And I'm afraid that Acid, and things like that, do open the doors in people's minds. It can be a naughty old drug and as much as it could harm you, each trip does something individual to each person.

Cocaine, thugh, is the only one I can't find a little pigeonhole for. You take it and go out socialising but it don't make you sociable in the right way. So it's counterproductive. At first it was the rarest of the drugs out there cos it was the most expensive and most ravers were poor. Sixty quid for a gramme of Charlie was a fucking lot of money for a raver, so it was more for the 'going out' crowd who had a few quid and could afford to buy champagne anyway. Coke is more of a woman's thing anyway. Testosterone and Charlie don't mix. It affects men and women completely differently: women don't get paranoid on it like men, and women can still feel sexy; on a bloke it don't have that effect.

It could lead people well astray as well. I know this fella who was really a straight businessman who'd gone and let himself be led down a wrong path and he had his head turned by temptation, and instead of just shipping snooker tables over to sell, which was his business, he started hollowing the legs out and bringing gear in. He'd actually got into it because of his missus. One night she got nicked with something illegal on her (I think it was a drug dealer) and the police brought her home to search it.

The husband weren't there so they asked her if she knew the safe's combination and like an idiot she said yes. The police opened it and found 4K of Charlie! So they nicked her, obviously. The husband then had to go down the nick and, in order to save her, own up and say it was his. And he got life. *Life*, for fuck's sake.

And if they described coke as it is: a white powder that will eventually empty your bank account, shrivel your cock and make you talk bollocks all night, then there'd hardly be a queue 'round the block of people wanting to buy it, would there?

And the spin-offs from coke are worse, like crack. Crack really is the proper mugging-your-granny-for-money kind of drug that the authorities like to portray all drugs as being. So for once your Uncle Dave says, Just Say No.

A scene I saw some years ago was probably crack-fuelled. It was at a Jungle rave on the outskirts of London and the atmosphere there weren't the happiest I'd ever experienced. It was when Jungle was still at a certain stage, very edge and attracting a lot of that gangsta crowd. It's mellowed out a bit more now, as things do.

But Jungle could be a bit of a moody fucking clubbing scene at the best of times. And at the worst of times was the thing I saw when I walked into the toilets. The door banged open just as I reached it and a fella ran out. When I went in the bog was empty apart from one guy scrunched up, down against the wall in the far corner and this other bloke stood over him with a long bayonet in his hands, plunging it in and out of this geezer's neck and face. He put all his weight into the final stab and slipped it right into the bloke's heart, pulled the blade back out (which was *pure* red), and then ran out.

Blood started squirting out like a high pressure hosepipe from this geezer's chest wound. And this was the red-red stuff coming out straight from the guy's pump. For a black guy he turned whiter, quicker, than anyone I've ever seen in my life. Almost see-through. When the spurts started hitting the ceiling I thought it was about time to fuck off.

Might have just been a case of wrong place, wrong time. Wrong drug. Who knows? Some people just are unlucky though, aren't they?

I mean, after Hitler shot himself some unlucky fucker was left behind to pay the gas bill.

14 Jesus Saves – Courtney Nets the Rebound

So Hitler appears at the Pearly Gates trying to get into God's gaff, Heaven. Saint Peter say's 'What the fuck are you doing here? You murdering bastard, you've got no chance, fuck off!' Hitler says, 'Oh go on, give us a chance'. Peter says, 'Piss off back downstairs!' Just then Jesus walks by and comes over to see what the row is about.

Hitler says, 'Any chance of getting in?' Jesus says, 'Not really, you were such a cunt to the Jews weren't you?'

'Look,' Hitler says, 'if you get me in I'll give you a medal, an Iron Cross!', and he shows him one. Jesus is fucking impressed by this and says he'll have a word with his dad and see what he can do. So Jesus tells God all about it.

God's not impressed by this at all so Jesus says, 'Yeah but dad, he said if I got him in would give me an Iron Cross.'

'What do you want that for?' God says, 'You couldn't even fucking carry the wooden one!'

And . . .

Jesus walks into this hotel, puts three nails on the reception desk and says, 'Can you put me up for the night?'

You see that's why I miss going to church, cos I used to get all the best God jokes from my local vicar. But then he went and got himself in trouble and had an affair with one of his married parishioners. The parishioner's wife was as shocked as me. We didn't even know he was gay.

The vicar's wife was even more surprised. I took her out for dinner and she tried to tell me all about it. But I had to say, 'Audrey, don't talk with your mouth full. And while you're down there lick my balls as well, will you?' She'd only gone under the table to pick up her fork and then I'd thought, well, now she's under there . . .

I think we got away with it. I don't think the waiter noticed, but he did seem to think it was a bit odd when I asked him not to put the salad down in the wet patch. He said to me, 'Did you find your steak agreeable?' I said, 'Yeah, but then I didn't want one that would fucking argue with me!' I'm not gonna have words with a bit of dead cow. I will *not* get dragged into it . . .

And I wanted a bottle of wine. The waiter asked if I'd like the House Red. I said, 'Leave my house out of it! It's white and it's staying white.' Bloody liberty. His brother-in-law must've been a decorator.

But the Bible used to move me to tears. When my mum hit me with it. I was so fucking glad when the paperback came out. I was gonna become an atheist until I realised I'd have nothing to shout out when I came – 'Arrggh . . . *nothing*!' Just ain't the same is it?

Any road, the story. The fucking story you're waiting for. Be patient, my children. Patience is a virtue. I could never be bothered to wait for it to develop, though. What a cunt. Must be nice to have genuine belief in God though. What a safety net that is when you go over the other side. Me? I'll just land on concrete.

It's nice when someone else has faith in you, and *for* you. I've had that.

I have the utmost respect for people who have faith, though. I don't know whether I believe or not. I know I'm making 'God jokes' here, but when I was locked up in 'The Unit' at Belmarsh, Posh Jon's parents, Val and John, sent me a beautiful Bible. And I read it and got something from it. No jokes.

Jennifer has big faith in me, of course. And Jen's mum did a blindin' bit of praying for me a short while back. It was around 1997, '98, when I had that big big importation charge against me. I was looking at about twenty years if I got a 'guilty' and they kept me on remand for a whole year in the High Security A-Cat wing at Belmarsh. I won't go into the full details cos they're all in *Stop The Ride I Want To Get Off* (fuck me, I'm shameless).

Jen's mum is a Jamaican lady who's lived over here since the 50s. She is a really really lovely lady. Very genuine and very religious. Always finds good in bad. Whereas me, I just always find I'm good in bed – completely different thing! But anyway, when I was on remand all that time Jen's mum said she'd pray for me. And when the actual trial began Jen's mum said she would fast for me.

She said you pray for someone, but if you fast it's like a shot going straight to heaven because you are sacrificing something for someone. I thought, Wow! Fuck me. Get *that* – a shot straight to heaven. Then I thought, I hope she don't get a bad ricochet and kill God! Would I have been fucked then or what? No, I'm just being silly now (so unlike me). I was genuinely touched by what Jen's mum said. I was really really moved by that.

Trouble was though that my trial ended up going on two fucking weeks. So Jen's mum was in a really bad way, really starving, for me. Thank fuck for both our sake's that I got 'not guilty'. I said I didn't know how I could thank her. She said not to thank her but to go to church with her one Sunday and thank God.

There's a few questions that even religion can't answer. Like what *was* the best thing before sliced bread? (And was it such a fucking hardship slicing bread in the first place?) And the geezer who drives the snow plough – how the fuck does he get to work? (Does he have to take it home with him every night just in case?) And if I had multiple personalities and I threatened to kill myself am I then in a hostage situation? And Donald Duck always wears just a jacket and no pants so when he gets out the shower why does he put a towel around his bottom half? And we know Pluto's a dog but what the fuck *is* Goofy? And if Jesus was so smart why did he befriend a geezer called Judas? Bit of a giveaway on the old grassing front that name, innit?

Anyway, a couple of weeks later after I'd made my promise to Jen's mum I came out of the Ministry Of Sound at ten in the morning. I'd been out since, about ... erm ... February, I think. Not sure of the year. It'd been a long one anyway, put it that way. I drove the Roller home, getting a flash from practically every single speed camera on the way. All those images of me taken from those cameras you could put together and made a fucking feature-length film. Call it *Speed*. Ha. Or *Get Courtney*.

I got in home and crashed out in the armchair and the phone went. It was Jen's mum, 'Hiya, David. What time you picking me up to go to church?' I'd forgot all about it. I told her I'd be there right away. I went to pick her up in dark glasses cos my eyes looked like marbles dipped in blood. They weren't exactly the kinds of things you'd like to see in church. Unless you were looking to do an exorcism.

We went to this religious convention in a church at Broxley Cross. We were in church for four whole hours and hearing the preachers shouting and singers wailing and the gospel choir right bang on it just made me come up big time. I was fucking buzzin', mate! Jen's mum was going, 'Praise the lord!' And I was going, 'Praise the lord!' Everyone was dancing and singing. I thought I'd walked right back into another club. That's what it was like, the buzz was as good. And everyone seemed to be able to sing as well, y'know, none of that wobbly warbling you get from white-boy Christians; this was proper full-on gospel-soul stuff.

I was right bang into it as well. I gave as many 'Hallelujahs' as anyone else in there!

And I haven't shagged a vicar's wife since.

But that church was as good as any rave or club I've been to, believe me. The naked geezer in the underpants nailed to bits of wood was a bit too S&M for my liking, but you can't have everything. The best churches are like good clubs and the best clubs are like churches.

Right at the beginning of raving people took to it like a religion or a cult thing. You only had to go once to get converted. John Lennon once said that the Beatles were bigger than Jesus, although how he knew how tall Jesus was I've just no idea. But clubbing took over that idea and became a religion.

I mean, if someone said that in the middle of the Sahara desert there was a prayer meeting in a church and also a big rave in a tent, which do you think is gonna be more popular? Ravers have hacked their way through the fucking rainforest to get to a rave there for fuck's sake. They've travelled to Australia. Gone up mountains. Walked through Brixton.

Clubbing vs Church was a no contest. You couldn't pull in a church, for one thing. Nothing human anyway. The church might've had us beat hands down on the decorations and venues, but it lost out big time when it came to uplifting emotion. In raving, each individual club was a temple with a DJ as your messiah. The disciples all wore the same gear (and took it) and their cup runneth over with Red Bull.

There was a group of rave promoters called Spiral Tribe who were the absolute bollocks and more than a little bit spiritual themselves. The tribal techno sound systems took off and Spiral Tribe did big outside raves and festivals, along with others like Headcorn, Sunrise, Energy and Orbital.

They were all the nuts but the Spiral ones were wicked. They were a freaky looking bunch of fuckers, though. Half of them were new age travellers – white guys with locks, that kinda thing – and the other half looked like Hari Krishnas; shaved heads, barefooted, the lot of them. Women as well. They were proper cosmic, Stonehenge-loving tree-huggers.

They had the knack of getting all the best venues for raves as well. Places like stately homes and manor houses in the country. Fuck knows how they did that. And when they first arrived it must've looked like Mad Max come to life.

They were just a big party of party people. Their raves were sexier because their favoured substance was acid. They were really into trips and trips are one of the sexiest drugs there is if you're man enough to take it and handle it. Viagra will make your cock go hard for longer than normal, and probably add half an inch to it, but it won't make you feel any sexier if you don't feel that way already. It's a body drug, not a mind one. But a trip, you can lose yourself in a trip. For days, in fact, if you're not careful.

Some of the outdoor events were like rave Glastonburys. And I know because I used to work Glastonbury doing the security. Metallica headlined one night, the Clash did a revival gig, and Ian Dury played, an old favourite of mine.

There was about thirty on my security team. They don't turn the whole of the festival over to one firm because that would give far too much clout into one company's hands. And then the sole security could make demands on the organisers, which they can't say no to in case the security walks out. So they've learned to break it down into cells. Now there's different firms for back stage, the perimeter, the VIP tent.

There wasn't much aggro there from the punters really. How much aggro can stoned hippies, pissed students and off-their-cake new age travellers cause anyway? The most ag came from drug dealer wars. They all wanted their own little patch, y'know? They make so much fucking money at Glastonbury it's a joke. Cos no one goes there that don't take gear, do they? It's actually like some massive annual, controlled experiment on drug taking! Imagine a Martian beaming his telescope down on earth and zooming it in on Glastonbury and thinking all earth people were like that. No wonder they've never invaded.

Talking of people from another planet. There's a load of undercover Old Bill there as well. They ain't exactly difficult to spot. Some proper hard-core substance takers would also help point them out cos they'd see their mates nicked after talking to them. So some security fellas, who shall remain nameless, took off their security jackets and went around chinning these undercover Old Bill. They were falling like fucking ninepins, mate. They all woke up sunburnt.

Big Brummy John was one of the fellas with me that year. We got tipped off that these dealers were giving the ordinary festivalgoers loads of grief so we went to have a word with them. They were just right lairy with us, told us to fuck off and went back in their tent and zipped it up. Now why they thought that little bit of blue nylon would protect them from John I just don't know. And the tent had a sewn-in ground-sheet so it was all enclosed.

John ripped out the pegs, picked up one of the corners and pulled forward. Then he leant back on his heels and started swinging this tent around like a big bag! They were all trapped inside, rolling around screaming and John, with his massive strength, was swinging the tent like a sack. It got up so much momentum that it lifted off the ground and when he let it go, fuck me, did that thing fly. It very nearly landed on the main stage and killed Van Morrison!

Another group of geezers who were causing untold grief were this gang of muggers. Glastonbury is a soft touch for those cunts cos everyone's so young and, generally, so out of it. And it would properly fuck up your weekend to get done over by someone wouldn't it? So we made a point of finding out where they were.

They had their little tents and sleeping bags more or less in the same little patch. One of them was even sleeping in an old toilet tent, y'know the little toilet tent they put inside the bigger one. Well this idiot was sleeping in one of them! No fear of having sweet dreams then.

Anyway, we got all these really long and thin elastic ropes from backstage. They use them to secure the scaffolding and light rigs together, because if they use nuts and bolts then the vibration from the music loosens them. What you might call real bad vibes, man.

So we got about six of these ropes, hooked one end of them to these muggers' tents and the other ends to the back of a Land Rover. Then we drove off. But because these ropes were elastic it took ages for them to stretch. We just kept driving! I thought we'd end up in the next field. Eventually they really tightened, went tense, then the elastic kicked in big-time and all the tents flew forward and started bouncing along the ground! It was like half a dozen ground-level bungee jumps.

We could hear them all screaming inside. To them it must've felt like the field had been tilted up and they were sliding down it. It did create some havoc. Especially for the pricks in the tents and any unlucky fucker who just happened to be innocently walking in the flight path! If you were one, sorry.

A Headcorn event in Kent was the single biggest rave I've ever been to. This one really was like the Glastonbury of raves. And it just went on forever. It was supposed to be a weekender but it just slipped into a weeker. People were conceived, born and hit puberty before this rave ended. Parents were getting letters of condolence from the organisers saying their son had been lost in action – 'We believe he put up a valiant effort in an attempt to storm the portaloos but perished on the hill.'

Not a bad way to go though, is it? I mean if you did pop your clogs at an outdoor rave. Breathing your last at a massive party surrounded by your mates dancing away under the sky. But, y'know, if you had to choose a way . . .

And then when you get to Heaven, do us a favour will you? Ask old Holy Hands up there to turn up the heat in Britain for us will you? No, it don't matter. I suppose I'll be having a word with him myself later. But if it's anything to do with me it will be very much much *much* later.

So all of the music, every single one of them on the scene when the scene started breaking up – House, Hardcore, Techno, Jungle, Trance, Garage, Drum & Bass – all had different names but were all sort of hypnotic and trance-like. Or, put it another way, the kind of music you could easily lose yourself in if you weren't completely straight. And anyone even a little bit buzzing could get completely lost in that repetitive music. An awful lot of black people can get into that mode in their normal everyday church. *And* white people in the southern states of America. They're fucking tripping on God those people.

It was very like that for ravers who weren't even aware it was like that for them. But you could actually go in there, in the club, or the rave tent, or even outside at night, and because it was dark it made it easy not to be embarrassed; and the tunes made you want to shut your eyes. It was very easy to lose yourself for hours.

Sometimes it is really really nice to lose yourself for hours, ain't it? You know it's true. And you could open your eyes and no one's looking, no one's laughing, everyone's smiling. And you thought to yourself, Fuck me, they want to ban *this*!

The right place, the right time, the right tune and, oh babe, you got religion!

15 The World's Most Dangerous Babysitter

And no, this chapter ain't about Louise Woodward or Fred West. It's actually about a nice geezer who was just a little bit of a liability.

Little Jimmy travelled 200 miles to try to find me. All the way down from Leeds. He'd seen me and Jennifer on *The Vanessa Show*. It was one of them 'Women Who are Married to Gangsters!' type of things. It started off with the audience being horrified, supposedly, at Jen being with a villain, or an 'ex' one as I was by then, but it ended up going really well, as it happens. I pointed out how Jenny was actually safer than most people because she was with me.

By the end of it even Vanessa, bless her, seemed to warm to me. She's not exactly my type, but there ain't nothing wrong with a hefty bird in my book. Slap it and ride the ripples, as they say.

Anyway, during the programme I mentioned my belief about always helping out mates or most people who came to me in trouble. I've always said that if I can't do anything myself I'll probably know a man who can. And I always wanted to be more Robin Hood than robbing cunt. So Jimmy's watching this and decides to hitch down to fucking London to see me. Just like that! Like it's the most natural thing in the world.

Now I've never been the most difficult person to find. I don't go around hiding from no one. I even gave the local Old Bill a key to my flat so they could visit without kicking the door off for the eleventh fucking time.

So, next thing I know, I got a call from the guv'nor at my pub the Albion (or what was my pub before the Old Bill started harassing me). He said there was this guy in asking for me. I went down to check him out and finds this young northern geezer in the bar waiting. Right off I could tell he was a nice enough kid. He didn't have nothing back home to stay for, he told me, and when he saw me on telly he decided to come to see if I could help him out.

I thought, Fuck me, what am I, the Samaritans? Then I thought how he'd come all that way just after seeing me on TV, which is some kinda compliment when you think about it. And you couldn't help but warm to Jimmy cos he was just so upfront and sort of innocent. I couldn't turn him away after he'd come all that distance on the strength of what I'd said.

So I put him to work on little jobs. Nothing major or dodgy. Just running errands and helping out and driving people, that kind of thing. He got to be a bit of a fixture round the place.

Trouble was that an awful lot of the things Jimmy did had a habit of going ever so slightly wrong. There always seemed some extra problem I had to sort out afterwards. He was like one of them people who swear blind that they know a shortcut, so you follow them and it takes twice as long! He always did things with the best intentions, though, which made it worse in a way cos I couldn't bring myself to tell him off. He'd say how he done what he thought was best to help me out. I thought, Oh fuck, what can I say to the geezer?

He reminded me of one of them characters in a cartoon that just walks along creating havoc without even knowing it – stepping over open man-holes without seeing them and walking out into the street and causing car crashes without noticing. That kinda thing.

But I trusted him enough to get him a flat in the block over the road from mine and to let him look after Jenson sometimes. Jenson was about nine and him and Jimmy got on well. So Jenson would go over and play computer games and stay over.

Anyway, this one night I decided to go out on the town. Well, it was either that or stay in and do my tax returns. Yeah, I was in a real fucking dilemma, mate, I can tell you. So I rung up my mate Brendan.

I'd met Brendan about eight years earlier at the Ministry Of Sound. I was sat on this back to back sofa in the VIP lounge, Brendan had blagged his way in and was sat behind me.

Apparently he'd double-booked birds (a common thing, I later found out) and this one bird caught Brendan on the sofa with another one and started kicking off, shouting and screaming. From behind me I just heard Brendan say, 'I'm sorry, babe, but you seem to have mistaken me for someone who gives a fuck!' I thought, Top line. I've got to talk to him.

So I saw him at the bar, completely off his face he was, and he began talking the most amazing amount of complete and utter bollocks I'd ever heard in my life. But he was so funny, really funny, that we hit it off right away. He was exactly the kind you'd want with you on a night out. Real value for money is Bren.

One time I'd come out of a club in Battersea, near the dog's home as it happens, and was driving home. Now round the corner there's another club called the Yacht Club and as I'm driving past this geezer comes staggering out into the road, looking completely the wrong way, and walks straight in front of the car. I slammed on the brakes and hit the horn. He jumped, spun 360 degrees till he was still facing the same wrong way (away from the car), held up his hands to an empty road and went, 'Hold it! *Hold* it now!'

I thought, Fuck me. Then he turned round and it was Brendan! Chances of that happening! Really I should have recognised the tartan velvet suit, to be honest. So I gave him a lift home.

I said, 'Where do you live again?' I'd known him a few years by this time and I still didn't know.

He went, 'Thamesmead Estate.'

'Yeah . . . where?'

He thought about it for a bit. 'It's . . . a blue door.'

'They're all fucking blue doors,' I said. 'You live in a council place, remember? What's the number?'

'I can see them but all the numbers are getting jumbled up. I can see a *seven* . . . and a five.' It was like talking to Mystic fucking Meg.

Anyway, when we got to the right area he told me to just drop him anywhere round there, it was close enough. Last I saw of him, when I drove away, he was flaked out in the sun on a grass verge with someone walking their dog stood over him like they'd discovered a dead body.

Next time I saw him he told me he'd eventually woken up in a flowerbed in someone's front garden with this pissed-off geezer from the house looking down at him. He'd asked Brendan what the fuck he thought he was doing.

Brendan said, '. . . nothing . . .'

'Well fuck off,' this bloke said, 'and do nothing somewhere else!'

Anyway, this other night was work not play. There was me, Brendan, Northern Billy, Big John and Jim, Kevin, Scouse John and Ravey, AJ, Slim, Billy, Jazz, Gilly, Chef, Boxer, Lawrence, John O'Keefe, Bal, Pike, Stephanie, Little Jenny, Mad Jack, Geordie Steve, two birds that Brendan had pulled at different clubs the previous week (another double booking) and about another hundred mates waiting inside for us.

So we're all having a good time, which ain't easy when you're out with a million mates in the biggest club in the country, high on life and whatever else comes to hand, whizzing on the dancefloor. It's a dirty job but, like they say, someone's gotta do it and I made sure my name was first on the list. People who know me know what I'm like when I'm out but others that just know *of* me seem to expect me to be stood in a corner doing the big gangstery 'I'm cool' bit. Bollocks to that. When I go out I like a fucking good dance, mate.

Some of the blokes from my walk of life wouldn't be seen dead doing that, out on the floor dancing, but I made a lot of good friends and allies out at play. More by accident than design but it's always better to work with mates, ain't it? You know how many deals are done on the golf course. Anyway, this night was just 24 carat, 100 per cent proof, havin' it large, bollocks-to-the-world fun. And I'm boogieing away when I clock some undercover Old Bill watching me. They're never difficult to spot if you've got a nose for it, but one of them in particular I recognised. I knew I was under heavy surveillance and it's a real bastard. Listen to this – a mate of mine's mother worked as a cleaner at a certain London nick and, through her, word got back to me about what was going on there.

Turns out they had a whole incident room put aside devoted to the surveillance on me! I thought, Wow! What a fucking compliment. Noticeboards full of information and pictures of me, like a little fucking shrine. And here's me thinking it'd be at least a couple of years before I got my own fan club.

They'd use the surveillance thing to fuck me in ways you wouldn't even think of. For instance, I'd only just been aquitted of a charge of importing coke into the country (fuck me, Pepsi I could understand). I was in the wrong place at the wrong time and got nicked. It weren't nothing to do with me, but the police used it to nick a year off me by putting me on remand in Belmarsh. And then they fucked my chances of bail by saying I was a leading suspect in a murder investigation. And that all came about through surveillance on me in a club.

I'd been in the Ministry that night and some geezer had come up to say hello to me. I didn't know him personally but his brother was a friend of mine. Months later the guy gets shot and the Old Bill pull me in on the strength of him being seen talking to me! But I say hello to hundreds of people a night!

And that was just their little way of stealing a year from me. And that ain't just paranoia cos one of the Old Bill actually told me that's what they were doing. Off the record, of course. So I'm putting it on the fucking record now.

This one copper that I'd recognised in the club was a proper cunt as well. One of them with an O level in sarcasm that you've probably been pulled over by. Obviously taken off the tit as a baby before he was satisfied and ends up in the police with a bag of chips on his shoulder.

Not that all this surveillance crap really bothered me (you can't let it get to you) but it does irk a bit when they try to have one over on you by spoiling a night out. And on top of that they're getting a fucking good night out and passing it off as work.

One time in the Paradise Club something funny happened. There was this dark tunnel, that leads from one bit of the club to another. If you walk straight into it you're half-blind before your eyes adjust. You'd see people hand-walking along the walls like Stevie Wonder in *The Twilight Zone*. Anyway, this copper starts walking over to go through the tunnel and I did, I must admit, get a naughty little thought popping into my head. One of those 'I wonder what if . . .' moments. Now you can either leave it at that or see what if.

Someone, who shall remain nameless, followed him into the corridor and chinned him. One punch – spark out. No witnesses cos no fucker can really see anything! Apparently other clubbers were walking into the tunnel and ending up on the floor after tripping over his body. He caused a serious multi-raver pile-up that geezer did. Then he was seen stumbling out the other end ten minutes later covered in footprints. Any you try getting served at the bar with 'Adidas-size 9' printed across your forehead. (Just one of the many trials and tribulations of modern-day policing, I guess.)

Anyway, back to the night at the Ministry. A good time was had by all (by all of us anyway) and we decided to go on to another club, and then another one and then maybe . . . oh, go on then, just one more. Touch of the old 'bleaching' came upon us.

It weren't exactly all fun either. Because in one of the clubs my trouser pocket sprung a leak. What happened was this. The diamond ring on one of my fingers had been gradually wearing a hole in the pocket lining. Which I wouldn't have minded if I hadn't got a grand in cash in that pocket. It was all dropping down my trouser leg without me knowing. I just thought I was the most popular fucker on the dancefloor, that's all, the way people were running up to me and diving at my feet! And it was the first fucking night so many people had actually bought me a drink. With my own money. Cheers.

So, anyway, two days after setting off we finally pulled up outside my gaff.

Me and Brendan at the head in one car full of people, another three cars full of ravers behind us and, at the back, a black Jeep full of dopehead surfer boys that no one seemed to know who the fuck they were, but they'd tagged along anyway.

So at about 12 o'clock at night there was a five-car convoy outside my house, including: a Jeep so completely filled with puff smoke it was coming out of the door locks, three cars full of sweaty, out-of-it club casualties still banging out tunes from the stereos, and me and Brendan and mates sat in ours. Course our car had to be the one with the fucked-up heater stuck on 'hot'. There was so much steam pouring off us it looked like we'd had the car fitted with frosted glass.

I was supposed to be just calling off at home to pick something up before going straight down to Hastings to another club I knew. I thought, Well . . . now we're out we might as well write the whole fucking week off. And my job as an outreach worker at the disabled donkey sanctuary would *just have to wait*!

I was about to get out when Brendan said, 'Hold it. Dave, they're onto us. I think that's Old Bill over there . . .'

'Where?'

'There. There's loads of them dotted about.'

I wiped a bucket of condensation off the windscreen and fuck me if he wasn't right.

I said, 'They wouldn't *dare*! Not in front of my own house!' I was fucking outraged. Even though we had a gun in the boot, a cosh under the dash, knuckledusters in my pockets and a convoy of complete nutters in tow – I was still outraged. I mean, *fuck* me, on a Sunday!

I got out, walked a few steps and suddenly all these red dots appeared on my body. Bit late in the day for measles, I thought, at my age. They were infra-red dots from the rifle sights that the SWAT teams use. All these armed police suddenly leapt out, loads of them all togged out in the gear, and came running over screaming at us. I nipped that little lark right in the bud. Defence often being the best form of attack, I walked right up to them.

'OK, OK! Hold it! I hope you've got a fucking good excuse for doing this to me in front of everyone,' I said: like I was out with the Salvation Army Marching Band and not half of London's walking wasted. They ran round the car pointing guns at everything that moved.

Brendan got out from behind the wheel. He's stood there in the street in the *brightest* green velvet suit you've seen, wringing wet and with his hair slapped to his head, eyes like dinner plates and looking every inch like someone who's been out for two days solid and – get *this* – one of the coppers turns to him and says, 'You're the cab driver, are you?'

Never one to turn down a good one when it's offered free, Brendan goes, 'Err . . . yeah. That's right. Problem, officer?'

Now I don't know which cab firm that copper usually used but if he could mistake Brendan – who looked like a big, green, totally fucked leprechaun – for a cab driver then I don't want to ever use them. The rest of our convoy were either sinking down in their seats trying to disappear or wandering about thinking we've driven straight on to a film set. Some of them were even coming out the cars saying, 'How long you gonna be then?'

Some of the neighbours were coming back home and walking straight into this three-ring fucking circus going on. All we needed was a clown car.

Which the Jeep at the back doubled up for, actually. None of those geezers emerged at all, I noticed. I just saw this hand reach up and wind the sunroof shut to stop more clouds of smoke coming out. The music shut off too.

Then what really freaked me out was what this copper said to me next. He shouted, 'Have you got a ten-year-old son?'

I thought, *What!* I'm stood here with twenty guns pointed at me and he's doing a survey. I just couldn't get my head round it. I thought, Am I tripping or what? I know they take being cheeky to teachers seriously these days but this was fucking ridiculous. Anyway, told him that yes I had a ten-year-old, Jenson. He asked me where he was. I said he was upstairs in fucking bed.

He said, 'Right – let's go!'

Now cos I live on the fourth floor I thought what *is* the thing to do in a situation like this when you've got a dozen SWAT officers behind you – take the stairs or squeeze in the lift? I went straight for the lift just for the laugh. As many of them as possible followed me in and the rest I could hear running up the steps. Fuck me, though, was that an uncomfortable one. You know when you're in a lift and no one wants to speak . . . and the others are all armed? No – I didn't think you would.

Anyway, on the way up I'm told that a guy had reported being attacked by someone who'd hit him with a gun and the geezer said Jenson had been with him. I couldn't fucking figure that one at all. Jennifer answered the door to all of us on the doorstep. Me and half the Mct's armed response units. She said Jenson wasn't at home, he was with Jimmy.

Hearing Jimmy mentioned made things a bit clearer along the lines of a molehill being turned into Mount Everest. Which is what seemed to have happened. The copper asked me where he was and I told him I didn't know. He said he didn't believe for one second that I didn't know where my son was.

I said, 'Hold it. I do know, *but* seeing as I now know who it is who's done wrong I'm not gonna grass him up. But I do know that Jenson's safe as houses with him and that's all I need to know.'

'Well, someone's told us,' the copper said, 'that he's in a flat across the road. So we're going in there.' Jenny jumped right on that one, though, quick as a flash. Put them right in their place.

'Where do you think you lot are going with all those guns when there's a kid in that flat!' she said. They all looked at each other like they were being told off by Mum. 'There's *no way* you're bursting in there with my son in there – I'm going with you!'

The lift back down was another funny one. On the way back down the older copper in charge said he couldn't believe that what they were looking for here was, basically, an armed childminder. He turned to me then and came out with a cracker.

'Twenty-five years in the force, Mr Courtney,' he said, deadly seriously, 'and I have never, ever seen such a dangerous babysitter!' That's a wicked line, ain't it? Fucking wicked line.

I was still laughing when we came out into the street to find a proper audience now. Neighbours out, dogs and cats watching, three cars with the doors open and everyone sat on the pavement or on walls; even the Jeep sunroof was open to let out smoke, and Brendan was leaning against the car trying to adopt some kind of 'cab driver' air about him. And failing miserably.

We all walked over the road in file, me and Jen at the head, then twenty SAS drop-outs behind. We passed right in front of my car and Brendan went, 'Erm, I *have* switched *off* the meter, Mr Courtney. In case you were wondering . . .'

I suddenly knew that Jen and Jim wouldn't be in Jimmy's flat and decided to go back to ours in case they returned. Jenny went on up to the other flat with the police and, sure enough, no one was there.

Meanwhile, when I got back to our flat the phone rang and it was Jenson. I said, 'Where are you?'

He said him and Jimmy were a few doors away from me, hiding in a neighbour's flat! Then he gave me the full wide-screen, Technicolor, stereo-sound version of events. Turns out that about half-an-hour before, near midnight,

Jenson and Jimmy had gone to the park to shoot Jimmy's air pistol. On the way back, this geezer had said hello to Jenson, but Jenson hadn't replied; Jimmy said he was rude for not answering but Jenson said he hadn't because he'd been told the guy bothered with kids.

When Jimmy heard that he went back and smacked the geezer. When he started putting up a fight, Jimmy pulled out the air pistol and hit the guy with it. The geezer then went and reported it to the Old Bill, who just heard the words 'gun' and 'Dave Courtney's kid' and mobilised the A-Team and Batman's brother.

Instead of running back to Jimmy's flat across the road, Jimmy and Jenson had come into our block and gone to a neighbour of ours. That's where Jenson was ringing me from. I told him everything would be OK and to come down to me.

See what I mean about Jimmy's heart being in the right place but it leading to major catastrophes!

So Jenny and the SWAT team had found Jim's flat empty and came back over the road to our place. Little did they know that I had already coached Jenson in exactly what to say. I opened the door with Jenson beside me. The officer at the front said, 'Ah, Jenson, we've been looking for you in connection with a reported incident. I need to ask you some questions . . .'

Right on cue – and bear in mind this is a nine-year-old kid – Jenson said, 'I'm sorry but I refuse to say anything until I see my solicitor.' The copper's face just froze in amazement.

I went, 'Yeah, he's right you know. And he's only nine, so you're not allowed to take him. Bye.' And I closed the door on them all!

Me, Jen and Jenson just went *YESSS!* Oh, fuck me, that was funny. A fully armed SWAT team fucked over by a nine-year-old boy smart enough to listen to his old dad.

When they'd gone, Jimmy came out of the other flat and down to ours. 'I only thought I was doing the right thing, Dave; looking after Jenson,' he said. Fuck me, I thought, what can I say to that? It was a typical Jimmy thing. He had done the right thing but not exactly in the right way, you might say. Only Jimmy could turn a walk to the shops into Vietnam: The Sequel. But Jimmy was such a nice geezer, really. Heart in the right place and all that. In fact, he was a whole *Vanessa Show* all by himself.

Then I thought, Right! That's it! Enough of this bollocks. I'm not gonna let a minor diversion like a Metropolitan Police Armed Response Unit fuck up my night act. So I changed my suit, went downstairs, jumped back in the car, everyone piled into theirs, the doors slammed, music went back on, joints came out and we fucked off straight to Folkestone.

We were out of it and laughing all the way. Brendan was laughing so much he forgot we were leading and the others didn't know where the fuck we were going and lost all the cars behind. I think by now he actually believed he was a cab driver – doing all the 'I own the road, I do' driving manoeuvres. Even slamming on the brakes at amber (instead of flooring it like usual) just to keep the imaginary metre ticking.

There was no sign of the others but I said not to worry, I'd leave a trail. I grabbed a pile of flyers off the dash and started ripping them up into pieces and dropping them on the road. We're doing ninety and I'm hanging out the window thinking this is a really good idea.

In case the others didn't make it I telephoned ahead to my mate Ricky in Folkestone and asked him if he could get ready for a night out. He asked me where I was.

'I'm on my fucking way down to you right now – wind in me hair!'

'You haven't got any hair,' he said (clever bastard).

'No, but I can feel the ones up my nose vibrating, all right?'

So we got there, eventually, after Brendan took a short cut he knew, which ended up being twice as fucking long (ain't that always the way). And most of those following us got there as well, which suprised me. I think it was cos everyone was caned to the exactly same degree; so they lost the plot, recovered it and then accidentally found themselves at the right place in the same way that we had.

Now Folkestone ain't exactly buzzing on a Sunday night. In fact, there's more buzzing around cow shit. It's sort of like a seaside cemetery with traffic lights. But my mate Ricky ran a brilliant event down there called 'Juicy Tunes' at the Parisienne Club (along with Martin). By the time the club was due to shut, there was nowhere else to go. No one fancied driving home cos we were all pissed.

I said, 'Right. Pick out someone in this club, anyone, and I bet I can persuade them to invite us back to their place.' And everyone picked out this right hard-looking black geezer, a proper face, pointed to him and said HIM! Oh cheers. Thanks a fucking bunch. Teach me to keep my mouth shut.

So I went up to this bloke and told him that I'd had a look around this little seaside place and he was the only one I'd seen that me and my few mates fancied having a drink with. I said that if ever he was up in London he could come to my place anytime. He said OK. I turned around and gave the thumbs-up and everyone came over – all twenty of them! Which was a bit of a surprise for him to see what looked like the whole cast of *Trainspotting* walking over. But I don't think he minded. (I later found out that he normally had more people than that back anyway. He was a top fella and we became mates.)

So we ended up at his house. Turned out he was a really nice geezer. We didn't take advantage or anything, we supplied our own puff and we sent out a taxi for booze and to stock up on grub. Which reminds me, I once paid for the country's most expensive pack of Rizlas. I was stuck in a hotel in Worthing on a New Year's Eve with some puff but no fucking papers so I phoned for a cab to go out and get some large ones, but he had to go to three garages. It weren't that far but you know New Year's Eve taxi drivers practically charge triple time and a blow-job, don't they? So when he got back it cost me seventeen bloody quid. And then an extra three quid cos no one wanted to blow him!

Anyway, back at this geezer's house in Folkestone we were all having a good time and there was this girl sat next to me. I didn't recognise her but she must've come down in part of our convoy. If Brendan hadn't been in the car with me on the way down, I'd have just put her down as some bird that he'd picked up in a club and offered her somewhere to stay for the night – i.e., on his face.

She was buzzing, this girl, and got in on the conversation, and suddenly she said that she'd had an operation last Wednesday. Then she asked me if I wanted to see her scar. Now I'm thinking appendix, something like that. Then she flipped her shoe off and she had no little toe. She'd had her little toe off! I thought. Is she really pedalling at the same speed as everyone else or what? (probably not, with only nine toes).

Now that ain't a scar in my book, that's a fucking stump. An amputation. And a proper little conversation stopper as well. No one knew what to say and she seemed to be waiting for a round of applause or something. Then she said, 'Do you know my boyfriend left me?'

'Oh yeah?'

'Yeah. And,' she said, 'he let me have everything back when I left the flat but he kept my toe.' She said he kept it in a jar and she'd asked for it back but her boyfriend wouldn't give her it.

I said, 'Well, that says something for your personality, babe, don't it? That he'd rather lose the whole of you and keep your toe.'

She weren't sure she'd heard me right cos I kept a dead straight face. But she was telling me about this toe like she thought I'd go get it back for her, like a debt collecting job. Y'know, we've got the place surrounded, let the toe go! Her boyfriend comes to the window with a gun pointing at the jar – 'Get back or the toe gets it!'

So I told her that maybe it was just a clever little plan by her boyfriend to get her back gradually, bit by bit. Next time he saw her he might cut off her hair, and then later smash her in the mouth to get her teeth, until he had the full thing.

On the way back from Folkestone the Roller started to die on us. I could hear the death rattle. We staggered on to the next service station. Everyone's getting pissed off now cos the fun's over and all everyone wants to do is get home. But as long as I've got a hole in my arse the fun is never over. So I took it upon myself, as leader and chief silly cunt, to keep everyone laughing.

I got out the car with a big fat cigar stuck in each ear. They were stuck out like boat oars. I went up to this geezer just getting off his motorbike and said, 'Can you help me out here, mate?' He looked out from inside his helmet and he saw me stood there with two Castellas stuck out my head at right angles. I could see he wasn't even thinking about a car, he thought I was asking for help with the cigars! I could tell he was thinking, 'I wonder if I can out run this lunatic . . .' so just before he bolted I pointed at the Rolls.

Looking at a massive Rolls-Royce engine is a pretty fucking daunting sight. I know cos the first time I opened the bonnet, just to put oil in, I had to go have a lie down. Even more daunting for this motorcyclist when he's got what he thinks is a skinhead nutter stood next to him. He looked it over and then he said, 'I can't say I've ever worked on a Rolls-Royce before.' I said, 'I can't say I have either . . . well, I could *say* I have but then I'd be lying.'

I was trying to keep everyone laughing so while he was looking it over I kept excusing myself, saying that I had a call coming through and then I'd walk away a bit, stand on one leg and start talking. Then I'd twist a cigar in one ear for better reception – 'Hang on, I'm losing you!' Shame we didn't have Nine Toe Girl with us to unleash on him as well.

Brendan got out of the car with a camera and started videoing the silly stuff I was doing. A guy who was sat outside the garage in his car must've thought we were making a film cos he got out and asked if he was in the way, and should he move his motor. I said that that would be great if he didn't mind. So he got back in, started it up, put it in gear, started to roll it forward and he'd only moved the car, literally, about two inches when I shouted, 'STOP!' He stamped on the brake. That's great, I said. 'Thanks a lot, guv. Much better!'

I think some kind of primitive self-preservation instinct must've suddenly turned the mechanic into a Rolls-Royce expert cos he got the fucking thing going! What had actually happened was that some hot oil had bubbled out on to the engine and Rollers all have a cut-out switch to prevent too much damage. Thank fuck for that.

When we got into London I pulled over the Roller and said, 'Excuse me?' This guy walked over. I said, 'They're not big and they're not clever!' He said who? I said, 'Little stupid people!' and drove off. Well, you've got to, haven't you. Who else is gonna do it if I don't?

I'll tell you something now, let you in on a little bit of a secret really that only my friends know. What actually makes all this funny for me, these stupid pranks, is that most people who see me out don't know me well enough to know that I fuck about all the time. I don't go out playing the Big I Am, and all that bollocks. But being who I am and what people know of me, and even how I look to people who don't know me (and there are still a few!), I just don't look like someone who is basically a joker at heart. So I can say things with a serious face and people don't say 'fuck off'. And my kick is making whoever I'm with laugh.

I went up to Manchester recently with Brendan to be interviewed on a programme called the *The Hot House* for Granada TV. This woman presenter was cuddling one of those Furby toys, annoying little fucking things. She said at the end of the interview she was gonna hand me the Furby and she wanted me to stroke it and show how the hard man had gone soft. I said I didn't want to do it, it made me look an idiot. And if anyone does that it's me not no one else.

Anyway, at the end of the interview she produced this thing and handed it to me on camera, expecting me to go along with it as most people would; like I said, people freeze on camera. But I've had things worse than cameras loaded with film pointed at me. I just took it, stroked it once, and then threw it at the wall and smashed it to bits. Her jaw dropped and nestled nicely in her cleavage.

After that we went out onto the *Coronation Street* set. It was dark but we just stumbled on it through some back entrance. The night watchman came out, one of those guys with an overall and a fully paid up limp, and told us we couldn't go anywhere down there. I said, 'I'm Dave. Y'know ... Dave?' like he should really know me, and he went, 'OK, as long as it's you!' *Touch*. It fucking worked! Talk about the power of self-belief.

I had a slash in Ken Barlow's doorway. Never liked him. Then we collared the night watchman again and I asked if he'd take a picture of me in front of the Rover's Return. Just as he pointed the camera I turned around and got my arse out. He took it anyway, probably out of shock, and in a real normal fashion I said, 'Thanks very much.'

Even as we were leaving stupid things were happening. As I was walking through the lobby of the hotel one of the security guards passed, saw me carrying bags and must've thought I was a porter and asked me if I'd hold on to his two-way radio for a minute. Fucking cheek, like I look like a bloody porter! So I nicked it. Obviously.

On the train back I called them on it. I could hear them saying, 'Who's that? Is that you, Frank? Who's fucking around on Channel 2?' I kept that as a memento.

Another memento came from when Brendan had to play football for his building firm's team. Now Brendan couldn't run to the toilet let alone the length of a pitch. And there was this silly fucker on the team who had something against Brendan and wanted to get him nicked. So, I went along and we're all there in the changing room and I sees this cunt and asked him if he had a problem with Brendan. He said he didn't. All of a sudden.

Anyway, match starts. The ball's going anywhere but near Brendan, which is a deliberate ploy even by members of his own side. Then, first touch Brendan gets and . . . he back-heads it into his own net!

I was on the touchline shouting and this linesman next to me was a scouser. He was complaining how bad they all were and saying they should give him a chance cos he once had a trial for Liverpool. Then he looked at me and asked who I was.

'Oh I'm their manager. And I agree with you. I want you to play. Yeah, straight up. I'm gonna use you as substitute!' So I called Brendan off, he swopped shirts with the linesman and this little scouser bloke sprinted on! We left right away, got in the car and drove off. Taking the linesman's flag with us.

Brendan's workmates rang him up afterwards and said they got hammered and the bastard who was the linesman cost them four goals. They were all offside but there was no fucker there on the line to call them!

And I've still got that flag.

Talking about mementoes, I recently got a call from this right nice fella called Andy Jones. Andy is a very good friend of Stephen Richards, author of Charlie Bronson's book *Silent Scream* (great book). Anyway, Andy was asking me for allsorts. I had to explain to him that I didn't sell liquorice (well, apart from that liquorice torpedo I once sold for a tenner at a rave). No, what he actually wanted was loads of souvenirs from me for a museum he ran called Crime Through Time. And he told me all about it.

This museum was in a Victorian building that had been an old magistrates' court and a police station. I felt at home already! Fred West was actually held in a cell there during his early days. Shame they didn't keep him in.

This museum had a big display of stuff from crimes in history like witch burnings, and things to do with torture, the holocaust, and more modern stuff. Personally, I liked the sound of the guillotine that was there. I could've put that in my back garden and used it to 'end' my Castellas whenever we have a barbeque.

Andy told me he had loads of gangster memorabilia from the Krays, Charles Bronson, Roy Shaw, Lenny McLean and Freddie Foreman but he hadn't got anything from me yet. I thought, Right, we'll soon sort that out, and I went on a souvenir–treasure hunt frenzy round the house.

I could tell from talking to him that this museum was a real passion for the geezer and he'd really look after anything he was given, so I didn't mind trusting him with some precious things of mine. Like the sword used in the infamous Chinese waiter stabbing that got me a three stretch, the hat I wore when I did security at Ronnie Kray's funeral, one of my oldest knuckledusters, a cosh, a suit, bail notices, a shooter, and loads of signed posters and books.

I think I got a bit carried away in the amount of stuff I sent him, to be honest, because after he'd set up the Dave Courtney display Andy rang me and said it's the only display now bigger than Hitler's! Is that a compliment or what? No, seriously, I'm asking you. *Is* it a compliment? Cos I couldn't decide. Fuck me, I thought, I've just topped the biggest serial killer in history. Shame I couldn't have topped him in 1939, ay?

I would still like that guillotine though . . .

16 Bushwacka!

Raving keeps you feeling young. They say you're only as old as you feel and I never feel anyone over 30. Although I do, of course, make a big exception for my Jennifer. She keeps me young.

Recently we went to the BAFTA film awards because a short film that me and Brendan were in was nominated. It was a blindin' little film called *Life of a Lighter* and what it did was trace the life of this disposable cigarette lighter that kept getting lost and found by different people along the way. I played one of the characters that find it in one scene. Good idea for a film, though, innit? Cos you sometimes do wonder where those bloody things disappear to and who's hands they end up in.

Inside the awards, me and Jen got very friendly with two singing sisters we met there. They were a cracking pair, young too. In fact, come to think of it, I've got knuckledusters older.

Afterwards we decided we'd all go back to this moored yacht of a mate of mine. While he was away on holiday he said I could use it. Brendan decided to do his bit to help young, nubile and needy dancers in the community and went on to Cherokee's table dancing club. That floats his boat every time, and we went to our own boat for the night.

Anyway, me and Jen and the singers were down in the yacht getting all ship-shape and shivering each other's timbers (whatever the fuck those phrases mean), when I heard this faint ringing noise. One of the girls heard it too and went, 'What's that?' I said, 'Oh, I always make that noise just before I come, babe. It's like the three minute warning before a nuclear explosion.'

Anyway, we carried on and out of the corner of my eye I saw some movement. I looked to the left and there was Brendan stood outside on the bedroom window ledge, which is only about six inches wide, trying to keep himself steady and have a wank at the same time! It was his mobile ringing, and that threw a big fucking spanner in the works for him, balance-wise.

He fumbled for the phone and lost his footing. Next thing, I saw him disappear from view and heard this splash outside. Man overboard! Don't panic! And we didn't, of course, we just carried on regardless in true British fashion, keeping stiff upper lips (stiff upper everything actually). Well, I knew he could swim.

The next night we went back out again, to the Gass, and he got so out of it I actually caught him trying to chat up a wall, for fuck's sake. Worse thing was he thought he was getting somewhere. Then when I saw him again at the bar he was laughing about something that had just happened. He said he'd found himself in this dark corner of the club, got out a cig but didn't have a light, and then saw this geezer stood against the wall. It weren't till he was halfway through asking this geezer for a light that Brendan looked down and saw there was a woman on her knees sucking the guy off. He said, 'The best thing was, though, Dave, the geezer actually gave me a light!'

I said, 'Yeah but I bet he had a *fuck* load of trouble getting it out his pocket.'

It weren't long after that that we met up at Stringfellows one night. Brendan brought a table dancer from another club with him and he'd somehow managed to persuade her to come out dressed as a schoolgirl. That's my boy. So there she was in a little skirt, white blouse and pigtails, the lot. She was a horny, naughty little thing this one. I don't blame the parents though, but Brendan would definitely thank them.

Trouble was that when she was pissed she was proper aggravation – loud and shouty and plain embarrassing. So we fucked off and left her there having a stand up row with the cig machine. And losing.

Ten minutes away Brendan remembered she'd left all her gear at his place so we went back to the club to pick her up. By this time though she'd been thrown out. We thought, Oh well, never mind, she'll never find her way back to Brendan's flat. But when we got there a brick had been chucked through the kitchen window and she was inside asleep on the settee bleeding from scratches on her leg. She'd got a rock from next door's rockery and done the window.

We just sat in the kitchen having a brew, deciding who'd wake her and throw her out. Brendan said he'd toss me for it. I said, 'You're not fucking touching me. We'll use a coin.' Next thing we knew this face appeared at the hole in the window. It was the next door neighbour.

He said, 'Morning.' We said, '*Morning!*' And we're thinking what the fuck does he want? Then he went, 'Erm . . . can I have my rock back, please?' *Fucking* hell!

Brendan picked it up off the kitchen table and handed it back through the hole: 'There you go, mate.' There goes the neighbourhood: property prices plummeted around there when Brendan moved in. And they had the biggest street party since the Silver Jubilee when he left.

I've been clubbing all over the country and cos I know people in all the major places there's always a little welcoming committee ready. One time I had some business to attend to in Newcastle. Nothing really to do with me, but a friend had asked me to go up and show my face at a meet with some people he was having trouble with. I was happy to do it; he'd helped me out in the past.

They were supposed to be faces up that way, so it was just a case of me walking in and being there to show he knew a few faces as well. Sometimes that's enough. I wasn't anticipating even having to say anything. Which is exactly how it turned out.

I thought while I was up there me and Jenny might as well make a weekend of it and called Brendan. He packed off whichever lapdancer he was getting a private show from, packed a spare velvet suit in case of an emergency and met me at the train station. We were also joined by Nutty Rob, Luke, Rod, Steve Whale, Wish and Boxer and Lone Wolf.

The business bit went as planned, as it happens, which left the rest of the weekend free. Steve Raith, who runs a lot of security up there, took us out and about.

Geordies are a fucking funny bunch, ain't they? Don't get me wrong, I don't mean that in a bad way, they're lovely people, but aren't they a fucking funny bunch? They're really hospitable and friendly and all that but the north-east ain't exactly the most cosmopolitan place on earth. A geezer told us he was gonna take us to a club which was a cross between the Ministry Of Sound and the Aquarium. I said, 'What time does it close?' He said, 'Two o'clock!' OK. That's not long after the time we're usually just setting off. That's probably why they have a better time than us in clubs – they have to cram it all in.

Twenty-seven pints, five fights, a triple-strength curry and a shag up an alley seemed to be a normal night out. And that was just the women. The men were even harder.

And oh but *fuck* me it was cold, mate. You could hear the balls of so many brass monkeys dropping it sounded like church bells. Most of these geezers were in short-sleeve shirts like it was the middle of summer. Do they put anaesthetic in the fucking water up there or what? 'Why 'eye, man – I felt nowt!'

Steve took us on the full guided tour of bars until we ended up in this nightclub. One of the Geordie fellas said to me, 'I used to work here meself as a DJ, y'know? But that was when it were proper DJing and yer had to talk between records, like.'

Then Gazza's mate, Jimmy Five Bellies, walked in. I said, 'Why'd they call you that then?' He said, 'Cos I'm fat.' Brendan went, 'I knew him when he was nothing. When he was Jimmy Two Bellies.' Very nice fella though.

This guy who looked like Lurch – six foot two and with a smashed nose – came up to me and introduced himself. He said, 'Guess what I am?' I thought, Don't tempt me. He said he was a private detective and gave me his business card.

He said to me, 'You couldn't have made a bigger splash in Newcastle, Mr Courtney, if you'd been Michael Jackson!' Oh great. Compare me to a skin-bleached, monkey-fucking, white-sock-wearing stick insect with a voice like Mickey Mouse. No, I'm joking. I took it as a big compliment.

One fella asked me who Brendan was. See, because Bren ain't a big geezer some people wonder why he's with me, as if I only hang out with brick shithouses. And this bloke wanted to know where exactly Brendan fitted in to the firm. I said he was my minder and the guy looked surprised. 'Oh yeah!' I said. 'He's a crap fighter but a fucking good *shot*!'

Most of the players of one of the big football teams were in there as well. I won't say which, just use your imagination here. Steve knew them all so we ended up seeing the night out with them.

Halfway through the night one of the players came up to me and confessed that he'd never had an E before but he'd just taken five! *Five*. Talk about going in at the fucking deep end.

He said, 'What do you think, Dave, man. Is five about right, like?' I thought, Well I ain't gonna burst your bubble and start an early come-down. I said, 'Well I've been doing ten a night for the last five years and it never done me any harm, mate.' That seemed to reassure him.

Half-an-hour later I sees him on the edge of the dancefloor, stood on this stage looking down. The whole of the floor was filled with all this foam that had been sprayed everywhere. This geezer's just looking into the foam, hypnotised. I thought, Oh no, I can see this one coming. To him it just looked like a big, soft pillow.

Seconds later he put his arms out and dived, and I mean proper *dived*, right out into the middle of the foam. He just went straight through, obviously, and – SMACK! – hit the floor. You couldn't hear anything cos of the music but I swear I felt that floor judder. He didn't reappear and everyone just carried on!

I kept watching people dancing through the foam over to the spot where he'd gone through and then they'd trip over his body and just vanish. Fuck me it *was* funny. They'd reappear a few seconds later rubbing their head. Then another one would come along and *bang*! same thing. Honestly, I could've stood and watched that all night.

Eventually, Mr Five Es came round and crawled out. I saw him pop up out of the foam, about fifty feet from where he'd gone in, with a faceful of blood. It looked like something out of a Hammer horror film rising from the swamp. He walked over to me, blood running down his face, and said, 'I'm sorry for that.' I said, 'It's all right.' Then some of my boys saw this geezer with a smashed face talking to me and thought something was happening so they all rushed over!

All the players ended up having one (or five) and by the end of the night they were all fucking cuddling each other. Back at the hotel one of them tried to kiss his mate (and no one had scored a goal so that wasn't on) and they ended up having a punch-up in reception. We all went into the bar and the conversation between these two geezers was priceless.

'I've known you for ten years,' one of them said, 'and you've never hit me before. And we've had loads of arguments over *women*!'

The other one went, 'It weren't over a women! You were trying to kiss *me*!'

'Gerraway!'

'You were! Youse were fucking coming on to me!'

We left them to it and got set to head off for this gaff above a pub that this geezer had got us put up in. Just before we left he came over to me and Brendan. He sort of motioned us into a little huddle as if he was gonna give us some secret information.

'Now lads,' he said 'When you knock you may think she's asleep cos she's a long time comin' down t'door, but don't fret – she's just putting her legs on . . .'

I'm looking at Brendan thinking, Hang on: did I hear that right This place cannot be as mental as that. They said that they knew we'd want to be low-key so they'd booked us into this pub bed and breakfast. When we got there I thought, There's low-key and low-key but this place is right off the fucking radar.

So I knocked, and waited for fuck knows how long until we heard this clumping sound. Brendan's already creased up just thinking it might be true. I'm thinking, Nah! Can't be.

The door swings open and stood there is this middle-aged lady in her pink nightie and fuck me sideways if she didn't have *two* false fucking legs. I swear to God. There was no mistaking it either cos in her hurry to get ready she'd got the bottom of her nightie caught in the tops of her legs! So she's stood there with this long nightie all tucked into her leg tops.

She went, 'I've been expecting you!' And we're just stood there with our jaws on the floor thinking, Fucking *hell*, we're staying with *The Addams Family*. But it didn't actually turn out that way. She was a really lovely lady who looked after us.

Brendan went into a massive faked coughing fit to try and disguise him laughing. It lasted all the way up the stairs. We could hear her clumping up behind saying, 'Don't you two canny lads mind me! I'll be up in me own time.' Oh, wicked! Our landlady was Douglas Bader's old missus.

What a weekend that was. Everything was so funny. Everyone was really nice people as well, and they bent over backwards to make us welcome. We had a wicked time. We couldn't even catch the train back without getting more.

At the train station Brendan saw these two Geordie birds walking down the platform with their bags. We had an hour to kill so he goes up for a chat. He said something to them like he didn't have time to flirt cos he only had an hour and was there any chance of a shag cos he hadn't had a bonk since leaving London. Yeah, the direct approach.

One of them said, 'Ey! What d'ya think I am? I want at least *two* hours.' They were proper down to earth, these girls. The other one told us not to let her drink brandy cos she'd start punching stuff!

'And don't let me drink whiskey cos I fart,' she said. 'And vodka, fuck me, don't let me have vodka . . .'

On the train back down one of us would suddenly start laughing for no apparent reason and the other would know it was just about the whole mad weekend up there.

It got better. The day after our night out, that team we'd been out with had a big cup-tic match. And fuck me if they didn't go out and win it about four-nil. The foam-diving geezer, Mr Five Es, rang me up afterwards. He thought they'd played so blindingly cos of the pills he'd had.

'I can't find the fella I got 'em off, Dave,' he said, 'but I wondered if you might know. Were they, like, special ones?'

I wish I'd seen that match. I bet the after-goal celebrations were fucking something else, mate. Doggie-style on the halfway line.

But there's nothing like getting back into London where people speak properly, don't eat their young, walk upright, and don't have to shave their backs. Excluding some of Brendan's birds, obviously. Oh *listen* to me, one that he pulled at the Ministry was a proper ape! I remember paying to go watch her swing on a tyre in the zoo. I told him that foreplay with her would be just combing her back.

But get a load of this one. When I lived in the flats he fucking woke me up at quarter to six one morning banging on the door. He said that he needed me to help him. He was obviously in some bother to wake me at that time, so I started running around throwing clothes on, looking for my duster and psyching myself up for a row with someone.

On the way down in the lift Brendan finally explained it. He said he'd pulled this bird last night and bonked her, but now he had to go to work and he didn't want to leave her in his flat in case she nicked things. I thought, What!? Just then the lift doors opened and he said, 'Listen. I've told her you're my chauffeur and can you drop her home in the Rolls?' Before I could say anything he stepped out, then turned around and went, 'Oh, can you wear the hat?'

He walked ahead of me to the car so I couldn't say anything about it. I was thinking, You cheeky cunt. She's already sat in the back of the Roller looking well pleased. Brendan fished out this chauffeur's cap from the door pocket that we used to joke around with. Just before I got in I said, 'You fucking owe me for this one.'

As I was driving this girl home she said to me, 'Have you been working long for Mr Courtney then?' Oh double *cunt*! He'd actually told her he was me! I just hoped he'd given her a proper good shagging and not spoiled my reputation. But I did get my own back. She said, 'I think it's really nice of you to drive me home.'

'Well I'm a bit pissed off, babe,' I said, 'Cos you're the third one this week.' I think we could call that a late equaliser in injury time, don't you?

And before we'd barely got over the Newcastle gig we went back up north to Manchester (and they're fucking normal up in Manchester ain't they!) We went up to a Garage Nation do at the G Mex centre. There was me, Terry Turbo, Adam, Brendan, George Abby from Tardis, Big John, Coventry Stuart, Wolfie, Seymour, AJ, Steve Low, Cowboy, Slim, Bal, Kenny, Danny Dolittle and Little Legs and Chris in a van and loads more following. We stopped to pick up this hitch-hiker and he looked really pleased until we kicked the back doors of the van open and he saw me, Terry and the rest of the crew staring back out at him. He just stood there, not knowing how to say 'No, it's all right fellas, you be on your way.'

So he came with us, we shared what we had with him and he had a blinding time for a few hours until he got out, tripping off his head. The last we saw of him he'd sat down on the grass in the middle of this big roundabout.

We walked into this posh place, the Grand Hotel in Manchester, and booked a suite. It really was the bollocks, this gaff. Looked like they'd nicked their chandelier from Buckingham Palace. I must've looked fucked already cos the guy on reception turned to me and said, 'Will Sir be requiring an alarm call in the morning?'

I said, 'No. Sir will not be requiring an alarm call because Sir will be *right* off his fucking nut by the morning.' Then this little porter fella in a uniform ran up and asked me if I'd like any help with my bag. I said if he went anywhere near my scrotum I'd deck him. Saucy cunt.

The suite was the fucking bollocks. We all walked in and straight off the bat I opened my case and on to the bed I tipped a handgun, a sawn-off shotgun and two machine guns. Terry went wow, Adam went Oh, Chris went white, Brendan went into hysterics and I went into the bog for a wank. I've just got this thing about guns giving me a hard on. Call me old-fashioned. (Anyway, they were all replicas; I was also doing a 'Gangsta Rap' photoshoot up there.)

On the way into the club we had to go through metal detectors. I knew we'd have to go through them so for a laugh I'd put one of the machine guns in a bag and stuffed it up my jacket. The metal detector went mental, flashing and beeping. I think I made it come twice. So the security came over and I pulled out the bag, took out the weapon and laid it on the desk and said, 'Erm . . . sorry.'

They all sort of stopped dead in their tracks about three feet from me. They started saying things like sorry mate but you can't bring that in here. Like I'd taken out just a camera or something. I said that was OK, I'd pick it up on the way out. They were absolutely shitting.

The G Mex centre is really massive and Garage Nation had packed the place out with 12,000 raving lunatics. It was fucking buzzing and the atmosphere was mental. We walked in and saw everyone going for it – people dancing on speakers and stairs, horny little club dancers on podiums, some blokes walking around on stilts, fireworks and the roof lit up like night stars. We just looked at each other and went Wow! *Fuck*ing wicked.

I did see one of the toughest looking barmaids I'd ever seen in my life in there, though. She was so hard she looked like she rolled her own Tampax.

By the time we got back to the Grand Brendan had some birds with him and before long they were banging in one of the bedrooms. We heard a smashing sound. Afterwards, Brendan told us that this bird who was right off her cake, spotted the champagne in the bucket and asked him to use the bottle on her. He thought, Who am I to argue? I am only here to please.

So he was shagging her with the neck of the bottle and suddenly it started to fizz! (the champagne that is), and really really quickly the pressure built up and the bottle just *SHOT* out of his hand, flew over his shoulder like a fucking rocket and smashed open on the wall behind. Amazing. And if that bottle had hit him in the face instead of going over his shoulder he swore it would've killed him. That would be a really tough one for your mates wouldn't it? – explaining to the parents how their son died: 'Well, there was this girl and this bottle of champagne . . .'

Anyway, after all that we felt a bit peckish so I rang up room service for some bacon sarnies. They said they couldn't do it, even though it was supposed to be 24-hour service, cos there was too many ravers here tonight and not enough kitchen staff. I thought what a pathetic excuse. And it weren't like we were staying in some cheap place either. I mean we even got bacon sarnies at the landlady's place in Newcastle, and very tasty they were too.

So we had this massive Catherine wheel firework . . . oh don't ask, we just happened to have it! And I thought, Wouldn't it be funny if we put it in the lift and sent it down to the lobby? And then I thought, Yes it would! It was about the size of a steering wheel this fucking thing and it said on it that it had a 25-second fuse. So Adam went down in the lift to time how long it took to reach the lobby. When he came back up we were just laughing like silly fucking schoolkids at the thought of this.

I nicked a steak knife off a trolley outside someone's room, pinned this big fuck-off Catherine wheel to the back wall of the lift, lit the fuse, stood back a few seconds, and sent it down. It was three in the morning so we knew it would go straight down. Or hoped it would.

Even from up where we were we could hear the commotion. From what we were told later by the receptionist, the lift doors opened, everyone heard the *ping* and turned, and just then the firework kicked off and started spinning and flaming and sparking to fuck in the lift. Right there in the lobby.

All the fire alarms went off and then the water sprinklers came out in sympathy. The fire brigade did get there quickly, though, you've gotta give them that. Those boys don't hang around when they hear about a firework in a lift, fuck me no. So we gave them a treat. We filled up these water pistols we had with strawberry milkshake and shot them from the upstairs windows as they left! What? Childish, us?

Like I said, raving keeps you young.

17 One Nation Under a Groove

I've lost count of the number of times I've met myself on the door of a club when I was doing the security there. People using my name to try to get me to let them in! Or pretend that they know me or that they're meeting me, or even that they *are* me. You can imagine how many I get, or used to get, working on a Saturday night. Once I was on the door of the Aquarium with Warren and Mikey and this geezer said to me, 'Is Dave Courtney here yet? I'm here to meet him.' I said, 'No, he ain't. He's at his Bible class.' This bloke started getting all cocky saying he was gonna set me on me! So I told him that I had something for Dave Courtney and could he give it to him. He asked what. I said, 'This . . .' and kicked him up the arse!

Another time when I was working on the door at the Ministry this geezer came up and claimed to be me. He was asking me to let him in. Which I didn't cos I know what I'm like. Worst of all this geezer was a little Chinese fella. With a beard. In a wheelchair. I had to lean down to slap him. No, only joking. I just let his tyres down.

When I worked the door at the Aquarium we had to throw this bloke out and he came back with four or five people and started asking for me. The other doormen said it was nothing to do with Dave Courtney but he started screaming get the cunt out here. He was going mad and people were trying to leave the club and I thought, It's a bit late in the day to start rolling around on the floor with this cunt. Clubbers at the door were four people deep so he can't get to me and I can't get to him. Or I couldn't until I took a fire extinguisher down off the wall, got hold of the black hose and used it to swing the big red bit like a club. It reached over everyone and came down right on the crown of this idiot's head.

You could hear the metal and bone go *DING!* He collapsed into a puddle, his mates ran off and everyone lived happily ever after.

Another time me and my partner Terry Turbo caught someone who was not wanted in the rave and the geezer obviously didn't know who Terry was and he started shouting that he was gonna tell Terry Turbo. 'Terry will have your bollocks on a plate, mate!' Terry's stood there hearing his own name being used to threaten himself!

So Terry said to the geezer, 'When you see Terry Turbo, tell him he's a cunt!'

Terry's the one who turned up at the Old Bailey to be a character witness for me during my big trial in 1997. My barrister took one look at Terry and said, 'Your friend Terry needs a character witness himself. He'd get two years just for looking like that in court!' I suppose he thought a big, shaven headed geezer known as Turbo wouldn't have gone down too well.

I met Terry out at a rave and we just hit it off. I wanted to do raves on a big scale and Terry had the same plans, and we both had loads of contacts. I was introduced to Terry by DJ Daniella Montana.

Now I'm a partner in a big club promotions company called One Nation with Terry. One Nation is now one of the biggest and best promotions in the country, and there's another three in the stable, Garage Nation and Rave Nation, and Dreamscape.

One Nation became the massive success it is now because Terry had more foresight in the field than most. He was always thinking big. And now it is. We've done Wembley, the G Mex, the Bowl at Milton Keynes, the Rex Arena in Stratford, Hastings Pier, Bagley's Film Studio, Ministry Of Sound and loads more. This year there'll be about 80 events by One Nation, Rave Nation, Garage Nation and Dreamscape; club tours and events abroad. Like this year when Garage Nation went to Ayenapa, Cyprus and played two of the biggest nights of the summer.

Before he took the One Nation name on as a promotion, Terry used to run this clubbing magazine, also called *One*

Nation, and he gave it away free to people. Then it got really big so it went full colour and he charged for it. And that's also partly how we met cos I started writing a page for the magazine. All the other magazines were too serious, so who did Terry come to when he wanted someone to write a page of complete and utter silly bollocks? . . . yours truly, of course.

Terry's mum did this funny agony aunt column for it. She called herself Aunt Trish and there was a photo of her in a wig and silly glasses. And he had this mad girl called Clare who did this nutty piss-take on Mystic Meg but it was called Mystic Peg.

So I started doing 'Dodgy Dave's Funny Page'. Which was mostly just all of the whizzed-up bollocks I came out with when I got back home from a club at six in the morning and found a Biro and a final reminder on the floor. Then I got put on remand for nearly a year in Belmarsh High Security Prison. But did that stop me writing? Did it fuck. And I'd like to see all those well paid newspaper columnists carry on their careers if they got banged up for a year.

So 'Dodgy Dave's Funny Page' just got renamed 'Not So Fucking Dodgy Dave Live From The Inside'. And instead of writing about going out I wrote about staying in. Not much fucking choice really. But I was banged up with Yardies, IRA terrorists, Animal Rights bombers, Eco poisoners, serial killers and all manner of naughty people so I had plenty to write about. I also started off a readers' wives competition through the *Scene* and I got the most unbelievable filth through the post. It was the nuts.

The letters I got from people because of Terry's magazine helped me out a lot. It's easy to feel like you've been forgotten when you're inside. Even Terry's mum sent me a copy of the photo of her they used for the Aunt Trish page in the magazine. All the other inmates had pictures of beautiful naked models and I had this photo of a 60-year-old in a bad wig and silly glasses. And knowing it was Terry's mum on the wall of my cell put me right off having a wank for a while. At least fifteen minutes.

So Terry was young and up-and-coming, loads of enthusiasm and knew the scene. He took over this one venue for the night and was doing the promoting, but these drug dealers were giving him a hard time. Terry was planning on having the club filmed inside for a TV programme and he had to cut down on anything untoward happening inside, but these dealers were demanding money if he wanted to get rid of them. He tried all ways of reasoning with them but they weren't having it, so I stepped in with some people. That solved it and I got to know Terry even better after that and we've been big mates ever since.

You see, in the early day there weren't the same protection and safeguards on the scene that there are now so people could get ripped off left, right and centre – punters, promoters, venue owners. It happened a lot in the first days until people wised up or got ahead of the game. Terry got mugged off by this club that said they'd had 1,500 people through the door when it had been nearer to 2,500. Terry's a very handy geezer himself, as it happens, does Thai boxing and all that, and he was considering getting some fellas togther and trying to sort it out. The other blokes had a big security company though, he wasn't sure who he was dealing with and you've got to know what you're dealing with before you walk in.

Terry started off MCing in the early days and his MC name, for some bizarre fucking reason, was Free And Easy (which reminds me of two birds I used to know). Anyway, free and easy are two things you cannot afford to be.

So Terry came to see me about the whole security thing cos he didn't want to get ripped off in future and we got together. I'd already been running my own clubs by then for years. And this was at a time when I had hundreds and hundreds of doormen at my disposal. It didn't hurt that I had a few police officers on the payroll as well.

So Terry ended up with the tastiest geezers in London working on the doors – proper hardnuts, ex-SAS, ex-marines, boxers, martial artists, mercenaries, boxers. And Warrior! Terry's girlfriend and dad ended up working with him at the clubs, and Terry's mum actually worked in the cashbox on some nights. So you'd definitely want handy geezers there to protect your old mum wouldn't you? That was our justification for having machine guns there anyway – gotta protect Terry's mum! Don't worry, Ma, we're getting the fucking bazooka out! Here comes the Panzer.

Trouble was that people who wanted to have you over at a rave would do a head count of punters, then look at the ticket price and start doing sums; 3,000 × 20 quid means 60 grand on the premises. Even one-third of that is enough to make some people go home and get out the sawn-off and that balaclava their granny knitted them for Christmas. Or one 60th of it for a crackhead.

I did give Terry his first duster, as it happens. Then I found out he didn't do housework so I gave him a knuckleduster instead. Always a touching moment in a man's life that. Brings a lump to your throat. And jaw. And nose. It was at a rave in the Temple I gave it him. Anyway, I'm walking around and I see the doormen carry this bloke by with is jaw bashed in. I know a duster whack when I see one cos I've carried one for twenty-five years. I see this geezer go past and I thought, Terry's only had that thing about twenty minutes! I went, 'Terry?!'

What it was was that the guy had been caught mugging people, nicking chains off kids. This was about '95 when the Jungle scene was still a bit dodgy. That used to be the big problem and one that you had to nip right in the bud early on. If your events got that kind of reputation then people stayed away, obviously. It killed the whole thing.

One time we were at a One Nation event at Wembley Arena. Jenny was MCing there. Anyway, this kid had been mugged so the security took him around to ID the geezer and then they brought this fella backstage. They said that they'd have to search him but he refused. He said he wouldn't be searched and he'd take any two of them on.

I was stood there, listening (nothing really to do with me) and I said, 'I'll have some of that.' The mugger went, 'What?' I said, 'Your little challenge; I'll have some of that.'

So I dustered him spark out and, by doing that, actually did him a favour, believe it or not. Because otherwise they were going to call the police and they would've found the nicked gear on him. And bruises heal quicker than prison sentences.

I always like the big, special event one-off raves. Me and Terry did a rave – one of the M25 raves – down in Staines called 'Love' in these two big circus tents. That was fucking wicked! Four thousand people having it in a big top. Even the elephants were on one! And this was the scene of another one of my public servicing of strippers. Well I consider it charity work, actually – giving to the needy. And these birds look like they needed it, mate.

What we had in the tent was this stage and the strippers came out dancing, stark naked apart from policeman's hats, Caterpillar boots and carrying truncheons and handcuffs. Convent girls, obviously. I was on the side bit by the microphones, and they'd made this lasso sticking out with wire that they jumped through. I had to go out and put the lasso down so they didn't trip over it. A job I volunteered for, funnily enough.

They were in full flow by now, stripping blokes off on stage, and when I went on they grabbed me and started playing about with me. A lot of the blokes up there were suffering from stage fright, as always happens, but I'd dropped a couple of blues and was right up for it. And not everyone can say they've been videoed in front of four thousand people fucking a bird dressed as Old Bill. Well everyone can *say* it, but then they'd most probably be lying. Afterwards Jen said that she hoped I hadn't embarrassed her, and that I had put in a good performance! So let's hope that publicly shagging a fancy-dress policewomen ain't ever made against the law cos I'd have to throw that video of mine on the fire. Mind you, it's a two-bar electric heater so a fuck load of good that would do.

That was the gig where I temporarily became my own phone company. It was one of them with 'No cameras, no recording equipment, no whatever' printed on the tickets; 'No breathing out', that was it, only 'in'. Anyway, there's all these thousands of people there in the tents and no phones. It was a 24-hour thing so everyone's trapped there. So I started hiring out my mobile for £5 a minute. There was people queuing up. And the last line that each one of them said was, 'Anyway, I've got to go, this is costing me five quid a minute!' Those phone companies have got it easy haven't they, ay?

And then when I'd done that I decided to go friggin' in the riggin'. The big top tents had these massive wooden poles holding it up, and eight-foot up the poles was this netting to stop people getting to the footings that led higher up the poles. But because my mate Warren is so tall I stepped into his hands and he helped lift me over the nets. Then it was easy cos the steps ran up the poles.

When I got to the top it was fucking high. A lot higher than it'd looked down there (but ain't that always the case?). And up there was a platform but to get to it I had to walk across this plank for about ten feet. Eighty foot up, walking across a plank. And you can't say 'don't look down' cos you have to look down to see where your feet are, so that was fucking scary. No safety net, either, just loads of skulls below me. Not exactly a soft landing.

When I finally got to the platform it was like, 'Top of the world, Ma!' It was mental. It only took a few minutes before everyone started noticing me and then they all looked up and started cheering! Something like fifteen thousand people looking up at you is a proper buzz. Next time I heard someone say, 'God', I said, 'No, just call me Dave.'

You could get a real messiah complex in those situations, though. No wonder those religious cult leaders like Jim Jones go right off on one through the adoration and start making their own communities and laws. I was only up on that platform for twenty minutes and already I'd started singling out the young females below for sexual initiation (sorry, bad example, I do that anyway).

Getting back down from up the pole was a real cunt. Getting up is easy, innit? Finding your footing coming back down is always a bastard.

The sexiest raves we ever did were the weekend ones at the holiday camps. Oh the fucking holiday camps! They were the horniest. Cos you're there Saturday, Sunday and Bank Holiday Monday, and the ticket actually buys you a chalet as well. And all the rooms that are there, the arcades and all the facilities. Very handy.

'Energy' in Skegness was fucking wild. I went to the first one and ended up getting laid about six times in one night. I went, 'This is amazing. I want to *live* here!'

Another event me and Terry did was at the Hammersmith Palais, and when I was in there this geezer came up to me and in a real posh voice asked me if I had any Es. I said I didn't but there would be some geezers around who had. He showed me this sovereign and asked how many he'd get for it! I thought, What is this the *Antiques* fucking *Roadshow*? So I said I thought he'd probably get about ten.

Then he said, 'How many would I have to take to get, you know, "out of it"? I haven't done them before you see.'

I said, 'I don't know. Depends on who you are, not just what you take. Take one and if that don't work take another, and if that don't work take another. And another.' You can see by that exactly why I failed my exam to be an outreach worker for the Just Say No To Drugs campaign! Actually that was our motto for a while – 'If anyone asks to share your drugs, Just Say No!'

Anyway, about an hour later I'm downstairs jumping around having a wicked time and this big commotion starts in the queue by the toilets. The door opened and standing there, pure drip white and crying is the posh geezer from earlier – Mr How Many? His trousers are half undone and he's looking about in a panic. He saw me and cos my face was familiar to him he locked on to me. I said, 'What the fuck's the matter? Come out here and let people in the toilet.'

He walked away with me, walking all funny. Then he said, 'I've shit myself! I've really shit myself!' I asked him how many of them Es he'd had and he said he'd taken them all. I said, 'Don't worry, don't worry about it. Everyone shits themselves at these things all the time. It just means you're relaxed.' I'm just trying to make him feel better about it. And he went, 'Really?'

The last I saw of him he was walking around, really stinking, and going up to people, saying, 'I've shit myself! I've shit myself too!' It was really fucking funny watching it cos you'd see people become aware of the smell first, because it reached them before he did. They'd be looking around thinking, Fuck me, smells like someone's shat themselves! Then this geezer would bob up, real proud of himself, and 'I've *shit* myself!' . . . and then he joined the police force and became Sir Paul Condom.

That was also the time we invaded Skegness beach. It was about 5 o'clock Sunday morning and we were all out of our nut. There was me, Jen, Terry Turo, Daniella, Seymour and Johnny Jacket all squashed in my Jag. We went out looking for a cafe, thinking we were still in London where everything's open all the time, and forgetting we were in Skegness where nothing's open no time. Let alone early hours in the middle of winter. It's the only place I know where the hospital has half-day closing.

Somehow I managed to get the Jag onto the beach. I don't know how I did it, I don't even know why I did it. But I did it. I think I thought, Oh fuck it, now that we're on the coast let's invade Europe! So we barrelled across the beach in the dark like modern-day gladiators with General Courtney at the head lashing the horses . . . and got stuck in the fucking sand. The back wheels dug right in. That fucked my little buzz up.

We got bits of driftwood to put under the wheels but it weren't happening. We needed a tow. We walked up to the road and there wasn't a car in sight. Not even a pissed, spikey-arsed hedgehog. Then I heard a car coming so I ran out to stop it. Everyone else ran behind me waving and shouting. The car just zoomed by. In fact, it seemed to accelerate when it saw us! Everybody was swearing and calling the geezer a cunt for not stopping.

I turned around, saw what we looked like and told everyone to just stop a second and take a look at ourselves. What the geezer in the car had seen coming out of the dark was this – a skinhead with a gold knuckleduster round his neck and a piece of driftwood in his fist, behind him a black woman in hot pants and a white bird with saucer eyes, both shouting; next to them a black geezer with locks, spliff in mouth, and behind him another big shaven-headed fella looking worse for wear and followed up by a geezer in a black leather jacket with one hand in his pocket.

I said, 'Look! *Look* at us. We look like The Invasion Of The Brain Gobblers!' The bloke in the car didn't see Dave, Jen, Daniella, Seymour, Terry and Jacket – he saw the Fred West sponsored Annual Coach Trip from Rampton Mental Hospital. Six Go Mad In Skegness. I'm not surprised that fucker didn't stop when he saw this bunch of proper wasted cunts staggering off the beach. I'm only surprised he didn't mow us all down in his Volvo.

Anyway, the only other person out and about at that time was the local milkman. And he couldn't get away from us cos milk floats only go 15 mph! So we overtook him on foot and persuaded him into giving us a tug out of the sand. We got a rope, a chain and another bit of rope and from the edge of the beach we got pulled out by this bloody milk float.

Some of the best times I've had have been at either One Nation dos or at Ministry Of Sound.

I did security at Ministry right at the beginning. Then after I organised and ran the security for Ronnie Kray's funeral the police came down hard on me big-style. They started threatening the clubs and pubs that used my security with loss of licences if they didn't stop using my boys. So, ironically, it was the Old Bill that fucked up what was then my major legitimate way of earning money. Thanks, boys.

Since then the Ministry door has been done by different security companies, the Simms, Carlton, Cirus, Nod and Humphrey, the Birmingham boys, Matthew, Big Bird & Co, Pete Thompson, to name but a few. They only tend to keep firms on the door there for a couple of years because they think they get to know too many people after that, and let too many in. When I ran it I actually worked the door myself at the beginning, as I always did when we got a new contract. Lead from the front, chaps! One time towards the end of the night there was only me and five doormen left behind. We had one quick last look around the club. I checked the toilets. I opened one of the cubicle doors and got smacked in the face by this fucking awful smell.

In this cubicle there was this bloke sat on the bog, trousers and pants down and head lolling on his chest with sick round his mouth. He was in a right fucking state. What I think had happened was this; he'd pushed too hard having a shit, got a blood-rush to the head, gone dizzy and then puked up and all down himself. Trouble is he'd thrown up between his legs and right into his own underpants and trousers.

This was definitely one of those times for showing leadership qualities. And telling-people-what-to-do qualities as well. So I told one of the other doormen to deal with it. He had to pull this geezer's pants up on him, full of sick, and then pull his trousers back up on him, also full of sick. Yeah, those undercover Old Bill were always the worse. Just couldn't handle their gear.

Another bad one was at one of the One Nation events. This geezer was sat on these stairs, *right* proper off his face. He'd obviously done a small chemist's worth of pills this geezer. He didn't fucking know which species of mammal he was, let alone the day of the week. And he was sat there holding an empty pint glass. All of a sudden he puked up straight into the glass, filled it with sick, and cos he's so out of it he started drinking his own vomit! Then this bloke, Les, who was stood next to him, sees this geezer drinking a pint of his own puke and that makes him turn around and puke up himself – right over the other geezer's mate.

The sights you see, though, are fucking incredible. Clint Eastwood would be really at home on the scene because talk about the good, the bad and the ugly. Not to mention 'the nutty'.

One time me and Terry were in the VIP room at a One Nation do at Temple in Tottenham (run by Timmy Ram Jam) and this bird in a mini skirt and no knickers started doing cartwheels for us. This was another nutty bird that made you wonder if she was pedalling at the right speed (like little Miss Nine Toes). Anyway, she came over and said she could do better than that. Me and Terry just looked at each other and then said, 'Carry on, babe!' So she started doing handstands. Knickerless, fanny-out, legs spread handstands. A geezer walked in off his face, saw her upside down and stopped dead in his tracks. I don't think he knew whether he was seeing what he thought he was seeing, or a midget with a goatee beard putting his arms in the air.

A lot of the geezers I'd known and worked with early on in the rave and club scene had gone on to much bigger and better things. Andy Swallow is someone I admire for what he's done. Andy used to be one of the Inner City Firm West Ham boys but raving turned his head another way and he started putting on raves, and then he formed his own record company, Public Demand, which is now really successful. He gives someone like myself a bit of inspiration in showing that it can be done. My mate Chris Paul moved out to LA to carry on DJing, started a rave company and is now working with Ice T, and his lovely missus Zoe Gregory Paul now acts and models for *Playboy*. No, I'm not even slightly jealous! Lou of the Aquarium was also from the early days. Timmy Ram Jam is one of the consortium that runs the Aquarium along with Paul, Tony and

Lou. They also run an organisation called Happy Daze and a club called Grace in the Old Kent Road. And Timmy started with me in the old Arches days. The manager at Ministry, Hector, I'd also known since the Arches days and he used to be the manager at the Limelight when I was head doorman there; then went on to become the MD at Ministry.

Hector actually studied a degree in pornography! What a touch! He did some kind of media studies thing at university and managed to talk them into letting him study porn for his thesis. I wish I'd known you could do that when my mum caught me having a wank over *Penthouse* – No, it's just research. It's fucking *homework*, Mum, all right?!

The Ministry, though, has always been somewhere I've wanted to play more than work, just because it's such a good club. It was always a winner, always a big club. I've tried to keep it as 'play'. The owner, James Palumbo, I've met a few times and got on well with. His background is very different from mine.

Yeah, so Ministry was always the nuts. But it was started with big intentions in the same way that Terry started One Nation, in a more professionally run way than other clubs. First, the size of it was huge, so you needed a big plan, and a long-term plan, to fill it. Right back when Ministry started half the people doing raves were still getting a kick out of other people getting a kick from it, y'know what I mean? Half the buzz back then – like at my Arches times – was from not getting busted, still going strong next week, still being in one piece, no one dying, the bogs not flooding, making new mates and watching other people buzzing as much as you.

What happened was this. Through government restrictions the authorities held out as long as they could, saying no no no and trying to stem the tide. All the time though they see it's gonna be a very profitable industry and, cos they've got the inside track on information to say what the future's probably going to be like, they start making plans for when it all goes legal. As soon as the plans were in place, all those bodies that were saying no suddenly found a loophole to open clubs until six o'clock in the morning rather than three.

So now, suddenly, it's legal to do what we've been doing for years and the scene went *schzoom*! All over the world, everybody raving, all on telly and the radio. And it happened because everyone wanted to encourage it; the clothing industry, the radio, the TV stations, the record companies, the venues, the merchandisers. Governments get swayed in their decisions by money, without a doubt. Even if it ain't a direct bribe, that's how it works. And the government saw the money to be made there and had businesses complaining of the money they would lose, so things changed.

All the bigger companies had hung back anyway, biding their time until things got more acceptable, and then they could go for dollar big-time without getting condemnation heaped upon them. As soon as that little opportunity appeared everything went BANG and raving spread overground like wild fire.

Then unbelievable things started popping up like raves for ten, twenty thousand people! It was mad. And that happened because all the people who had been objecting to rave, the big fuck-off leisure companies, suddenly saw the money they could've made. So they tried to make loads at the start to make up for lost ground. Then you had some cunt putting on a rave for twenty thousand people! What is that all about?

I remember a fucking circus tent on Margate Pier. Not just a room on it but the whole pier. It was mental. And that was people trying to get back, money-wise, what they'd never had. It was never going to last but it burnt into the map of the music industry.

But then after twenty thousand people had all been having it large under one roof – black, white, young, old, hardnuts, divs, rich, poor – all barriers knocked down dead for a pill; the authorities had to somehow convince all twenty thousand of them to 'Just say No To Drugs!' To which the twenty thousand replied FUCK! RIGHT! OFF!

See, the local authorities and big companies and corporate bodies and all the other cunts wanted the money but they didn't really want the scene. They wanted to fuck the bride around the back of the church and still marry her a virgin.

Clubs like Ministry Of Sound beat them at their own game and opened up the first superclub. And pretty fucking super it still is too.

Then when it all started going legal and overground and commercial *that* was when the cunts started coming down heavy on the people who'd actually help create the scene – like Wolfie. You have to remember that back then even London mostly closed at two o'clock, and only a few clubs at three. An awful lot of people didn't want to go home at two or three. Nothing worse than a buzz cut short, is there?

So when I first did the Arches and then my other clubs I stayed open until . . . just about whenever I fucking wanted, mate, actually! Usually about ten in the morning. I had all the fucking limos down from Stringfellows asking to buy bottles of champagne at any price! I remember thinking, Fuck me.

Bit by bit things started to change and when more class and comfort came into clubbing you lost the free and easy feeling that you could smoke puff. Which is where it all began. A lot of the lovey-dovey stuff had gone out the window. Business always hardens up a scene.

The superclubs now make more off merchandising and releasing compilation albums than anything else. But one of the sweetest moves that some of these clubs came up with was one you wouldn't even think of. They made everyone queue. And they made everyone queue for a long time. One – it made the club look busier and better, and Two – everyone then knew they had to wear a coat. You can't stand in a bloody queue in this country for very long before kissing goodbye to fingers, toes and nose. So no fucker was gonna stand there coatless. Especially in the kind of gear clubbers wear.

So the extra money from the cloakroom was two quid times, say, fifteen hundred people. No one really thinks of the two quid either. £15 to get in? No, it's actually £17. So that's between three and four K a night, four nights a week. Between £12,000 and £15,000 a week from hanging coats on hangers. Pop a geezer in the cloakroom for thirty quid a night. Then there's the ice pops they buy by weight for a few pence each and sell for a quid a piece. Thousands a week. That's fucking good business, mate.

Personally, of course, I always wear a kagool in the queue so I can roll it up really really small and save two quid. Oh *shut* up. I very rarely queue cos I really hate queuing. Sorry if that's snobby, but I do hate it. I once queued for Stevie Wonder's autograph. It was shit, I couldn't even read it. What is he, blind?

Which reminds me of something – well it would, wouldn't it? I can hear you saying – well, just *shut* up! And fucking listen, you cheeky monkeys. Anyway, I once found this blind person's white cane in Dulwich. I suppose they must have dropped it and then couldn't find it again. Makes sense. So I got some cheap 99p sunglasses and went into this pub called the Forresters in Lordship Lane, with my mates Peter and Keith Eves, Big Lee, Bez, Steve Low, Bal and Frank and Linda. I started swinging the stick about, knocking drinks off and hitting people. I was saying sorry, sorry . . . so sorry. Then I ordered a pint, missed my mouth and poured it down my shirt. This place was like an up-market wine bar gaff, which made it even more enjoyable.

Everyone was sat outside as well cos it was a nice day. So I stumbled out to the car, with everyone watching, got in and started it up. I drove off really slowly, holding the stick out of the window and tapping the pavement. It was like a Mr Bean sketch.

Oh listen, just remembered. At Ministry there was this geezer called Colin who used to go there. Me and Jen called him Belly Dancer Colin cos of the way he'd twist and twirl on the dance floor. Anyway, he right liked us and our little crowd. He didn't know anyone quite like the little naughty-ravey gang of ours. So one night he asked us back to his house for a drink, but meaning just me and Jen. I said OK but then decided I didn't fancy it and thought we should have more company. About fifty more.

So in one of the offices in Ministry I photocopied this piece of paper he'd given me with his address on. And then handed them out – Come people, come! Come to Colin's! There shall be wine, dance, song and McVitie's chocolate digestives!

By the time we actually got to Colin's all the road was properly jammed with cars and people, and people on cars, people in cars, music blaring out, cars bumped up on the pavement, people going in and out of Colin's house. Fucking madness. Colin himself was stood on the pavement having fucking kittens and practically crying.

'No, God no! Dave, do something!' he was saying. I thought, Ooops! It's a hell of a lot fucking easier to invite fifty people than uninvite them. I could've always put on Mud's 'Tiger Feet' and called Mad Jack, I suppose.

Once in 'The Tardis', George's place, I saw this bloke walking about with one of them Teletubby bags on his back, a Teletubby rucksack. The yellow one, I don't fucking know its name – Divvy, I think. Anyway, my mate Mickey Taylor got a knuckleduster, walked over and whacked the Teletubby on the head! It was really funny. He was just swinging at it, knocking its head about. The bloke spun round like it was him being attacked. So Mickey just kissed the Teletubby better, the big E'd-up softy. It was George from the Tardis who introduced me to Andy McNab, the ex-SAS guy, and my opinion of him was wrong cos he's a nice fella and a really smart operator.

But two of my favourite things that ever happened at raves were both at One Nation events. First one, we hired this blindin' lookalike of the Queen: and she was the spitting image as well. If you held a tenner up next to her she was bang on. I got a little lady-size knuckleduster made for her but she said she wouldn't wear it. Well, I bet she beats up old Prince Philip lookalikes most nights so I suppose she's got to have one night off from wearing a duster. I also asked her if she'd come with me to a court appearance at Bow Street Magistrates' Court – if I was gonna be there at Her Majesty's pleasure, I thought I'd take Her Majesty along – but she refused.

She came down to the rave in a chauffeur-driven black Bentley with flags on the front and then, at 1 a.m., she walked out on stage in front of 5,000 Drum and Bass raving lunatics! The place just fucking erupted – all these ravers off their heads going, 'Look! It's The Fucking Queen!' Then she started dancing around with the club dancers on stage. *Go Liz!*

She did a perfect little white-gloved wave when she left. I bet that performance fucked a fair few heads up that night.

The other good one, you'll like this, was when One Nation blew up a police car on stage. Yeah, you *know* that! I knew you'd like that one. It was at one of the Wembley gigs as well, absolutely massive. On the stroke of midnight the music stopped, which is pretty unheard of itself at a rave, ain't it? If you're gonna stop the music you'd better fucking make sure it's justified by something wicked.

The stage went dark and out of the speakers this voice said, 'This is what One Nation think of the Old Bill!', then the lights came back up on a proper Rover police car on stage. Then it just blew up! It blew right up. It was wired with loads of fireworks and there were sparks and flames all over it. The whole thing just went up in smoke and everyone in there just went mental. Some people began having flashbacks to the Brixton riots and started running round, looking for TV shop windows to put through. And I could have sworn I saw Warrior run past doing a war cry!

Then the lights dropped, the music banged back on and everyone went back to it with a little more fizz to their buzz. You could still smell the smoke in the air as you were dancing.

I got a bit of déjà vu watching that car blow up. Took me right back to a scene about twenty years ago when I got paid to blow up a car. The geezer owed money or owed the car, I forget the details. But I haven't forgotten the sight of that gold Cortina 1600E with a black vinyl roof blowing itself to bits. Try claiming that back on third fucking party. Bet he had a conversation and a half with his insurers, especially when they asked him where the car was and he had to say, 'Up on the roof of my house!' Afterwards, I rang the bloke who wanted the job doing and he said he knew we hadn't done the car cos he'd just seen the geezer driving around in it. Turns out we'd done an identical car in the same area.

So at the One Nation event I was only disappointed we didn't get the Queen lookalike to explode the car. Or better still, me. At least I couldn't have done the wrong one!

See you there next time.

18 Carry on Abroad

I had a really funny bonk in Tenerife once. Or was it twice, No, I only did her the once but it was a good one.

We were out on the water on a pedallo in the middle of the night. She was leaning over, bending forward over the back of the seat and I was behind her, but my feet were on the pedals. So as I was bonking this bird my feet were pushing the pedals around. But cos it was double pedallo and I was only pushing one set of pedals we ended up going round in circles. It's the only time I've ever had to stop mid-shag cos I was fucking dizzy! No, on second thoughts, there was that time once on the whirling waltzer . . .

Years ago I went to Tenerife with my mate Rory Bullen. It was when we were still teenagers and we'd both run away from home. We didn't do things by halves and just run off to Margate, or somewhere daft like that, we left the fucking country, mate. Let your mum try and find you hundreds of miles away. Bit of a test on the old parent-front that one, ay?

Anyway, we were just dossing around out there. We hardly had any money or anything but we didn't give a fuck cos being penniless on a beach in Tenerife is a thousand times better than being at school in Peckham with loads of pocket money. And on the beach, at night, these two removal lorries would drive up and out of one they'd take out loads of petrol go-carts. One lamppost would be propped up on the beach with the cement bags and about half a mile away they'd put the other one, and make a track between with the tyres. Next day the track would be open to tourists.

You were supposed to leave your passport as security but because me and Rory had lots of nicked passports anyway we got around that one. So we got in a go-cart each, did a few laps and then shot up off the beach, got onto the road and just drove off! We went buzzing about twenty miles until we reached the other side of the island. And those go-carts don't half seem fast when your arse is only six inches off the floor.

That was the same holiday where I fell asleep on a lilo. We didn't really sleep properly anywhere, and I was also pissed, so when I got on this inflatable lounger on the water I just drifted off. And drifted off and drifted off. When I woke up I couldn't see land! I absolutely fucking *shat* myself. I thought, What the fuck do I do now? Navigating by the sun has never been a strong point with me. There weren't a lot of call for it in south London, know what I mean? If I wanted to get home I'd generally just jump on a number 122.

It was do or die now. I thought I may as well choose a direction and start paddling. There was a bit on the horizon that I thought looked a bit vaguely like land so I went for that. Hours later I washed up on the beach like big, burnt, shipwrecked sausage. There was everyone else just laid there sunbathing and I staggered out the water half fucking dead, saying 'Water! Water!' I'd kept my sunglasses on all the time so when I took them off I had two big white circles round my eyes. I looked like a fucking panda. People started offering me leaves for breakfast.

Years later I'd go out there clubbing in Tenerife, also taking a Happy Hardcore group called Bass Construction with Danielle Montana, Roschelle and Freaky. They played at a club called Club Ecstasy, along with my Rude Rude Courtney Twins. That was the first time Jen had been out there. Nigel Benn DJ-ed at the gig as well.

I also took out a band called The Business. The lead singer was Steve Whale. Steve and the *Sun* writer Gary Bushell used to be in the same band, a sort of skinhead-punky band. Trouble was that if they weren't on stage playing then they just looked like a group of hardnuts, and they got in loads of fights because they looked like a firm of geezers so other geezers would kick-off with them. Which right fucked them off cos they were just on holiday to get sun, sea, sand and sex like everyone else! They all grew their hair after that.

In February of this year I went back out to Tenerife for my birthday. There were so many of us we chartered a whole plane. So imagine what the stewardesses were thinking when they saw us lot, all suited-up, approaching the plane. It weren't so much *Reservoir Dogs*, more like *Reservoir Crufts*. There was a whole dogs' home of us.

I wore my gold knuckleduster on a chain going through Customs. When they saw all the people with me one of the Customs officers said, 'You do realise, Mr Courtney, that people have invaded countries with less than this?'

Bear with me for a minute will you, while I give my little Tenerife army a shout. There was my One Nation partner Terry Turbo, DJs Carl 'Tuff Enuff' Brown, Chris Paul, Daniella Montana, Mickey Finn, Nigel Benn, Ben Jammin', Steve and Andy B, Dreamscape's Steve Foster, The Flying Crew, singer Mark Morrison, the pop group Unique, Normski, actors Gary Love, Bill Murray, Mark Bannerman and Spider, boxers Prince Naseem and Julius Francis, footballer Lee Chapman, Oliver Skeet the showjumper, Miss Moneypenny, Mickey Biggs, writers Marcus Georgio, Norman Parker, Carol Clarke, Tony Thompson, Steve Wood, David Hurst and Gary Bushell, photographers Jocelyn Bain Hogg and Eamon O'Keefe and sons Jamie and artist Kevin Nutter.

It wouldn't have been the same without: Aquarium Lou, Brendan, Seymour, Wolfie, Lone Wolf Dave, Dean, Danny Dolittle, Laurie Scott, Christian, Andy, Adam Saint, Jack Adams, Big Albert Chapman and Keith from Birmingham, Big Brummy John, Tommy Harrison and his boys, Welsh Bernie, scousers Johnny McGee, Robbie, John and Jim, Wish, Zak, Kevin N, Rod, Mohammed, Coventry Stuart, Ray Bridges, Scouse John, Ravey, Boxer, Big Willy and Memmy and the Glasgow boys, Limelight Rose, AJ, Slim, Gary G, Gary Love, Steve Richards, Gummidge, Big Mel, Dave Quelch, Scarface Danny, Butts, Hak and Tarkan, Gravesend Matt.

Not forgetting: Harry Holland, Kenny and Dennis Lucas, Norma, Lance, Micky Mack and Co, Mick Colby, Matt, Mickey Finn, Nicky, Michelle and Paul, Mo and Jill, Neil O'Brian, Frankie Baby, Fred and Kerry, Dave the builder and sunbed Joyce, Steve Low, Andy Hanson, Gary Baron, Steve from Mirage, the girls from Sunnyside, Steve Raith, Mitch, Jarvis, Blackwood, Tyson, Garry Ditton and Fireman Steve, Moley, Abby, Steve Holdsworth, Lamb, Belfast Brian, Big

Luke, Kevin Jenkins and Daniella Westbrook, Steve Whale, Hammer, Reese, Chops, Darren from Showsec and Lee Brown.

And last but not least: Barking Zena Flashpetal, Zoe Gregory Paul, Susan and Wayne, Paddy and Mel, Frank and Linda Todd, Roy Schnell, Peter Ross, Rob the barber, Chris Huxford (Forum), Ginger (Hippodrome), Toby von Judge, Tinpan George, my driver Ebo, Jamie Foreman and Ian Royce, Paul Dolphin, Rod Davies, Gary Eastwood, my pal Mick (not 'Unknown'), Sheffield Ben Joynes and Lindsey, Lee and Lianne, Little Jenny, Charlie Dixon, Bernie, James McDonald, Faz and Cookie, Pard, Del, Lee, Big Colin and Fast Trevor, Docherty, Mechanic Jim, Denis Firman, brothers Tony and Danny, all the staff of the Orange, John Colbert and James Cohen.

My good friends from the Hell's Angels were there too. We've helped each other out in the past and the Angels are good people to know. I'd like to name them all but don't want to get anyone in trouble – they know who they are.

And Val and John, Jonathan Evans' parents, flew out there to see me as well.

OK, done. Sorry about that (I feel a bit listless now). Wait a minute, what am I apologising for anyway, you didn't even fucking read it, did you? You just scanned the list looking for your own name you little publicity seeker you! Well, I forgive you.

Oh, but there's one big name I have forgotten – Her Royal Majesty The Queen Mother. No, course she weren't there, but if I mention her name they'll put it in the index at the back of the book. Then when someone's stood in W H Smith's scanning the index they'll see her name and think, Fuck me, the Queen Mum ain't mixed up with old Dave Courtney, is she?

Having said that, I *did* actually get a telephone call from Buckingham Palace a few months ago. Now I know what you're thinking: here comes another corny Courtney quip, like – it was Prince Charles on the phone asking me where he could pick up a cheap saddle for Camilla, I said ride her bareback like everyone else. No, I said Charles, you've got it wrong, everyone says she's a real *dog*, not a horse.

Truthfully, it was my mate Eamon calling me from Bucky Pally. Eamon's got his own really successful business which does work by Royal Appointment. So he was actually at the

Queen's gaff for a meeting. While he was there he just started buzzing off the idea that one minute he can be hob-nobbing with the Queen and the next eating McVitie's hobnob's with Dave Courtney. From Buckingham Palace to Camelot Castle.

So he got out his mobile and called me from inside the palace! He said, 'Dave, you are not gonna believe this but . . .' And if it had been anyone but Eamon I wouldn't have believed it. Mad Jack, for instance, would have had great difficulty in convincing me he was having tea and crumpets with Her Majesty. Now if he called and said he was having porridge at Her Majesty's Pleasure, that would definitely be more believable.

The other big reason why me and everyone were out in Tenerife was because I was doing another 'Evening With Dave Courtney'. I'd done a lot of these 'Evening Withs' back home in Britain after the success of *Stop The Ride* . . .; in Liverpool, Birmingham, Glasgow and three nights at the Talk Of London theatre, organised by Neil O'Brian. And I did take that as a big fucking compliment that I was invited to a place called 'The Talk of London'!

My mates Joe and Les bought a nightclub in Tenerife and we stayed with them. They have a beautiful gaff as well, this white villa with hanging baskets. I don't really agree with that, actually – hanging baskets. I mean, what if they later turn up some evidence that proves they were innocent?

The 'Evening With' in Tenerife was held at Happy Days 2. Frank Carson opened the show. As well as all my crowd, it seemed like every ex-pat in town wanted to be there. But you find that over on the islands. Everyone leaves England for this supposedly dream life in the sun but when you've been there a year or two it can start to lose its shine. So everyone jumps on anything that's from back home.

On the night all I had to do was sit on stage with a microphone and talk about myself, tell jokes and answer questions. So what a tester that was. Not. When you've been in the smiling and talking racket for a while it comes as second nature. And I'd been in that racket for the last forty-one years. No, make that thirty-nine, cos I didn't speak till I was two.

So I went down a storm, even if I do say so myself. We went to Barry's Bar and the Happy Days 2 club as well.

After the 'Evening With' Lineker's closed their doors so we could have a private party and the next night so did Bobby's Bar, Leopard Lounge, Busby's, Boobs and Marco's place. There was just me and my people and some punters who'd bought tickets.

At about three in the morning when everyone was well on their way to getting pissed, Jen turned to me and said, 'Come on, babe.' I asked her where we were going and she said she had a surprise for me for my birthday. I was thinking – spacehopper? chopper bike? slinky? – what could it be that I haven't got?

We drove back to the apartment and Jen ran in. When she came back out looking hornier than the Devil, wearing her PVC dress and boots. Oh that kind of surprise. Then she directed me to this club she said she knew. So we pulled up outside and I saw what it was. 'That's a brothel,' I said, 'Fuck me . . .'

'Yes it is,' Jen said 'And yes we are going to . . .'

When we got inside it was really dark and cos I was in there to shop Jen put the lights up. Which made you realise why the lights had been down in the first place. There were some scary sights on offer. Proper milk-curdlers. Some of these birds had got a few miles on them and I didn't want an MOT failure breaking down on me. But there were some cracking ones as well so I had a really wicked birthday.

Also in there was the photographer, Jocelyn Bain Hogg, there with us for *GQ* magazine, and he took one of the best photos of me that's been taken, and I've had a lot taken. Outside the Paradise Club hotel where my lot were all staying there was a big pool with a white bridge curving over it. I saw it and thought it would make a blinding shot with me and the boys all stood across it. So I told everyone that if they wanted to be in the picture to be there bright and early(ish) the next morning. That night we had a bit of a booze up.

Next morning everyone's feeling wrecked so some didn't make it. And how they regret that now. We all lined up over the bridge. About thirty geezers all in black suits and me in the middle wearing my gold one! Below us is the white bridge and bright blue water, which just happened to have a dozen plastic policemen's helmets floating in it. I wonder how they got there.

There were little signs on either side of the bridge saying it weren't made to take above a certain weight, which was about the same weight as my mate Lance just on his own. So we ignored that, obviously. Toby von Judge expressed a bit of concern about the big-geezers-to-bridge weight ratio. Or, as he put it, in his own unique manner; 'Don't you think, David, it might be a trifle risky to overload the construction?'

I said, 'Oh, not the old "trifle risky" ploy, Toby! Fuck me, don't hit me with risky trifles at this time in the morning. In fact, I'd rather have a custard tart. Anyway,' I said, 'don't matter if the bridge does give way because we can all walk on water.' Ha *ha*! Stick that in your pipe and smoke it, officer.

But the photo is the absolute nuts, mate. Jocelyn really produced the goods with that shot. In fact, for the last year he's been following me and some of the other chaps around, taking pictures for a photo book that comes out this year. And as I said in the magazine, I had to be sure that Jocelyn could handle himself among 150 shaven-headed, flat-nosed, scarred geezers, and I was right: he could. And after having him around for a little while he does become invisible. Which is quite something for a six-foot, clumsy bastard!

I also flew off to Brazil for Ronnie Bigg's 70th birthday party in Rio de Janeiro. Honestly, work, work, work! It's all go, innit? I was just about to kill myself when the invite dropped on the mat. I thought, Oh, go *on* then. If I must.

I went out with the usual big family gathering, including Roy Shaw, Bruce Reynolds and his son Nick, Tony Hart and a reporter called Bahan. We booked in at the Hotel Gloria and had a rare old time. It was a real honour to be there. I met Ronnie's son Mick, Jon Pinkerton, Ronnie's best mate and Ronnie himself is doing very well, thank you very much. Don't let anyone else tell you any different. His house up in Santa Teresa is the bollocks with a swimming pool, snooker room and maid, he lives in permanent sunshine and, most important-ly, he is FREE.

He said to me, 'If anyone tells you that for one second I sit here wishing I was back in Old Blighty, it's crap.' Everyone out there treats him like the president, calling him 'Senore Biggs'. People flock to Ronnie's gaff to see him and he entertains tourists all day long with stories. After meeting Ronnie, I can say I am a Ronnie Biggs fan. The man is, without a shadow of a doubt, unique.

Rio is a fucking peculiar place though. It has a real air of danger about it. It's so falsely glittery on the surface but there's almost a visible line where you can see the façade end and the reality begin. And real poverty is really unpleasant to see. You can go to Copacabana Beach and at the end of the beach is a four-lane motorway. You cross the motorway to get to this club. The front of the club is all gold and glittery and down the side you can see where the fancy tiles run out and the bare plaster begins. A bit further down, by the time you're at the back of the club, you're in danger of being murdered. The pretence is that blatant, that obvious. It really is unhidden.

Sex is the only weapon and pleasure and earning potential that a lot of them have. They can't even afford to buy, say, an apple to sell it on for a small profit. So the women have a way of earning a living – the share price in pussy never drops does it?– but the men don't have that way. Which makes it even more dangerous.

I'll tell you what really epitomised it for me. When we were there the local politicians had a meeting in parliament to try to pass a bill saying that people just HAD to stop at red traffic lights! And that was because drivers weren't stopping cos if they did they were literally a sitting target, and they got mugged or kidnapped or car-jacked. In your car. At the lights. Some cunt would run up and bash the window in, or bash your head in, or shoot you, or chop your hand off with a machete to get your Rolex (and what a cunt if you'd only been wearing a fake!) So drivers were just slowing down a bit, having a quick look and then flooring the accelerator. Bit like me in the Rolls driving through Woolwich, come to think of it.

Mind you, I only saw Rio. The country as a whole is probably not like that. But I'll tell you one thing they've got absolutely bang on. It's the only country that really, truly, does not recognise racism. The people naturally range from the very dark skinned to almost white, and every colour in between, but, they're all Brazilian. The colour in the middle of that range though, is a sort of honey brown which is just fucking beautiful; they look like a mixture of Pocahontas and Miss World.

And every one of them does a blindin' impression of Ursula Andress when she came out of the sea onto the beach, dripping wet, in the James Bond film *Doctor No*. I was laid there thinking, Yes! I *am* James!

In the same way they don't wait around to kill you, they don't wait around to fuck you either. They ain't got time for flirting. They just walk up to you on the beach and pull their thongs to one side to show you what they've got. The women bleach their pubic hair blonde and shave little shapes out of it, like a heart or a star or a Nike tick! I thought, if I see one with a knuckleduster shaved into her fanny I'll have a fucking heart attack on the spot. Yeah, they come up, pull the thong aside and say do you wanna play with this? I said, Listen, I'd sell my fucking house for that!

There's a place there called 'Help' and it's a fucking good place to go if you need your ego boosting up a bit cos when you say the women are on you, you wouldn't know – unless you'd been to Thailand – what 'on you' meant. You have not experienced a woman 'on your case' unless you've been to a place where, twenty-four hours a day, seven days a week they are professionally on men. You can't get rawer than that. No time for romance, which is why Jen packed the Durex for me.

So the whole Strip is like that but the other side is dangerous. The men don't have that work opportunity so you can imagine what kind of desperation that breeds.

Another thing. Until you've been on holiday to a place on the other side of the world you ain't really ever been on holiday. Until you actually see the night stars from another continent, or the sky from a much farther away country. You can go to Spain but it ain't the same. But if you've done Australia or America, for instance, and you look up at the sky at night – it looks bigger and more full of stars. And it's clearer, as if the heat from the country has blown a hole through all the crap that usually fogs up the sky, and made it crystal fucking clear. Sorry to sound like an old hippy but it is amazing.

So I'll be making more trips back out to Rio and Tenerife. As I always say, it's nice to be wanted by anyone but Scotland Yard.

19 Bang up to Date

I've always been used to being watched in clubs, either because someone knew who I was or just cos of the way I looked. I'm aware of it but I don't mind it. I love it. You see, when I was only about 22, 23, I got a job on the door at Tattershall Castle club and that was the first time I'd worked under CCTV cameras. Something happened and we got took to court and they played the CCTV film of it.

Now that don't sound like much but it was a moment of change for me. From that minute on I decided to behave as if I'm always being filmed, and act accordingly – with as much style, panache, wit, or sometimes even silliness, that I can muster.

So I'd do the things like the 'kicking the copper up the arse' stunt that I've told you about before; or the saying silly things in court to the judge and on police tapes; to even doing stuff in clubs when I know someone's watching me. It all counts. It is my *duty* to entertain!

Another thing made me realise the power of the right words at the right time. It was years ago when I did my first bank job with a mate. We burst in with a sawn-off; everyone had their backs to us cos they were queuing for a window, and my mind suddenly went blank! I couldn't remember what the fuck I'd planned on saying. My mate looked at me, so I improvised. I shouted out, 'All right, everybody get down on the floor! I'm gonna make a very large withdrawal!'

Word of that remark got 'round and people talked about it for ages afterwards. Made me think: next time I'll do one of those on purpose. My bank job days were pretty short lived though. I weighed up the odds on that little game and decided that, for the amount of bird you got against the amount of money you got, I could earn almost as much doing something which would get me much less bird.

They weren't always the smoothest plays either, my adventures in self-banking. Yeah, that's a phrase they use now innit, 'self-banking'? Meaning that the banks make you use wall machines and drop-off boxes and computers so they have to do less. Lazy cunts. Well, I was doing my own version of self-banking years ago. Helping myself in banks.

But, like I say, my raids didn't always go to plan. One was a betting office that I did one Saturday afternoon. I knew it'd be busy then and have full tills. So I got outside, adrenaline pumping, rolled the wool hat I was wearing down into a balaclava, unbagged the sawn-off, and kicked the door in. It bounced back and slammed shut! I thought, What the fuck . . .? and kicked it again. It flew open a bit, I heard loads of noise, then it slammed back shut again! I couldn't figure it. So I shouldered the door and pushed it in.

Inside the place was fucking rammed to the walls and right up to the door with punters, all screaming and shouting. Shoulder to shoulder, no breathing space, and every one of them facing away from me and watching the Grand National on a TV screen. Oh, fuck me, Grand National Day! So I'm stood there like a cunt, trying to make an impression with the sawn-off and none of these fuckers even knows I'm there.

So I fired into the ceiling. Call me old fashioned but that's always a good attention-getter. Everybody stopped dead. The crowd parted like the Red Sea and made this path for me to the counter. When I say 'everyone stopped dead' . . . not quite. There was one geezer stood at the end of this path, and directly beneath the telly, still shouting at the screen and geeing his horse along.

I thought, He must have a fuck load of money on that nag not to care that I'm behind him with a smoking shotgun. I told him to shut up but he just carried on. I shouted again, 'Oi! Shut the fuck up. Shut it!' He just ignored me. I walked over and tapped him on the head with the barrel. He turned around and jumped, saw the gun, saw the ceiling hole, and then started babbling away at me. I could hardly tell what he was saying and that's when I realised he was deaf and dumb.

I've had some right misunderstandings with the old deaf and dumb brigade haven't I? I wonder what happens if one of them ever gets called as a witness. Maybe it's like charades in the witness box and you have to guess from the mime – three words, sound like . . .

So, anyway, I do have some fun with the knowledge that when I'm out there's always someone watching me. Now that more people know me after *Stop The Ride . . .*, if I'm in a club and I look up, I see about twenty heads suddenly turn away.

There was one little gag that I used to do when I was out raving. I'd stand and make a joint, real careful like you have to be in a crowd, crumble the puff, roll the joint. Then, just as I went to lick the Rizla I'd lift it up instead and run the edge of the paper right across my head, wetting it. And *then* roll it up. All the time knowing that people watching have clocked that and are either laughing or going 'fuck me'.

Another good one was one that I actually nicked off Funny Glen. You had to do this one at the end of the night just as you were getting ready to leave a place. People with me would start finishing off their drinks so I'd pick up mine, open the top pocket of my jacket and pour the drink straight in. It just gushed all down the jacket! Then I'd pat the pocket like I was checking the drink was safe. No one in our group would bat an eye and I'd keep a straight face. I'd turn to leave and see loads of really baffled faces around us.

A serious advantage that came from being watched was that it made me not make mistakes. It don't half keep you on your toes.

I've always got a good reaction from all the ravers and Clubby people; always got a good reaction from people if they've taken the time to get to know me. Cos I know how people look at me when they look at me. And it's really pleasant to watch that go away, to dispel that worry that people have. I like doing that: have them walk away and know they're thinking, Hey, he's all right – I've got in and out of his rave without being beaten up. I've took a Rizla off him, I've danced with his missus, he shook my hand, introduced me to another ten geezers and said 'See ya later', and I've survived!

If the truth be known it is this: I ain't hanging around with any gangsters at the moment. But I've done the real thing and got out of it, and if any cunt wants to fuck around with my credentials I would challenge them to do half of what I've done in real life.

I don't have to prove myself now. The police know that. Well, you'd think they would. Ain't stopped them from moving in surveillance cameras over the road from me though, has it? First they went to this Asian geezer who lives bang opposite me, and asked if they could put cameras in there. He said they couldn't. Then he came to tell me that they went next door but didn't bring the stuff back out.

You would really think they would fucking learn, wouldn't you? But I truly believe the Old Bill think I'm still right bang at it. How could I kick in someone's door when anybody who saw me, even if they didn't know my name, would just say, 'It was that fella off the telly, the one who's wrote the book.' Having your face up on a fucking roadside billboard don't exactly do wonders for your anonymity.

But you can have a bit of fun having the police just over the road watching you. Yeah, I can see you're gonna take some convincing on that one. Actually, it's a cunt being watched: not cos I'm doing anything wrong; just knowing they're there.

So when I got back from Tenerife I got all the undeveloped films I'd taken on holiday, put them in a bag and took them over the road to Spy Towers. This geezer opened the door and I handed him the films. 'When the Old Bill come back to pick up their films,' I said, 'could you ask them to develop these for me at the same time. It'll save me a trip to Boots. Cheers.'

He just took them and went back inside. Notice that he never said that he didn't know what I was talking about, did he? Which you would if you didn't have one of the Met's videos screwed to your bedroom wall.

I love the thought that whichever spotty-faced plod is given the job of picking up their films will have to go back to the nick with my holiday snaps and say, 'Sarge . . . you won't guess what Courtney's done now!' Yes! Result. And the fact the photos showed me having a fucking good time as well is just the cherry on the cake. And the fly in their ointment.

They're a persistent bunch. You got to give them that. Not long ago this happened: a girl got caught with something going into a club. Most geezers used to give their puff or pills to their birds to carry. Not cos they're passing the blame but cos it was much less likely that the women would get searched. The police cottoned on of course and now both are likely to get it. Old habits die hard, though, and this geezer gave his bird four Es to put down her knickers. She got searched and they were found.

The story I was told is that the police had a speech ready for her. They said that they could nick her on the spot, but they didn't do that. She and her boyfriend claim that the Old Bill said they would just give her a caution *if* she would say she'd got the Es from me. She had never been in this position before and was way out of her depth but the boyfriend jumped straight on in and said the Es were his. He was nicked but got bail.

He got in touch with people that knew me, came round my house and told me all about it. He did that for me and I'd never seen the geezer before in my life. When he saw what was happening, he thought, That's wrong. Top man.

Stop The Ride I Want To Get Off was, and still is, a big big success. It stormed into the top ten before making itself at home in the top five of *The Times* bestseller list, and then refused to budge. It even had a row with Delia Smith's cookbook and battered it!

I got 'Book Of The Week' by Craig Brown in the *Mail On Sunday*. That made my day. When I first heard it was gonna be reviewed in a very very conservative paper like that, I did wonder if they'd slag me off. So I'd like to reassure Mr Brown that the contract on him has now been cancelled! Cheers.

So thank you all very much – all those of you who bought it. And to all those of you who didn't – I hope you get the 'flu *and* diarrhoea and then sneeze in a crowded lift and shit yourself. Just before the lift breaks down. Not that I bear a grudge or anything!

Anyway, I've spent the money wisely on a new biro, shooters for all the kids (playgrounds are so tough these days), a bigger knuckleduster for me, a Jacuzzi for the Roller, a lifetime's supply of head moisturiser, finest puff, and loads of stamps and Jiffy bags to send signed copies of the book to all the chiefs of police. I haven't had one back yet so either they all liked it or they're slow readers.

One of the best things that happened as a consequence of the book – and the bit that, personally, chuffed me most – was when I was at another seaside dance do, down at the Radio 1 weekender put on by Steve Low at Pontins, Camber Sands. This woman came up to me, looking all emotional. I thought, Oh no, here we go: she can't believe it. I'm even more devastating in the flesh!

She just came over and held my hand. She was nearly crying. I asked her what was up. She called her husband across. She introduced him and then she said, 'I've never been in trouble in my life but, had I not read your book – which I never would've by choice but my husband there kept laughing in bed when he was reading it, so I had to read it – but if I hadn't I'd be in trouble now. Two weeks later me and my husband got arrested for being "knowingly concerned" over something that's nothing to do with us. When the police took us it was fresh in my mind what you'd said about how to behave when you get arrested. They separated us and all the time he was worrying about me, but I said nothing and played it by the book. Your book.'

'Yeah?' I said. 'What happened?' She told me they got 'not guilty' last week! I said, 'That's fucking wicked, babe! Well done, mate.' I shook her old man's hand. He was a bit more reserved about it cos of the 'man' thing, y'know, not showing too much emotion and all that. But his missus was just so open about what it meant to her.

And it meant loads to me. No one could give me any bigger or better compliment on earth than to say my book stopped them from getting nicked. Wicked. What a recommendation. I want that on the next book cover.

And since becoming a regular columnist for *front* magazine I've even been made a member of the National Union of Journalists. Not bad for someone who left school at six, which I thought was good of me cos it closed at half four. The editor, Piers, now a good mate of mine, and bosses Sally and Andy, stuck their necks out a bit in asking me to write for them. Some people are put off by my reputation but they weren't and it's paid off for us all. So big respect to Piers & Co.

Working for *front* is a real touch though. I mean I actually get paid to write about being me. Which is easy cos I know what I'm like. I even look like myself! I also get to interview my mates like Tricky, Nigel Benn, Bez, Mark Morrison and Steve McFadden. Ain't life hard?! And *front*'s just asked me to go out to Ibiza to write about MTV's club weekend. (I'd love to tell you about when me, Steve McFadden and the boys went out in Steve's VW Camper Van but, unfortunately, I can't. Tease, ain't I?)

One of the weird things about being in the mag is that readers do actually send you letters. I thought that was all made up, but it ain't and I love it. Such a novelty for me to get a letter that don't have a police crest on it. I even get begging letters, so I'd now like to take this opportunity to say, 'Please stop sending them, Mum. I don't care if you do think you overpaid me in pocket money, you ain't getting a refund!'

One letter I got that really touched me was from a lady in Derby who was suffering from cancer. She said she really enjoyed reading the magazine and my column cos it made her laugh. She said she'd appreciate a signed photo of me. I thought, I can do better than that!

I rang my mate and driver, Ebo, and said, 'Fire up the Courtneymobile, we've got a mission!' Half-an-hour later we were cruising along at an altitude of two feet in Mercedes E-class Airways. Got to Derby, knocked on the door, she answered, and I went, 'Da-*daaa*! Surprise, surprise!' After me and Ebo had revived her with the smelling salts, I had a really good day. I sat on her bed and we talked. I signed loads of stuff for her (we had a bit of difficulty holding the cat still, though). I had a cup of tea with her mum. We just had a really nice time and she was a lovely lady.

And the very next morning the police raided her house.

No, that ain't a misprint. The police raided her house. Because, at the moment, I'm under investigation for something which I'll tell you about later, and they'd followed me going up to Derby. Next day they raided her house! They were saying, What was Dave Courtney doing here? What is his association with you? Don't tell me he's driven all the way from London to Derby just to sign photos for you!

She rung me up as soon as they'd left and told me about it. She thought it was amazing! She started thanking me cos it was one of the most exciting things that had happened to her! What a great lady.

And what a shitty thing for the Old Bill to do. I notice they didn't publicise that little episode too highly did they?

Did you see me on Channel 5 end of last year? I was doing the weather, which is piss easy. I said if you want to know what the weather's doing in your part of the country . . . look out the fucking window, you silly cunt – what are you, blind? And if you are blind, just open the window and stick your head out. If it comes back in wet, it's raining. Or the geezer in the flat above you is pissing off the balcony again.

No, really, I was on a programme called *The People Versus Jerry Sadowitz*. Jerry's a wicked comedian and a bit of a top magician as well to boot. He's very Scottish but we won't hold that against him, even if they did have to transmit the show with subtitles.

The show is the bollocks actually, there ain't anything else like it on telly. All the other programmes you can understand. Jerry sits behind a desk on stage in front of a live audience and people take it in turns to go on stage, sit with him and talk about whatever the fuck they want. If you're good, or got bit tits (women only), he lets you talk. If you're boring he rings the bell and you're off.

Because the show can sometimes get a bit hostile and cos Jerry ain't the most diplomatic geezer in the world – 'Fuck off, you cunt!' was a favourite – they decided to have an on-stage minder. Guess who? Yeah, Julian Clary. I was absolutely outraged! So I challenged Julian to a dual, dusters at dawn. I whipped out my best gold, diamond-studded duster, and he got out a Jay cloth.

Anyway, I took the gig and we started touring the show, going to Cardiff, Manchester, Liverpool, Glasgow, Birmingham, and just the one place where they actually spoke English, Oxford. It was the nuts, mate. On tour in a big coach with the crew, staying in hotels, aftershow parties, seeing all my mates in whichever town we were in. It's a proper buzz and a laugh being on the road. No wonder The Rolling Stones never stop touring.

The shows were just mental, though. I didn't know there was so many nutters off the leash. Was there a mass escape from Rampton Institute that I didn't hear about? I think the show's producers must have put a massive industrial strength magnet on the top of each venue just to drag in anyone with a metal plate in their head. And it worked.

One geezer got up on stage and took out a glass jar with his foreskin in it. He said that when he'd been circumcised his mum had kept it. My mum didn't even keep my birth certificate, let alone bits of my fucking body! I said to the audience that I didn't think it was his foreskin cos there'd be no end to this prick.

We seemed to get an awful lot of people in leg braces and walking frames too. The scrap value alone of half the audience must have run into thousands. That magnet really *was* strong.

Liverpool was the bollocks. Top people there. It was all going well until this geezer came on and started verbally abusing old Jerry, which is fine – that's what he's there for. But when this bloke turned around and had a pop at me! I heard the words 'fuck', 'off', 'bald' and 'cunt', in that order. So I grabbed him, lifted him, and threw him through the set, in that order. He ran off, his mates jumped out of the audience, everything went a bit mental for a second (I heard a leg brace hit the floor!), but order was restored when I walked back out on set, lit a cigar and said, 'Ay, *all right*! Calm down, *calm down!*'

Jerry got the colour back in his face, which didn't take long. Cos his colour is *white*. Honestly, he is the whitest geezer I've ever met. He makes Chris Evans look suntanned. Thank fuck he's funny. I did offer to book him a course on a sunbed till I realised I'd only be able to afford the first year!

Anyway, we carried on the show and filming was nearly finished when the Old Bill burst in and arrested me. Turns out the cheeky little cunt from earlier had gone and reported me for assault. I was taken outside to a squad car but, get this, loads of the audience ran out into the street and started protesting that they should let me go! Wow. It was like that favourite scene of mine from *Spartacus* where the crowd stop him being taken by the Romans. And that happened to me in the streets of Liverpool. I was touched. (But then my psychiatrist says I always have been.)

All of this, by the way, was captured on camera. The film crew just left the cameras running and filmed me being taken out to the police car. A fucking Astra it was as well. I had a good mind to complain. A man of my stature being nicked in a Vauxhall!

So they took me down the local nick, St Anne's. When they realised who I was and ran my name through the computer, they were practically jumping for joy. Every copper in the nick came out to have a nosey. They didn't realise I took it as a compliment. Silly bastards. One of the coppers actually said to me, 'We've done what the London Met couldn't do in twenty years, Courtney – nicked you!'

Then, in my jacket pocket, they found a photo of me sat at home surrounded by guns. That got them jumping around again and they nicked me for firearms offences. Worried? *Stop* it! Jerry ain't the only magician that can hide an ace up his sleeve. I had a full pack up mine, mate. As you'll see.

The geezer who'd insulted me and that I'd thrown off set quickly dropped the ABH charges. Which was mostly down to the police giving him a full rundown of my history. Cheers, chaps. That poured a bucket of piss on their first bonfire but they kept the firearms charge though, and took me down to the cells.

Now, I ain't bragging here, really I ain't, but when I was sat in that cell nearly every copper in that nick came down to have another look at me through the little cell door window. But then they started to get embarrassed about the obviousness of it, y'know, that they were just getting a kick out of seeing me. So they'd use the excuse of asking if I wanted a cup of tea.

'Yes,' I said to one at the window, 'I would like a cup of tea; as I said to the last *seventeen* of you that's fucking asked me!' That caused the little shutter to slam shut. I shouted after him, 'And it's two sugars and a chocolate digestive please, mate!' Well, if you don't ask, you don't get.

When I was sat in the cell for hours I knew exactly what was going on up top and later, when everyone told me about it, it had gone just as I'd said it would. They sent an officer back to our hotel to search my room for further photographs of me with guns. My son, Beau, and writer, Marcus, went upstairs with the officer and, lo and behold, what did he find? A whole bedside table of pictures of me and some other geezers holding AK47s, a Magnum, a machine gun and an M16. Ooops, how careless of me!

Back down in the lobby, Sean, a London Weekend Television producer, had a word with the officer and told him that LWT were filming a documentary with me called *Guns in Britain*. He said that they had asked me to get loads of replica firearms for the filming. Which I had.

I really do wish I could've been a fly on the wall upstairs when that copper came back and had to say, 'Guess what, Sarge? The guns are replicas . . .' A few hours earlier on I'd thought I'd heard the sound of champagne corks popping, now I could hear the thud of jaws dropping. Clang! Oh dear, I think someone's just dropped a bollock. Or two.

When they let me out, the scene upstairs in that nick was completely different. It'd been like a party when they brought me in. Standing room only. Now when they were letting me go there wasn't a single one of them to be seen! Just me and the desk sarge to sign me out and give me back my belongings.

On my way out I said to the officer behind the desk that I was gonna complain. He said that the arrest had been legal. I said, 'No, not about that. It's just that I think the room service here is fucking appalling!' You see I never did get that cup of tea.

And that was all at St Anne's nick in Liverpool, for all the locals around there who want to make the odd light-hearted joke with them. Ha.

That following Sunday the *News Of The World* ran a page on the whole thing – COMIC'S GUEST GAGGED – with pictures taken from the video footage. They quoted a spokesman for Merseyside police saying: 'The custody officer refused the charge because, for one reason or another, there was not enough evidence to proceed. I don't want to speculate about what happened but maybe when the complainant got to the police station he had second thoughts.' Oh *yes*! Fucking wicked! I nearly came on the spot when I read that.

Then it quoted me saying, 'I was there as a minder and, when he got lairy, I minded!' I've always been a good worker!

I was also asked to go on a programme called *Cosmic Challenge*. I thought, What's that then? You ask some hippy out for a fight? Top. Count me in. No, actually, what they do is choose someone to be analysed by a tarot card reader, a graphologist, an astrologer, clairvoyant and a palm reader.

They see how accurate they can be about your personality and life. And, if they guess that I'm a celibate, pacifist Christian working as High Court judge and with a full head of hair and a limp, then I'll be asking for a fucking recount!

The film crew filmed me at home, a bit like *Through the Keyhole*. More like Over the Drawbridge. One of the crew, Sarah, said that the clairvoyant fella had taken a piece of her jewellery, a ring, held it for a minute to 'get the vibes' and then told her things about herself. She said he was spot on. I said that he probably meant something else when he said he wanted to finger her ring.

And what a fucking good programme that would make, ay? If they had an arse-ologist on the panel. Well they have palm readers and even head-bump readers so why not an arse reader? The arse-ologist could stand there, blindfolded; some celebrity comes on and bends over, and he has to guess who it is by sticking his finger up their bum.

Fuck me, I'm sure that would beat *Through the Keyhole* in the ratings, wouldn't it? 'Through The Arsehole'! Imagine Lloyd Grossman introducing it, 'Annnd who's rectum could this be?'

I would've been easy to guess, though, cos as soon as his finger got anywhere near me it would've been snapped sideways. 'Arrgh! . . . is it Dave Courtney?!'

My best one yet? Listen to *this* . . .

As if I haven't got enough to do, I entered the race to be Mayor of London this spring. Yeah, I know it's a bit of a step down from being King, but beggars can't be choosers. All was going really well: the newspapers went mad for the story and I was getting loads of publicity. I had backers for the £10,000 fee, I had loads of support from people and I knew if only my mates and people who'd bought my book voted for me, then old Ken Livingstone would have to settle for second place. Because they estimated that only about 19 per cent of Londoners would vote, and I had little chance of persuading any of that 19 per cent to change and vote for me. But, between the fourteen candidates, the winner might only get 5 per cent of that 19 per cent and I know more than 5 per cent of London already! And another 5 per cent of people – young, ravey, clubby, fuck-you people – would have voted for me as well.

Then all the *Stop the Ride* . . . buyers who just wanted to fuck with the system. I'm tellin' you, it was a real possibility.

And they can't say they weren't worried about me winning. Well, they can say that, but they'd be lying. The reason I know why is this: a very good friend of mine was one of the chief reporters at the *News of the World* at the time. So one night him and his boss, and the editors and top reporters of all the other newspapers were called to a late night meeting at Scotland Yard. And, I was told, it was called late at night because it's so difficult for the people who were there to get a free hour at exactly the same time. So they had it after work hours.

There were copies of all my press spread across a table. At one point, one officer was walking around looking at one of my flyers and saying, 'He can't win . . . can he?' As this friend of mine sat there and heard what was being said about me by the inspectors and chiefs from the Old Bill, and how scared they were of what might happen, he knew he couldn't keep it to himself. So he left the room for a minute and called me from his mobile. He said, 'Dave, you're not gonna believe this. Listen . . .'

Then he went back in the room with the phone still on so I could hear it all. Listen, when I heard the stuff they were saying, properly scared of what could happen if I ran, I swear I came twice on the spot – a hands-free multiple orgasm.

And that is why I know it can't be dismissed as paranoia or conspiracy theories about why they tried to stop me. It was a bad case of Stop Dave Courtney He Wants to Get Back On.

In my London, puff would be legalised, clubs would be open till eight. Rizlas would be free, and the homeless and elderly would be better looked after. The sign of a good society is one that protects its weakest. The strong can always look after themselves.

Another serious policy of mine was this: if legalising smoking puff was too much for Britain to take, then at least legalise it being smoked in prison. For this reason. When you're doing bird, you can be piss-tested at any time; if it's positive, you get more time banged on your sentence. Now, puff stays in your system for about twenty-eight days, heroin for about two or three. So people who usually smoke puff (and would never have dreamed of heroin) turn to heroin to chill them out instead. Who's going to risk getting extra bird for a joint they may have smoked three weeks ago? So prison is turning out heroin addicts.

I also had a hundred thousand full-colour flyers printed up with a picture of me in Mayoral robes and the words, CAN YOUR WORST NIGHT MAYOR BE YOUR NEW LORD MAYOR? – YES! VOTE DAVE COURTNEY. YOU KNOW IT MAKES SENSE. I thought a little helicopter drop over London would've gone down very well, thankyouverymuch.

Then the Greater London Council lost my application form. Oh very convenient and not the least bit suspicious, ay? So I sent another one by Recorded Delivery and they said they'd lost that one! I rang them up and pointed out that the Post Office had recorded it arriving. They said they'd check again and, whadda'ya know, they found it. What a surprise.

So everything was going well. The press were coming to the house in droves (whatever they are) to interview me about it all. I asked them to form an orderly queue.

Then the Old Bill stepped in with their size 10s and objected to my running for mayor because of my past. I got a letter from Michael Toyer on the GLA Election Team saying that I was not eligible because I'd been convicted of a criminal office in the last three years and that was against a GLA Act. Which was completely wrong cos my last conviction was over three years ago.

So, like 'good upstanding citizens' are supposed to do, I played it by the book. I wrote to my MP John Austin and the Prime Minister. I got a reply from 10 Downing Street to acknowledge my letter, and one from John Austin after he'd made some enquiries. I wrote back to the fella at the GLA, Michael Toerag, sorry, 'Toyer', and said 'Would you please send another excuse why I cannot be mayor because that last one doesn't work . . . I would appreciate a hasty reply as I'm a very busy man (and intend to go for world domination after I've become mayor). Thank you.'

The letter I got from Toyer said, 'I was under the impression that you had been convicted in the last three years . . .' Now I wonder who gave him that impression. The boys in blue maybe.

Anyway, his 'impression' was fucking wrong and why should I miss out just because he's made a mistake? He didn't seem to get any wrong 'impressions' about any of the other candidates did he? He didn't even get an 'impression' that Jeffrey Archer was bent. Funny that though, ain't it? I tell you, my sides hurt.

So the voters of London were going to be denied their democratic right to vote for whoever was standing for mayor because of an 'impression' about one of the candidates by one of the GLA. Even Rory Bremner doesn't do that many bleedin' impressions.

So, just when I'd cleared all that up and I'd proved I was eligible and ready to run – and that I had the best gaff out of any of them (with cracking new murals by my artist mate Kev Nutter) – the Old Bill stepped back in with one last ploy and said that I was on bail, which was true, and that finally fucked my chances.

Sorry, people, but I did try. You can't say that I didn't do that.

The story behind the thing I was on bail for is a whole book in itself. Which, funnily enough, is being written right now under the title of *Wrongly Accused*. I can't lay the whole story on you now, but I ended up being charged for conspiracy to pervert the course of justice along with a couple of the Old Bill.

The police know I haven't done anything because one of the officers has *said that to them already*! But they don't like me because of who I am. Their aim was to put me on remand for a year until the trial and nick that time off me.

So, on the morning of 8 November last year I turned up at Bow Street Magistrates' court in a blacked-out Jeep and followed by a convoy of seven Mercs with Seymour, Terry, Marcus, Dean, Piers, Brendan, Kev, Zak, Rob, Tucker, Costas, Little Legs and son Jamie, Terry, Sell and Dubey, Don Crosbie and Al Benson, Baz, Big Lee, Barry, Christian, Joey and Johnny Moore, Charlie Dixon, Builder Dave, Luke, Kevin and Chrissy the Greek, Ken the Dog, AJ, Slim and Gilly, Gravesend Matt, Derek, Albert Chapman and Johnny Magee and Coventry Stuart. Just a small selection!

Brendan had £50,000 bail money in cash in a carrier bag. Everyone was black-suited up, half of them wearing shades, and when this little army of naughty geezers got out of the cars all the press camera flashbulbs went off at once. I was still in the Jeep and thought it was the flash of a nuclear bomb. I thought, Fuck me, whatever happened to the four-minute warning?

But that little display was nothing to what happened when they saw what I was wearing when I got out.

Because the whole case and trial and them trying to drag me into it was such a big fucking joke, which I never tired of pointing out to people, Ed at *front* suggested I wear a jester's outfit. I didn't think little court jesters came in my size but they did find one. The same one used in the film *Shakespeare in Love*, as it happens. So I got right into character and got my balls out. Well you've got to juggle. Be fair.

So I stepped out to meet the press in a red, green and gold medieval jester's outfit – fancy jacket and pantaloon pants, pink stockings and pointed pixie boots and pointy hat with bells on. The full monty. For a second the camera flashes turned me into an X-ray. You could just see my skeleton and two dusters. I hadn't dressed this stupid since I last went to a fetish party as the Gimp! And even that didn't have bells on.

We all walked into the court building and who did I see but the lying bastard that's trying to fit me up. I did a quick side-step and an Ali shuffle and lamped him right on the jaw. Different parts of his body all said goodbye to each other and he collapsed and puddled out on the floor. Bit of a mini riot broke out then, shouting and scuffling, and I was led away by a couple of police.

They took me to one side. One of them turned to me and went, 'First off, Dave, good shot.' Then he pointed out that in a magistrates' court, on camera and in front of witnesses I'd just committed a serious assault. I pointed out that me and him shouldn't even have been in the same room together. He accepted that point and said that if I got rid of all my boys from the building, then they'd forget about the knockout. Done deal.

But I refused to appear in the same court, at the same time as the others accused, as it is fuck all to do with me so I'm not gonna get painted with the same brush. The court officials rearranged the schedules so there wouldn't be a rematch.

There was a big debate then about whether they'd let me in the court wearing the jester's outfit. I said I could take it off but I'm not a pretty sight in just a leopard-skin thong. They suddenly agreed that the jester's outfit would be better. Then Brendan stepped up with the cash. The *South London Press* reported it like this: 'Magistrate Graham Parkinson expressed his horror when the man standing bail, Brendan McGirr, casually carried in £50,000 cash in a bag. As everyone gasped, Mr Parkinson warned, "This is a public court and everyone here now knows how much is in that bag. I do worry for your safety."'

Ha-ha! 'I do worry for your safety'! Top line. Who the fuck did he think was gonna mug Brendan with us lot there?

When I came out on to the court steps, I said to the assembled media, 'I'd like to say that I have faith in the British justice system and that, as long as I have a hole in my arse, I will knock that geezer out wherever I see him. Thank you.'

Not a bad one to get away with though, ay? A knockout, in court, in front of the Old Bill, and all the while dressed up like The Lunatic That Time Forgot. And I played it in such a way that I got away with it. Now I'm getting hard just talking about it again!

Another thing that got me firmed-up was getting an award with Terry Turbo for drum'n'bass Promoters of the Year at the MTV music awards. We got up on stage, someone stuck a microphone in my hand and asked me about the drum'n'bass scene. I said, 'It's the absolute *bollocks*! Nuff said!' and everyone cheered. Was that a little buzz or what?

Brendan had a little buzz before he got to the show. On the way there, he pulled over somewhere quiet and bonked the bird he was with on the bonnet of his car. At the time, he just laughed about the white stain on the bonnet where his bird had been laid, but two weeks later the geezer at the car wash couldn't shift it! He said to Brendan, 'What is this, mate, bird shit?' Brendan went, 'You could say that.'

I had a little buzz of my own before the show that night. I was in the Mitsubishi Shogun with Jenny, Big John, Seymour, Lone Wolf Dave and Wolfie and we were playing this track I'd first heard the week before when I was in Sheffield going to the club Gatecrasher with Jen, Marcus G, Ben J and Lindsey,

Lianne Wellings and Lee. This tune had come on that went, 'God made me funky! And I'm glad he blessed me that way!' I thought, oh, yes! Proper war cry music it was. If I was on the way to some ag and that tune came on, you'd be in big trouble. It was real speeding-through-lights music.

And that was playing when we pulled up outside the MTV awards show, so I felt fucking naughty, mate. Anyway, outside the building, it was completely jammed with cars, no room. But the middle lane of the road had been coned off for building work and inside there was a low-loader trailer that a JCB had been on. I thought, Right, let's get off the beaten track, drove over the cones, killed a few, spun the Shogun round and reversed it up the ramps and on to the low-loader. All the doors opened simultaneously and all us geezers in dinner suits got out. The nightshift workers doing the road just stood watching us, gobsmacked. I asked how long they'd be here and they said all night. I said we'd only be a few hours and asked if it was OK to leave the car there. Apparently it was OK, or they didn't want to argue. *Touch.* One of my better entrances I think (not counting that last bonk).

Oh yeah, nearly forgot – the bit after the awards was blindin' as well. We went on to China White's club and I met loads more mates in there. So there was tons of us, half in dinner suits feeling like the old doormen and really buzzing as well. We were ready to invade, mate.

Anyway, so in comes this guy with heavy-shouldered minders, know what I mean? Might not have been intentional, don't get me wrong, shoulder pads can be difficult to control. But some of my fellas were getting pushed out of the way and turned to look at me as if to say, 'How much of this do you want me to take?' I was saying, be nice, everyone smile; then I thought, Wait a minute, though. Cos I was in a right naughty mood. A real *naughty* mood.

So I got these two big South African geezers that were with me to go up to this guy and say, 'My boss Dave Courtney thinks you are a *wanker* and he's waiting for you in the VIP lounge.' You can imagine it sounded even better in a mental South African accent. You could see him then whisper to his bodyguards, and they looked over at us and they didn't fancy it at all, mate.

Then, just to be extra naughty, I sent the South Africans back over to say, 'Mr Courtney don't like to be kept waiting.' It was like something out of a James Bond film. And it was bloody funny. We thought so anyway. He left pretty soon afterwards. Oh well, if he leaves, he *leaves*.

What else has happened since the book? Well, I've done loads of interviews, and not one of them in a police station with a tape recorder going! *Boom boom*. One of my favourite ones was by the absolutely gorgeous Jo Guest on Bruno Brook's Radio Storm show. I think that station is the best in the world.

Colin Butts, who wrote *Is Harry on the Boat?*, and Dave Hurst have written a book with a character based on me. Just give me a bit more hair, will you, lads?

My promoting of the UAO Martial Arts Tournaments is going great guns with Crew Danny and Lloyd. It's becoming Britain's most successful. At the last do I met Ian Freeman, the World Freestyle Fighting champion and presented him with his heavyweight award. He said, 'I don't want a trophy, I just wanted to hurt the bastard!' Top line.

Some other big geezers came out with me to the Ministry. A good friend of mine, Andy Frost, was looking after the top WWF American wrestlers. So we took them out clubbing. I looked around at one point and thought, What would I do if this little lot suddenly kicked off? I was stood next to The Rock, for fuck's sake – even his shadow looked heavy!

Then we went for a little private drink at my new local bar in Greenwich, Million Hares (owned by the Hares), run by my pals AJ, Bill and Darren. Find me there.

Oh yeah, get this: I got invited out to New York by Quentin Tarantino, the original *Reservoir Dogs* man himself. I did an 'Audience with . . .' with him and Tricky in Central Park in front of twenty thousand people. What a buzz! I thought I was gonna fucking take off and dive bomb the Empire State Building.

I was all lined up to play the character Brick Top in the new Guy Ritchie film *Snatch*, the follow-up to *Lock, Stock and Two Smoking Barrels*; did a read-through and everything. Then some of the money people behind it got a bit twitchy about using me when they saw some of the press surrounding

Stop The Ride. So that project didn't happen. Guy Ritchie explained it to me cos he's a straight geezer and it weren't his fault, but there really wasn't anything he could do. Anyway, the actor who got the part of Brick Top, Alan Ford, is a great actor. I'm good at playing Dave Courtney but he can play anything.

And did you see the TV version of *Lock, Stock?* Course you did. The character Miami Vice was played by this bald-headed geezer in a suit, with a diamond stud earring, gold jewellery, a cigar and a white Rolls-Royce. Who could that be I wonder? I was pondering that as I shaved my head, put in my diamond stud earring and adjusted my rings; then I lit a cigar and went outside to sit in the Rolls to think about it some more. I know he looked bloody familiar . . .

People were calling me up all night when the first episode was on, saying, 'Dave? Have you seen Channel 4?' So all night long I was saying, 'Yeah, I know, I *know* . . .'

I was happy that my mates Big Marcus, Lone Wolf Dave and Birmingham John were in it. When Marcus had first started filming, he rang me one day from the set to say that he couldn't believe he'd just seen a mini-Dave on set. Lone Wolf Dave also has a good role in *Snatch*.

Anyway, I've got a great writer of my own, Mr Steve Wood, working on the screenplay for a television adaptation of *Stop the Ride I Want to Get Off*. It's going to be in four, hour-long episodes.

But what about the film, Dave, I can hear you shout. Well, never fear, Courtney's here. And mister Quentin Tarantino's on the case. We got on great guns (an AK47 and a Magnum). After we've filmed my life story – with me playing me, who else? – we're gonna make a film showing that some gangsters have a softer side, y'know, that sometimes they're just big pussycats. It'll be called *Reservoir Mogs*. Sorry, couldn't resist.

But he is Gangster Director No. 1, old Quentin, ain't he? Who better to have on my side? See you at the premiere!

More likely, though, I'll see you in a club. And if you see me before I see you, come up and say hello. (Just don't ask me for Rizlas, please.)

20 Two Tigers Walking Down the Street

Raving definitely broke down barriers. Even the dress was cleverly devised as some kind of uniform, like at a comprehensive school where the rich kids were the same as the poor kids cos they all wore the same uniform. Ravers made the fashion casual for everyone. Baggy trousers, T-shirts, trainers.

And it was an easy set to get into. It was driven by the working class but the middle-class got into it and started putting on raves. So how it actually evolved was like this: there was this building where everyone, rich and poor, black and white, could smoke puff and take Es, and no one wanted to lose that love feeling in the middle. No one wanted it to get segregated. So the fashion evolved to make everyone acceptable to everyone else. The poor kids didn't feel inferior, and the rich kids didn't feel out of place.

That was more important to the working class kids, really, cos when they left that building they were second-class citizens, and felt it and looked it. But in the rave everyone was one. That was addictive. The middle-class kids always had their safety nets though, so it didn't matter much if their little excursion into another lifestyle didn't come off. In fact, I think they actually ended up envying the street kids.

And while it took a long time to accept the mixed race and relationship thing, that ten-year block-rockin' period of raving force-fucking-fed acceptance. Until nearly every white kid knew a black kid. Then they weren't scared of them. And they started dressing like them and getting into their music.

You're frightened of something if it's kept from you. So raving did the old rock'n'roll thing of stealing the country's youth, but not to fuck them up as all the parents thought; it took them away for a while and sent them back better!

But births are always traumatic, ain't they? Whether it's the birth of a baby or of a new music scene. You probably scream more as a just-born baby than you will ever again for the rest of your life (not counting piles, fuck me). Life in general gets quieter, don't it? Must be a sort of natural wind down, I guess, preparing for The Big Sleep. I suppose if you were raging and raving right to the end and then just dropped dead at seventy – *bang*! – it would be a much fucking big shocker for everyone. Although, having said that, I am planning on living like that! Stick around and prepare to be shocked.

So, the rave scene emulated that rock'n'roll thing that happened in the Fifties. Like in the film *The Wild One* – 'What you rebelling against, Johnny?' And he says, 'Whaddaya got?' And if that don't give you a bit of insight into young people then nothing will.

No one really knew that at the time, I ain't saying that, because everyone never stopped dancing long enough to really think about what was happening. And why should they? Everyone was having a fucking good time and good things were coming from it as a sort of . . . by-product, if you like. Everyone bangs on about the 'side effects' of drugs and all that, but no one seems to mention the much more massive beneficial side-effects of the rave scene.

The influences of rave culture can be seen everywhere you look in films, clubs, cafes, clothes, the charts, my bloodstream. Loads of things. Fuck me, even young police officers go there now!

Funny thing was that although raving was advertised as the loved-up, love drug cultural thing, what actually happened was shagging went right down! The fact that the club was open till six meant that you came out fucked but didn't get fucked. It was always light when you came out. You'd go home and where was the shagging time? Or your dick was shrivelled on whizz or your head out of it on acid.

But you were often quite happy not to shag cos you'd had such a blindin' time anyway. And if you did happen to cop off and find somewhere to have a shag, and you'd both had an E, then you had a really blindin' bonk. Which, again, is addictive.

Because normally he might be nervous, and she might be shy, but look at them go there!

Then try convincing that geezer, who's just had the shag of his life, or that girl, who's never felt emotion like that before during sex, that Es are a bad thing. You've really got your fucking work cut out there, mate.

Different parts of the rave community made stars out of people. It made stars out of certain DJs (some of them superstars), it made stars out of certain doormen and, for the time they lasted, certain dealers. This was a music that took its stars from the street – the DJs. Street kids and council estate kids. Their music, their neighbourhood, their street. At the beginning it was fucking raw.

And because there weren't so many clubs the actual DJs of those clubs became cult figures: Danny Rampling, Paul Okenfold, Pete Tong, Nicky Holloway, Brandon Block, Fabio & Grooverider. There's millions of places to go now and millions of DJs so it's difficult to get that famous now. But the ones you remember are the ones who had this cult thing.

A lot of the organisers who had the first illegal raves, the raving 'speakeasies', became famous. Legends. If they didn't get caught when the authorities went all Pamela Anderson and started doing big busts, they got away and got into doing European and world dance things, events and festivals. These are a lot of the geezers who own the clubs you got to know.

Because that little period of change from illegal raving to promoting to make a living was over something like a five-year period, in that time people got addicted to going out.

And all that I've just said, even though it harks back to things that have already happened and might sound sort of nostalgic, all the ideas about how people *felt* still applies today. To all you sixteen-, seventeen-year-olds who are bang into it now and can't, wait to get out to your club or get on a plane to the Balearic Islands.

Things stay the same it's just the names that change. Or is that just on my passport? No, I mean when things get banned you have to rename them and shove them back out there. Like Es are banned and now called Class As and you can get nicked for them, so they now bring out something called Viagra (or a V). Which basically does the same thing, and has caused the same kind of stories in the press as Ecstasy did, y'know, 'The bonking love drug'. Which don't sound like a bad thing these days, does it? Sounds like a good selling point to me.

Bit of a tip here for any geezers out there that fancy taking a V but are too embarrassed cos you think people might say you can't get it up. That's not what it's about. It ain't about fixing something that's broke. You don't have to be hungry to eat a Mars Bar, you do it for the pleasure.

Explain it like this: if you were gonna drive 90 miles down the road you wouldn't just put 90 miles' worth of petrol in the tank, would you? You'd put more than a bit of a drop extra. That's what a Viagra is, and, like the old Esso petrol advert on the telly used to say, 'Put a tiger in your tank!'

Which reminds me. Two tigers walking down the street. One turns to the other and says, 'Fuck me, there aren't many people around for a Bank Holiday Monday, are there?'

21 At the End of the Day . . .

When raving first started, and before big money got involved and spoiled parts of it, it was just done for the love of it and the experience. And it grew you up, in a sort of way.

Talking about me personally, I draw things from experience. Everyone should cos really that's all you've got to teach you. Reading a book about something can only take you so far, know what I mean? I even mean that about this book.

So what I want you to do after you finish reading this (apart from having a wank cos it's excited you so much), and what I want you to do *especially* if you ain't ever done it before, is to go out somewhere, doesn't even have to be a club, and just have a fucking good time. And it don't just have to be like the kind of times you've read about me having – don't jump in at the deep end!

If you're having doubts about doing it, you shy ones out there, then do this: write down a big number, say 'one million', then times that by the same again, and then keep doing that forever and that's how many days you're gonna be dead for. But if you are, say, about twenty years old, then you've only got around fifty or sixty summers left before you die.

Sorry, didn't mean to do your head in with that, but we all need a kick up the arse now and again and that's yours from your Uncle Dave. So if you ain't already – Get living! Because at the end of the day . . . it gets dark.

My boy Beau is a DJ now, even playing at some of my old haunts. He's a chip off the old block, Rockin' Beats is my Beau. So now my son's involved in the club scene I can't get out of it even if I wanted to. Which I didn't anyway, by the way, so there you go. I'll still be going strong even when Beau *and* Beau jnr are still clubbing.

Going out is good for the soul, raving keeps you young, and it helps you stay sane to get involved in a bit of lunacy now and again. You *know* that.

So stay lucky. And remember, never look a gift horse up the arse . . . cos that's the wrong end, you silly cunts!

Index

Abby George, 216
Adam 216–17
Adams, Bryan 62, 86
Adams, Jack 239
Adams, Terry 62
Adrian Age 48
AJ 195, 216, 239, 260, 263
Albion, The 192
Andrews, Bob 101, 171
Andy 239
Andy, *front* 251
Andy B 239
Andy the Cab 63
Aquarium, The 86, 212, 220
Aquarium Lou 86, 99, 156, 230, 239
Aquarium Paul 86, 230
Aquarium Tony 86, 230
Archer, Jeffrey 1, 260
Arches, The 23–5, 29, 31–4, 37, 39, 44, 91, 135, 171, 231
Arches (Terry 'Ram Jam') 2, 86, 156, 172
Ash, Amon 15, 127, 158
Ash, Johhny 83
Astoria 86
Austin, John 259
Ayenapa, Cyprus 221

Babushka's, Elephant and Castle 86
Bagley's Film Studio 221

Bahan 243
Bal 195, 216, 234
Bald-headed Bill 174
Bannerman, Mark 239
Barking Zena Flashpetal 240
Baron, Gary 239
Barry's Bar, Tenerife 241
Barry, Christian 260
Bass Construction 238
Baz 260
Becks beer 152
Belfast Brian 239
Belly Dancer Colin 234
Belmarsh, HMP 185, 196, 222
Ben Jammin 239, 261
Benn, Nigel 87, 97, 101, 238–9, 251
Benson, Al 260
Bermondsey Boy 36, 46
Bernie 240
Betts, Leah 72
Bez 63, 234, 251
Big Barry 63
Big Bird & Co 229
Big Brummy John 189, 239
Big Chris 15
Big Colin 240
Big Jim 88, 91, 195
Big Joe 128
Big John 87, 89, 93, 95, 195, 216, 261
Big Larry 158

Big Lee 63, 234, 260
Big Marcus 119–21, 123, 176, 264
Big Mark 63
Big Marky 158
Big Mel 158, 239
Big Mick 63
Big Noel 62
Big Norman 28
Big Scotty 15
Big Willy 239
Biggs, Mickey 239, 243
Biggs, Ronnie 243
Bill 263
Billy 158, 195
Billy the Car 158
Birmingham Boys, The 229
Birmingham John 88, 91, 264
Blackwood 172, 239
Blind Beggar, The 61
Block, Brandon 25, 101, 156, 171, 267
Blonde Simon 158
Bobby's Bar, Tenerife 158, 242
Bogat, Steve 15
Boo 83
Boob's, Tenerife 158, 242
Boogie 172
Bootleggers 112
Boris 101, 105–6
Boulevard, Ealing 83–4
Bowl, The, Milton Keynes 221
Boxer 195, 211, 239
Boxer Baz 127
Branson, Richard 15
Brendan 45, 63, 79, 82–3, 85, 93, 103, 107, 193–5, 197–8, 200, 203, 205–7, 209–12, 214–18, 239, 260–62
Brett 158
Bridges, Ray 18–21, 23, 29, 63, 168–9, 239
Bronson, Charles 207–8
Brookes, Bruno 263
Brooklyn John 176

Brown, Carl 'Tuff Enuff' 25, 101, 239
Brown, Craig 250
Brown, Lee 240
Builder Dave 260
Bulldog Dean 63
Bullen, Rory 237
Busby's, Tenerife 242
Bushell, Gary 238–9
Business, The 238
Butts, Colin 87, 156, 239, 263
Buzz club, Charing Cross Road 85, 158

Capital Radio Roadshow 168
Carlton 15, 229
Caroline 87
Carr, Roy 172
Carson, Frank 241
Carter Street police station 30–31, 163
Cecil 172–3
Chapman, Big Albert 239
Chapman, Lee 239, 260
Chef 195
Cherry Tree, Stoneyford Lodge 117
China White's club 262
Chocolate Candy Box 99
Chops 240
Chris 110, 216–17
Chrissie 172
Chrissy the Greek 260
Christian 239
Christina 118
Circus, club, Ireland 155
Cirus, security company 229
Clarke, Carol 239
Clary, Julian 253
Clash, The 188
Clay, Johnny 19–20
Clink, The 40–41, 137
Club Ecstasy, Tenerife 238
Club Manumission, Ibiza, see Manumission

Cohen, James 240
Colbert, John 240
Colby, Mick 239
Colin 87
Continentals club 79
Cookie 240
Corbit, John 63
Cornell, George 61
Coronation Street 206
Cosmic Challenge 256
Costas 158, 260
Cotterell, Selwyn 62
Courtney, Beau 160–62, 255, 269, 270
Courtney, Chelsea 36, 137
Courtney, Drew 82, 160–62, 164
Courtney, Jennifer 49–50, 55–63, 75, 78–84, 86–9, 91, 99, 107, 110, 112–15, 118–19, 122, 130, 147–9, 152–5, 160–2, 164–6, 168, 185–7, 192, 199–201, 209, 211, 224–5, 227–8, 238, 242, 145, 262
Courtney, Jenson 82, 160–62, 193, 199–201
Courtney, Levi 36
Courtney, Tracey 56, 139–40, 168–70
Coventry Stuart 216, 239, 260
Cowboy 216
Cox, Carl 'Tuff Enuff' 25, 101
Crazy Mondays, club nights 25, 49, 95–8, 105
Creed 63, 83, 101, 129, 158
Crew Danny 263
Crime Through Time museum 207
Crosbie, Don 260

Danny 95
Darlington Dave 41, 43–4, 63
Darren 263
Darren from Shosec 240
Dave 87
Dave the builder 239
Davies, Rod 240

Deamscape 239
Dean 239, 260
Dean, Tango Man 74, 75, 76, 77, 140, 147
Dean, DJ 128–9
Death Ray 125, 126
Del 240
'Delicious' club night, Boulevard 83–4
Dennis 95
Derek 260
Devious D 48
Dhalia 104
Ditton, Garry 239
Dixon, Charlie 87, 240, 260
Dobs 87
Docherty 158, 240
Dolittle, Danny 63–4, 107, 127, 158, 216, 239
Dolphin, Paul 240
Doncaster Dave 137, 140
Dr Jim's 21
Dreamscape 221
Drury, Ian 188
Dubey 260
Dukey 158
Dungeon, The 118
Dungeons, Lee Bridge Road 48
Dunn, Dave 15, 95
Dyke, Danny 141, 147

Eamon 240
Eastwood, Gary 240
Ebo 240, 252
Ed, *front* 260
Elliot 95
Emporium 174
End Club 174
Energy, promotions 188
Errol 83, 172
Evans, Chris 254
Evans, Jonathan (aka Posh Jon) 141–3, 145, 147, 149, 185, 240
Evans, Val 141, 185, 240
Everton 87

Eves, Keith 234
Eves, Peter 234

Fabio & Grooverider 25, 156, 171, 267
Farquar, Angus 151
Fast Trevor 240
Faz 158, 240
Finn, Mickey 239
Fireman Steve 239
Firman, Dennis 158, 240
Fitness Centre, The, Southwark Park Road 46, 48, 50, 75
Flighty, Steve 101
Fling Crew, The 239
Floyd 83
Ford, Alan 172, 264
Foreman, Freddie 8, 167
Foreman, Jamie 240
Forresters, The 234
Foster, Steve 239
Francis 175
Francis, Julius 239
Frank 234
Frank (Spain) 165
Frank and Sheila 158
Frankie Baby 239
Fraser, Frankie 8, 96, 175
Freaky 238
Fred and Kerry 239
Fred the Fuse 63
Freeman, Ian 263
Frog and Nightgown, The 87
front 251–1
Frost, Andy 263
Fulvia 172
Funny Glen 41, 46–7, 62–3, 95, 131–2, 137–8, 248
Futures club, Deptford 25, 49, 95–8, 102, 104–5, 117

G-Mex, Manchester 221
event 216–17
Garage Nation 221
Gary 132

Gary G 239
Gass, The 86, 93–5, 128, 147, 149–50, 158
Gatecrasher club, Sheffield 261
Gazza 212
Geordie Steve 195
George 235
Georgio, Marcus 239
Gilly 260
Ginger 61
Ginger John 18
Glasgow Boys, The 239
Glastonbury 188–9
Glen, Slough 62–7, 160
Glen 83
Goldie 63
Goldtooth, Mickey 127
Gordon, Steve 172
Grace club 86, 175, 231
Grantham, Leslie 47
Gravesend Matt 239, 260
Green, Mickey 15
Grove Vale depot 18–19, 23
Guest, Jo 263
Gummidge 239
Guns in Britain 256

Hak 239
Hamed, Prince Naseem 239
Hammer 240
Hammersmith Palais 226
Hanson, Andy 239
Hanson, Robert 63
Happy Days 158
Happy Days 2, Tenerife 241
Happy Daze 231
Hards, Ricky 121–2
Harrison, Tommy 239
Hart, Tony 243
Hastings Pier 221
Hayward, Billy 96
Hayward, Harry 96, 97, 100, 102, 103
Headcorn 188, 190
Heaven 15, 17, 86

Herbie 15
Hickorys club (Deja Vu), Swanley 119
High-Roy 172
Hippodrome Ginger 132, 238
Hippodrome, The 61
Hogg, Jocelyn Bain 239, 242–3
Holdsworth, Steve 239
Holland, Harry 239
Holloway, Nicky 267
'Hot and Spunky' club nights 117, 156
Hot House, The 206
House club, Forest Gate 117
Hurley, Ray 101
Hurst, Dave 87, 239, 263
Huxford, Chris (Forum) 240

Ice T 230
Independent 32
Is Harry on the Boat? 263
Isaac, Billy 15

Jack 107
Jacket, Johnny 63, 95, 107, 132, 227–8
Jackie 63
Jaimie 239
Jamie (little Legs) 260
Jamie 127
Jarvis 239
Jay 95
Jay, Ian 101
Jazz 195
Jenkins, Kevin 240
Jimmy Five Bellies 212
Joe 41
Joe, Tenerife 241
John Boy 9–10
Johnny 158
Jones, Andy 207, 208
Joyce 87
Joynes, Sheffield Ben 240
JR's, Catford 96
Judge, Toby von 240, 243

Keith 15
Keith, Birmingham 239
Ken the Dog 15, 260
Kenny 216
Kenny (DJ) 48
Kerry 63
Kev 260
Kevin 195, 260
Kevin N 239
King John 21
King, Rodney 69
Kingsey 87
Koo Club 93
Kray, Charlie 8, 63
Kray, Reg 5, 60, 208
Kray, Ronnie 5, 60–61, 208, 229
Ku Club, Ibiza 158

Labyrinth club, Dalston Lane 48
Lakeside 117
Lamb 239
Lambert, Dean 101, 128, 156
Lambert, Mark 22
Lambrianou, Tony 8
Lance 95, 239
Lawrence 195
Lee 240, 261
Lennon, John 187
Leopard Lounge, Tenerife 158, 242
Les 165
Les, Tenerife 241
Lester 172
Lianne 240
Life of a Lighter 209
Limelight 24, 42, 110–11, 117, 156
Limelight Rose 239
Linda 234
Lindsey 240, 261
Linnekars 158
Little Jenny 195, 240
Little Jimmy 192–3, 199, 201
Little Joe 128, 200
Little Legs 158, 216, 260

Livingstone, Ken 257
Lloyd 263
Locations 86
Locks 95
Locks, Dennis 172
Loft, Shepherds Bush 84
Lone Wolf Dave 15, 211, 239,
    261, 264
Love, Gary 239
Low, Steve 158, 216, 234, 239,
    251
Lucas, Dennis 239
Lucas, Kenny 239
Luke 83, 211, 260

M25 raves 224
Mad Jack 127–31, 140, 158, 195,
    234, 241
Mad Pete 176
Mail on Sunday 250
Manny 95
Mansion 118
Manumission 156
Mapp brothers 158
Marco 158
Marco's, Tenerife 242
Marcus 255, 260
Marcus G 261
Mark 83
Marks, Howard 53
Marky Mark 132
Martin, Folkestone 202
Mason, Gary 97
Master P 61
Matt 128
Matthew 229
Matt 15, 239
Maximus 59
Mayfest, Glasgow 155
McDonald, James 240
McFadden, Steve 252
McGee, Johnny 239
McGirr, Brendan, *see* Brendan
McLean, Lenny 208
McNab, Andy 235

Mechanic Jim 240
Memmy 239
Metallica 188
Michelle and Paul 239
Mick (not 'Unknown') 240
Mickey Mack 239
Mikey 220
Million Hares, Greenwich 263
Ministry of Sound 4, 58, 86, 127,
    156–8, 186, 193, 196–7, 212,
    215, 220–1, 229, 231–2, 234,
    263
Miss Moneypenny 239
Mitch 239
Mo and Jill 239
Mohammed 239
Moley 239
Montana, Daniella 63, 83, 101,
    107, 221, 227–8, 239
Moore, Joey 260
Moore, Johnny 260
Morgan, Hugh 34–5
Morrison, Mark 239, 251
Morrison, Van 189
Mr Universe 62
MTV, music awards 261
'Mums The Word', club nights 86
Murray, Bill 239

Nashers 105
Neil 95, 132
News of the World 256, 258
Nicky 239
Nod and Humphrey 229
Norma 239
Norman 41
Normski 239
Northern Billy 195
Nutty Rob 211

O'Brian, Neil 239, 241
O'Keefe, Eamon 239
O'Keefe, John 127, 195
Okenfold, Paul 267
One Nation promotions 221, 223,

231
events 224–5, 229–30, 236
Orange, the 240
Orbital promotions 188
Oss, Peter 240

Paddy and Mel 240
Palumbo, James 231
Paradise 47, 58, 85, 125, 196, 242
Pard 240
Parisienne, Folkestone 202
Park Club, Kensington 88, 91–2, 124
Parker, Norman 239
Parkinson, Graham 261
Paul 83, 158
Paul, Chris 230, 239
Paul, Zoe Gregory 230, 240
People Versus Jerry Sadowitz, The 253
Phil 110
Phil (Mansion) 118
Piers, *front* 251, 260
Piggot, Lester 98, 100–101, 103
Pike 195
Pinkerton Jon, 243
Pinto, Jennifer *see* Courtney, Jennifer
Pinto, Julia 49–50, 59, 61
Pit Bull 132
Place, The 79, 81–2
Pontins, Camber Sands 251
Porkpie Martin 179
Post Office Tower 117
Public Demand 230
Pyle, Joey 8, 167
Pyle, Joey Jnr 63

Queen's (The Queen Mother Reservoir Yachting Club) 9–12, 15, 36
Quelch, Dave 239

Railway Signal, The 21
Raith, Steve 211, 239

Rampling, Danny 25, 267
Rat Pack 48, 171
Rave Nation 221
Ravey 195, 239
Rawlings, Ned 158
Reema and Tony 158
Reese 240
Rex Arena, Stratford 221
Rex 174
Reynolds, Bruce 156, 243
Reynolds, Nick 156, 243
Richards, Stephen 207, 239
Ricky 43, 98
Ricky (Folkestone) 202
Ritchie, Guy 263
Rob 260
Rob the barber 240
Robbie 15
Robinson, Colin 76
Rock, the 263
Rocky 83
Rod 211, 239
Roschelle 238
Ross, Nick 143
Royce, Ian 240
Rude Rude Courtney Twins 119, 155, 238

Sadowitz, Jerry 253–5
Saint, Adam 239
Sally, *front* 251
Sandy 87–91, 93
Santry, Michael 82
Savile, Jimmy 97, 123
Scarface Danny 239
Schnell, Roy 240
School Dinners 85, 99
Scott, Laurie 239
Scotty 110
Scouse Jamie 174
Scouse John 195, 239
Scouser Jim 239
Scouser John 239
Scouser Robbie 239
Scully 127

Steve (DJ) 239
Sean (LWT) 255
Sell 260
Seymour 63, 92, 107, 216, 227–8, 239, 260–61
Shaw, Roy 8, 208, 243
Shoom 41
Sidcup rave 45
Silent Twins, The 151
Simms 229
Skeet, Oliver 15, 239
Slim 195, 216, 239, 260
Smith, Tony 174
Sol 174
Special Patrol Group (SPG) 30–31
'Spectrum', club night 15
Spider 239
Spiral Tribe 188
'Splash' club nights 156
'Spreadlove', Dominic 95, 101, 129
Spud 127
Stephanie 195
Steve 41, 43, 158
Steve (from Mirage) 239
Steve (Newcastle) 213
'Still Buzzin', club night 84
Stormin' Norman 42, 46–7, 63, 131–2, 134–6, 140
Stringfellows 210, 233
Sun 48, 238
Sunbed Joyce 239
Sunnyside, the girls from 239
Sunrise, promotions 188
Susan and Wayne 240
Swallow, Andy 95, 230

Taggart 151
Talk of London theatre 241
Tank 156–7
Tarantino, Quentin 263–4
Tardis, The 216, 235
Tarkan 239
Tasco's Warehouse club, Woolwich 171

Tattershall Castle club 9, 246
Taylor, Mickey 127, 235
Temple club 86, 230
Terry 'Ram Jam' 156
Terry, Croydon 110
Thompson, Chrissy 23
Thompson, Pete 229
Thompson, Tony 239
Timmy 'Ram Jam' 86, 99, 230, 231
Tinpan George 240
Tobin, Mark 22
Todd, Frank 240
Todd, Linda 240
Togs 127
Tong, Pete 267
Tony 83, 132
Tony, Croydon 110
Tony, Underhill Road 18
Tooting Common rave 44
'Toucan Club', Bootleggers 112
Toyer, Michael 259
Tracey 44
Trevor 158
Tricky 251, 263
Tucker, Ian 101, 147, 148, 260
Tucker-Tate killings 174
Turbo, Terry 127, 132, 156, 177, 216, 221–4, 226, 226–8, 230–1, 239, 257, 261
Turnmills, Clerkenwell 175
Tyson 239

UAO Martial Arts Tournament 263
Uncle Frank 140
Unique 239

Vanessa Show, The 192, 201
Vince (Spain) 165
Vinoo 10, 11

Warren 15, 131–2, 134, 220, 225
Warrior 176–7, 236
Warwick 63, 106

Webb, Big Terry 158
Wellings, Lianne 261
Welsh Bernie 239
Wembley Arena 221, 224
Westbrook, Daniella 240
Whale, Steve 211, 239
Wilson, Linda 21
Wilson, Paul 21
Wilson Peter 21
Windows 95

Windross, Norris d'Boss 25, 101
Wish 158, 211, 239
Wolfie 11–16, 24, 26–7, 30, 33–6,
    95, 107, 216, 239, 261
Wood, Steve 239, 264

Yacht Club, Temple Pier 86–7

Zak 239, 260
Zens Club 141